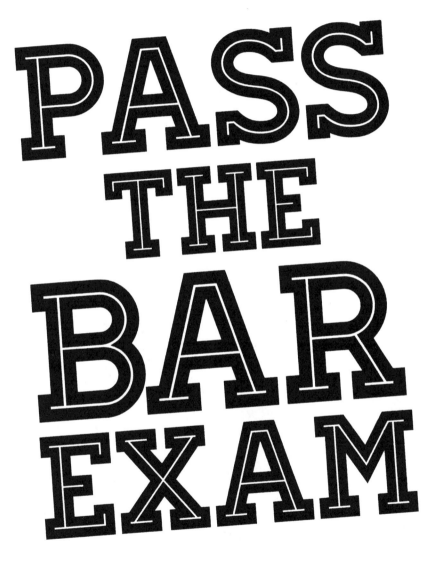

A PRACTICAL GUIDE TO ACHIEVING
ACADEMIC & PROFESSIONAL GOALS

PASS THE BAR EXAM

SARA J. BERMAN

Cover design by Kelly Book /ABA Publishing.

Printed in the United States of America.

17 16 15 14   5 4 3 2

Cataloging-in-Publication data is on file with the Library of Congress.

ISBN: 978-1-62722-238-9

Discounts are available for books ordered in bulk. Special consideration is given to state bars, CLE programs, and other bar related organizations. Inquire at Book Publishing, ABA Publishing, American Bar Association, 321 N. Clark Street, Chicago, Illinois 60654-7598.

www.ShopABA.org

DEDICATION

This book is dedicated to Julia and Daniel,
who make everything worthwhile.

CONTENTS

ACKNOWLEDGEMENTS

There are so many people whose work contributed to shaping my ideas about bar exam success that I hesitate even trying to name names for fear of leaving people out. I will nonetheless thank certain people below, reserving the right to belatedly thank the many others who are not specifically noted.

First and foremost, my students (former, present, and future); it is all about you.

Next, my passlaw partners, who have influenced much of my thinking about teaching and learning: Steve Bracci, I will never be able to express the extent of my gratitude. I learn from you every day, and I admire beyond words your ability to simply explain even the most complex concepts. Craig, thank you for bringing me into the 21st century and continuously keeping my focus on both the best and worst uses of technology. And, Bruce, my gratitude for demonstrating true experiential learning, merging law practice into law teaching, and lawyering from the client's perspective.

I must acknowledge Professor Arthur R. Miller as the first bar review voice I ever heard, a voice I have come to know as the clearest and strongest at the highest levels of legal scholarship, the most fundamental understanding of law for lay people, and everywhere in between.

An enormous thank you to all the clinical legal education pioneers at UCLA Law School including David Binder, Albert Moore, Carrie Menkel-Meadow and most especially Professor Emeritus Paul Bergman who both opened the door to teaching for me and was the first person to support my passion for bar review. I thank you, Paul, as well for always reminding through word and deed that humor has its place in life and law, as do kindness, humility and common decency.

Thank you to the original BarPassers faculty including Steve Bracci, Jack Goetz, Robert Hull, and Laurel Liefert. Thank you to everyone on the Concord Law School faculty, including but not limited to Dean Greg Brandes, Dean Emeritus Barry Currier, Dean Stephen Burnett, Dr. Martha Siegel, and Donna Skibbe, as well as the many alumni who have generously served as bar mentors. Many thanks to everyone at

Kaplan Bar Review. And, a special thank you to the Whittier Law School, especially Professor Tina Schindler and Dean Penelope Bryan.

Infinite appreciation to all who helped make this book as useful to readers as possible. I thank ABA Publishing and specifically my amazing editor Erin Nevius. Thank you to Kathi Cervi, JD and Professor Michele Tobenkin, Esq. for their eagle eyes, ever-present support, and saintly patience. For their candid critique, I thank colleagues and friends Julie Baumgartner, Ira Berman, PhD., Lori Cooper, Craig Gold, Esq., Michael Jewell, Yvette Lloyd, Esq., Ross Mitchell, Esq. and Desiree Navarro, Esq.

And last but furthest possible from least, thank you to Donna Skibbe; you confirm at every turn that bar passage and success in general have as much to do with being the best person one can be as they do with knowledge, preparation, and skill.

INTRODUCTION

This is not a rule book. There are plenty of those. This book's focus is on practical success training. You may use this book to help prepare for any bar exam in the nation or to master techniques that will allow you to achieve almost any goal you set your mind to. Read it while you are in school, and return to it when you begin a new job, try your first case, or even embark on a fitness mission. Many of the success steps are the same. And they work.

WHOM IS THIS BOOK FOR?

If you are in law school, this book is *written for you and to you*. It is an interactive guide. Think of it as a conversation with a mentor or supportive professor who is sharing advice, stories, worksheets, quizzes, and planning tools. It will discuss professional, life, and study skills that will help you with bar prep and beyond.

Knowing that what you do and how you think now will pay dividends of success for decades to come will help sustain you through the struggles and challenges of bar prep. Seeing the positive results that flow from hard work will make you want to take on new challenges. I hope the strategies inspire and propel you toward a lifelong cycle of success!

The book's text and tips apply to all law students. Selected comments will address those who are struggling, but do not skip them even if you are doing exceptionally well. These notes have universal applicability.

If you are at the top of your class in law school, you may not *need* this book. (You are likely either already doing much of what is suggested or are getting reliable advice elsewhere.) But you will *want* this book to provide reassuring mentoring and help you maintain your success.

Most law students do need to take deliberate, affirmative steps to ensure bar passage. The sooner you know what to do and how to do it, the easier it will be to create and implement a plan. Let this book be your success manual.

In addition to law students, the following people will find this book helpful:

- Families, friends, spouses, and partners of law students. Many of you are or will be confused, even offended, by the behavior of your son, daughter, mom, dad, husband, wife, partner, or friend. He or she may seem inordinately stressed out, or to have virtually disappeared. You may think, "How hard can law school be?" and "Isn't the bar just another test?" (Law school is *very* hard, and the bar is *not* just another test; this book will help you "get it.") As a key player in the support network of someone taking the bar exam, your help is critical. Learn how you can lend a hand, or back off, as needed.

- Practicing lawyers taking the bar exam in another jurisdiction. You may think because you passed one bar exam and have been practicing law that passing another bar should be easy, and that you do not need to prepare as thoroughly as other applicants. Wrong. In many respects, you need to set aside your practical knowledge, forget for a moment that you are a lawyer, get back into the mind-set of a student, and follow the exam advice and strategies in this book.

- Law school professors and administrators. This book will help your students and assist in improving bar pass rates. There is also a Teacher's Edition guide— containing lesson plans, syllabi, and an updated section on online bar support and mentoring—which will particularly interest faculty and administrators in Academic Support (ASP) and Bar Support.

- Prospective law students. This book will help balance the negatives you may hear about legal education and see that, despite the great challenges, enormous rewards await. I hope it helps you decide to go to law school. If you do, the text and tips will aid in both law school success and bar passage. The book will help you start good habits from day one.

- Experienced attorneys who work with new lawyers. This book will help you understand some of the concerns facing prospective law clerks and new associates. It may assist you to become a stronger mentor and be more effective in integrating new lawyers into law practice. Today's attorneys face generational divides. Baby Boomers encounter challenges when managing new grads who are Millennials. Second- and third-career law students also face their own challenges, as well as awkwardness on the part of some seasoned lawyers who find it uncomfortable to supervise new lawyers who are older and have more life experience.

- Students working to achieve any academic goal, from high school to graduate school. Much of the stress and many of the challenges described here are not unique to law or the bar exam. Replace the words "passing the bar exam" with "doing well on final exams or midterms," or "getting a high score on the SAT, LSAT, or other standardized test," or "completing almost any professional training," and you will find success strategies to achieve your goal.

NOTE TO 1L STUDENTS: YOUR FATE IS NOT SEALED AFTER FIRST YEAR

While it is true that opportunities for certain big-firm jobs may be fixed with first-year grades, bar passage is not. Too many students act as if bar passage were predetermined by one or another first-year grade. If first year did not go as well as you had hoped, do not withdraw or give up. Get help. Throw yourself in. Determine what went wrong and how to improve. Use your upper-division years as opportunities to make the changes necessary to ensure first-time bar passage. Read some of the many excellent books on success in law school. (Ask your ASP faculty or your school librarian for suggestions, and note selected sources in the Bibliography of this book.)

Be brave enough to confront the situation, and talk with a supportive professor or mentor. (I know; you don't want to appear stupid or weak by telling someone about your struggles. You hope they will just go away, next year will be better, and no one will have to know.) I am not suggesting you broadcast your concerns to the entire school, but that you find someone smart and empathetic who can help you recognize the changes you need to make. The key is realizing what you need to do differently. Once you do, making the necessary changes may not be that difficult.

So, if you have struggled in school, tackle your concerns head-on. Do not delay. The longer you wait, the more you will suffer. Break through the pride that is holding you back. I assure you: you are not the only one with challenges. But you will be the smart one if you seek help. Get on the success path today.

WHY WAS THIS BOOK WRITTEN?

Over drinks or coffee, most lawyers will tell bar exam horror stories. Many will describe the exam as a "hazing ritual." Older lawyers took and passed it, so you have to also. Some will say they still have vivid bar-related nightmares. But dig a little deeper, and you will likely find that almost everyone learned a lot from the process.

Studying for the bar exam does not have to be the "torture" some refer to it as. You can choose to view it that way and be miserable for several months. You can even let it get to you so much that you never figure out how to pass, thus paying the price for years, if not decades, to follow.[1] Or you can view the bar exam as an extraordinary opportunity not only to master a large amount of law and critical lawyering skills, but also to embrace the process of attaining academic and professional success. At the end of the day, you might even look back on the whole thing as a positive experience!

Are you balking? Do you think anyone who could possibly regard this grueling exam as having redeeming qualities must be nuts? I get it. And I may be nuts. But for more than two decades, I have helped thousands of people pass the bar, and I am convinced that training for this exam is a paradigm for succeeding in anything. So please, keep reading.

Throw yourself into bar preparation, and it will teach you indispensable life lessons. Among other positives, you will become more determined and more confident, you will learn to see the benefits of struggle, and you will understand that you can work hard enough to thrive in the face of virtually any challenge. I hope to convince you that embracing bar success can become an incomparably powerful turning point, one that will guide you to a lifetime of success.

EVENTUALLY THE FACT PATTERNS LOOK LIKE PUZZLES; THEY'RE CHALLENGING AND FUN!

The teaching moment I most look forward to is about ten days before each bar exam when, inevitably, a student sheepishly inquires, "Is it really weird that resolving these questions has become . . . fun?" The minute one person asks this, other students pour forth admissions that they are also (finally!) starting to enjoy the practice tests. That makes me smile. (Even when I teach online to students miles away, they know I am smiling.) That's because it's now apparent that the students have worked hard enough, and they are ready. They are not weird at all; they are on target.

I hope that before your exam, you will also declare with conviction, "Bring it on! Throw any fact pattern at me, on any bar subject. I can break it apart and say something intelligent about the issues. I may not remember every detail of every rule, but the examiners are not expecting me to. The exam is a pass/fail, minimal-competency test. I am not writing an amicus brief for the Supreme Court. In the real world, I will almost always be able to look things up. (Most of the time, I will be required to look things up!) On the exam, I will be relying on what I know and the reasoning skills I have developed. I will read the facts they give me, think logically, and explain my reasoning in a straightforward manner. I can do this. I am ready to prove myself."

Beyond the "hazing ritual" critique, many view bar exams as useless wastes of time and money. I will not dispute that the process is costly, but your effort and investment serve numerous important purposes.[2]

- The bar exam is empowering. If you prepare the way you should, you will develop more skills and possess more knowledge than ever before. Picture the powerful athlete who has trained for the Olympic Games and is poised to run or swim when the starting gun sounds. That will be *you* when you are told you may break the seal, open your booklets, and begin the exam. Visualize yourself as strong and smart, ready to logically approach any fact pattern the examiners might throw at you.

- Bar preparation brings clarity. Studying for the bar provides an opportunity to review what was covered during law school, as well as to learn material that wasn't taught. You spent endless hours focusing on minutiae, concentrating on the veins in the leaves on the branches of trees—or thousands of disparate legal rules—sometimes without ever seeing the forest. During intensive bar studies, you are given the opportunity to pull it all together. You will see connections and parallels in different subjects that previously had no link in your mind. Imagine a photo that is out of focus finally becoming clear. Law school blurs information, sometimes intentionally, to prepare you to handle the gray areas in people's lives and problems. Bar review simplifies and clarifies. It boils things down to straightforward rules. Once you have completed the training process, you will just read the facts carefully, apply rules you have mastered, and draw upon reason to reach logical conclusions. Bar review lecturers do not "hide the ball" the way law professors do. You can enjoy a short respite from the mystification before things again become real-world murky.

- The bar sharpens your ability to reason. Ideally, you will be applying the rules you have learned (and by the exam will have memorized) to hundreds if not thousands of different fact patterns. You will not be delving as deeply into the complexities and subtleties of law as you did when studying appellate cases in school, but you will be reasoning through a far greater volume of factual scenarios that extend into many different areas of law. Your brain will become a power tool. Once you know your stuff, you can go into the exam looking forward to those new fact patterns. They will have become fascinating puzzles that you have the ability to solve. Train well, and your mental muscles will welcome the challenge.

- The bar exam levels the playing field. There is, of course, a hierarchy of prestige among law schools and class rank within particular schools. Nonetheless, this objective measure certifies that *every* passer, regardless of race, gender, or alma mater, possesses the requisite competency to practice law. This opens up access within the legal profession and is particularly important for graduates of third- and fourth-tier law schools. And, despite the criticism of bar exams as being barriers to entering the profession, they are an undeniable equalizer for every lawyer who can honestly say, "I passed the same damn bar exam you did."

- Bar preparation can help you master the critical skills of organization, calendaring, and concentration. Some people have these down by the end of elementary school; most of the rest of us are still working on them. The more effective you are at these, though, the more successful you will be as a professional, and quite likely in life generally. Our complex world has simply foisted great time-management demands on us all.

CALENDARING

A 3L student asked to meet with me the following week to go over an exam. I noted the time and date of our appointment, and as he walked away without writing anything down, I asked him if he would remember. He laughed and said he had never kept a calendar and so far had done just fine. I told him he should start. He chuckled again and said, "I'll be there; you'll see." He kept his appointment with me, but several months after the bar, he phoned to tell me that he had missed a meeting with colleagues at his new job. The partner indicated his displeasure, noting that he might well have been fired if it had been a client meeting. He said I was right about the need to calendar and wished he'd gotten into the habit earlier.

- Bar study gives you a reprieve from, and helps combat, the endless pressures to multitask and hop superficially from topic to topic. Developing a sufficient command of the law so as to readily analyze numerous new fact patterns demands significant mental engagement. While not as deep as the level of reflection required when called on in class or writing a law review article, your thinking must be more like that exercised when analyzing a novel than when skimming Twitter, Instagram, or Facebook posts. It is important, and it is good, to give yourself time for real reflection and learning. Too many of us are used to reading on when something does not make sense, hoping that context clues will help us understand what we really do not. Part of being a professional is having the integrity and persistence to figure things out, to drill down until you truly understand whatever issue you are wrestling with, and to help others do the same.

Again, I am not unmindful of the many and varied criticisms of bar examinations and the calls to reform or do away with these tests altogether. By all means, once you pass the bar, lobby for any changes you believe are needed. However, because bar exams are fixtures for the foreseeable future, I find it far more productive for applicants and educators to focus on their benefits than to complain about them. Applicants, use your bar preparation as a time to embrace the qualities of a trustworthy and thoughtful professional. Educators, recognizing that graduates today have more debt and face greater difficulty finding suitable employment, let us offer more energy, more resources, and a greater focus on helping students pass these exams.

Many concerns about bar exams are warranted; yet even within these, one can find learning opportunities. Take the claim that bar exams are outdated; stated otherwise, "No one needs *memory* in the digital age." Applicants spend time being angry that they have to memorize rules they will be able to look up on their tablets or smartphones when practicing law. My response: even one minute spent stewing over this is a colossal waste of time and energy. Why? First, you will walk into that exam with only your brainpower and a laptop or pen, with no access to outside resources. Accept it. Bar exams will not be eliminated any time soon, and, aside from the performance-test portion, they are closed-book. So stop thinking about it until after you pass. Also, despite our smartphone culture, you will *not* always have ready access to needed information or time to look things up "in the real world." (I hate that expression. There is nothing unreal about school or bar prep. It's real, if you take it seriously.) Second, it is wonderful training to be free for even a short while from our dependency on machines. Even when you can readily look something up, the human brain sometimes makes subtler and ultimately more useful connections than machines. Machines do not reason. They tell you a rule, but *you* have to put the rule in context and apply it to particular facts. You also have to know when and how to gather additional facts. A scene from the James Bond movie *Skyfall* depicts such a moment when human thinking trumps a computer's ability to search for information. The much-younger Q is working frantically to find the location of the villain. Although equipped with the most modern, sophisticated software and programming savvy, Q does not obtain the answer that the older Bond does as the result of having connected the dots using memory and reasoning.

HOW WAS THIS BOOK WRITTEN, AND HOW SHOULD I READ IT?

This text is based entirely on my experience teaching in law schools and bar review for more than two decades. (All the stories are real, though I have changed the names, genders, and other features of certain students to protect their privacy.) I consulted nothing other than my own prior writings until I completed my first draft. After that, I undertook limited research into studies and publications relating to bar passage and found that much of my experiential knowledge is confirmed in the scholarly works addressing this subject. (References to selected bar-related sources can be found in the Bibliography.) As law school faculties embrace bar support, more research opportunities will arise. In the Teacher's Edition supplement, I suggest a number of inquiries that merit further research.

Most law student readers will start with Part I to plan for a successful exam outcome and then read Part II on repeating the exam for a hefty dose of preventive medicine. If this is your first bar exam, do everything in your power to avoid the enormous burdens of having to retake the exam. (It is critical to be able to honestly look at yourself in the mirror and know you did your very best, no matter what. You never want to say, "coulda, woulda, shoulda.")

Readers who are repeating the bar exam might start with Part II for specifics on the unique issues you face, and then read Part I to guide you to success on your next exam.

TERMINOLOGY NOTES

Traditional and nontraditional students. The term *traditional law student* in this book refers to those students who enter law school in their twenties, either just out of or soon after college. They may be working part time, but are generally not working full time. Law is typically their first career. The term *nontraditional student* refers to students in their thirties to sixties. They are often working full time or caring for young children, aging parents, and sometimes both. Law will likely be a second or even third career for these students.

These terms have limited value and can be both over- and under-inclusive. A twenty-five-year-old traditional law student may have a parent dying of cancer or other grueling family demands. And a fifty-year-old nontraditional student may be financially stable, have grown children, and have a spouse or partner who takes care of nearly all of his or her needs. Neither group has it easier. Everyone struggles with something. (And these days, most every student is oppressed on some level by the weight of financial worry.) Acknowledging their limited usefulness, the terms are still helpful to reveal common denominators with certain groups of students. I will highlight those. I will also occasionally provide notes to particular subsets of nontraditional students, such as those with young children. I do encourage all readers to review all passages, even those targeted to people in "different boats." You might be surprised to find that your own challenges are similar, and that the advice helps.

July and February Takers. This book refers to first-time bar exam takers as *July takers.* If you graduate in December or for another reason are taking a February bar as your first exam, just replace *June* with *January*, and *July* with *February*. Yours will be a winter rather than a summer time line, but what you do during the months prior to your exam will largely be the same. (The bar exam is offered twice annually, and although there are myths about one exam being harder or easier than the other, they are just that: myths.)

This book assumes that most readers will take one bar exam at a time. But many students take (and you may be taking) two bar exams in the same administration. For example, applicants may sit for the New York bar on Tuesday and Wednesday and the New Jersey bar on the same Wednesday and following Thursday (the multistate bar exam [MBE] counting for both exams). Anyone taking two bars may find helpful hints on endurance and stamina in references to three-day bar exams, such as in California. Just being "on" for three days straight is exhausting. And, while many state bar exams require a knowledge of state law and federal and modern-majority rules, taking two bars often requires knowledge of state law in two states as well as knowledge of federal and generally applicable modern-majority principles. (You will want to pay particular attention to memory strategies so that you can learn and easily recall the multiple layers of and distinctions between these rules.)

1L, 2L, 3L, and *4L.* The first year of law school is often referred to as *1L,* while *3L* and *4L* refer to the last year of law school: 3L for students in a full-time program and 4L for students in a part-time program. (This nomenclature was popularized in the 1977 novel *One L: An Inside Account of Life in the First Year at Harvard Law School* by Scott Turow.)

Intensive bar review, early start, and *bar planning.* I use the phrase *intensive bar review* to refer to the two months prior to the bar exam when law students traditionally hibernate, do nothing but study, and, typically, prepare with the assistance of a commercial bar review course. *Early start* refers to the last year of law school, especially the four-to-five-month period before formal bar review courses begin. Early-start work may be done independently, in law school extracurricular programs or curricular bar support classes, or with a review course. Early start is essential for many students—especially nontraditional students who are working or have significant family obligations while studying for the bar, as well as traditional students who have struggled in law school. *Bar planning* refers to a range of actions, from gaining familiarity with the exam to researching and enrolling in a suitable bar review course. Bar planning ideally begins on day one of law school orientation.

STATISTICS AND PERCENTAGES

This book occasionally refers to bar statistics, but *you* are not a statistic. I teach some students who have a 99 percent chance of passing based on the most reliable indicators of bar passage, law school GPA, and, to a lesser extent, LSAT scores,[3] and I teach many others whose chances of passing are statistically much lower. Students who are nearly certain to pass often feel just as much anxiety as do those who are statistically much less likely to pass. But there is one critical difference. The nervousness of those more likely to pass is countered by a belief that they *will* ultimately pass, whereas bar applicants from pools with typically lower pass rates harbor deep concerns that they

xx   PASS THE BAR EXAM

may not. Thus, a primary mission of this book is to change attitudes along with study approaches—to give bar applicants, no matter their statistical chance of passing, more tools *and* more confidence. But let me be very clear: this book is *not* about bestowing false confidence or giving hollow pep talks. It is about the determined belief that if you work hard and sensibly, and remain doggedly motivated, you can trust that you will succeed.

WHEN SHOULD I START BAR PREP?

If you are approaching law school graduation, success is nearly yours. You can practically taste it. The bar exam felt so far off in 1L. Now it's here. *Commencement* may have seemed to be a strange term after high school and college. After all, you were celebrating the fact that you were *done* with this part of your education. But after law school, not only are you not finished, you are facing the biggest test you will likely ever take. So expect law school graduation to be anticlimactic. If you are burned out by or before graduation, find a way to recharge your batteries. (Bar review usually starts right away.) You will need to be in the highest gear you have ever been in to give June and July your all.

TAKE OFF TIME IF NECESSARY TO GEAR UP FOR BAR REVIEW

A student e-mailed me about a week into intensive bar prep: "I hate bar review. I am fried. I cannot seem to get back any of the energy I had even last year." We talked. I urged her to take some time off, clear her head, and return ready: "The bar is the last lap in the legal education marathon. Picture Olympic runners, how tired and wiped out they look. Yet their jaws are somehow set, their steely determination far stronger than their fatigue. The sweat drips; you know they are aching as they move toward the finish line. Then, pure elation when they break through that ribbon! This is your last lap. Of course you're tired. You have every right to be. Take a short break. Change your scenery for a day or weekend. Or take a mental break with a movie marathon and lots of popcorn. Do whatever you need to get back into high gear with the energy to finish the race. Break out of feeling trapped in slow motion. You did not start this to give up. You owe it to yourself to cross that finish line. So step away from the stress for a moment. Get off the treadmill, rest and recharge, and then get back up and ready to run!"

If you are beginning 3L or 4L, get a head start. Use the tools in this book, and take practice exams. Your school may also have a bar support course or extracurricular bar-prep program. Starting early will help prepare you to get the most out of bar review and significantly increase your chances of passing the bar exam the first time around. (I compare early start in bar review to priming the pump to get the water flowing in a well, or painting a base coat before adding layers of color.)

If you are still in 1L or 2L, you are doing yourself a great favor by reading this now. If you are working or have significant family responsibilities, planning ahead is critical. And if you are a full-time law student, you will serve yourself well by cementing the good habits you will need and making the necessary improvements to your skills before it is too late. Focus also on physical, mental, and financial readiness. Put money aside in a bar fund if at all possible, starting on day one of law school. By knowing what to expect and planning for it, you will free up an enormous amount of energy, likely do better in school, and possibly have more time in 3L for internships and other extracurricular activities to round out your resume.

Wherever you are in the process, the bar exam is a light at the end of the tunnel. It is the main event. When you get there, you will need to give it your all, just as you will when you are trying your first case if you are a litigator, starring in a Broadway show, or climbing an enormous mountain peak. (I refer to the bar exam as the "law student's Mount Everest" so often that one former student sent me a copy of "The Man who Climbed Everest," addressed to his favorite "Sherpa," after he passed it.)

Do not dread this process. But do not underestimate how much it will take. Climbing this mountain will be tough, but exhilarating. Use every last ounce of energy. Don't hold back. Learning to commit 100 percent, with total focus, marshalling all your resources and working really hard to achieve what you seek will serve you well for the rest of your life. It will help you achieve future goals that you set your mind to.

When you express doubts or bitterness about having to take yet another test, remember: you do not just wake up one day and decide, "I'm going to take a bar exam." You *earn* the right to sit for the bar. When you walk into the first session of the first day of your bar exam, know that you *worked for* your seat in that room. You sweated and sacrificed. You made an enormous investment. To even be allowed in the door, you toiled—in both high school and college. You went through countless application mazes. You took SATs and LSATs. And you survived the trying and competitive years of law school. You earned your Juris Doctor (J.D.) degree, and you earned the right to take this test. And you are *fortunate* to be there; you are among the most educated people in the world. You are working for a license that will give you possibilities that many people will never even dream of, let alone attain.

PART I

FIRST-TIME
BAR PASSAGE

INTRODUCTION TO PART I

Part One of this book focuses on first-time passage. Bar exams differ in various juris-dictions. Some last two days, others three days; some include thirty-minute essays, others full-hour questions.[4] But all have common denominators. They are all *tough*. A lot rides on passing them. Just to get in the door to *take* the exam requires years of study, months of intensive review, and thousands of dollars invested on top of all your student loan debt. They are a big deal.

Many students fail the bar exam. Sadly, many *expect* to fail. Too many of you believe that statistics will dictate your fate. You are not a statistic. Demystify the bar exam, learn to set and achieve goals, and start working now to replace any trace of self-doubt with what will become a well-worn path of hard work and strategic training. Ban thoughts such as, "Sure, I'll try" or "I can take it again if need be." No way. From now on, doggedly pursue passing the bar. Do whatever it takes to succeed.

Equally dangerous is the trap of expecting to *pass*. Maybe your school's grades are inflated and you have a false sense of competency. Maybe you figure that since the bar exam is a pass/fail test, it can't be that hard. Or perhaps you just know you often get by without working that hard. The bar exam is different. You don't "get by." There is a good chance if you pass 1L and graduate from law school that you can pass this exam, but *only* if you work really hard, understand what it takes, and plan ahead.

Others fall somewhere in between. You may not *expect* to pass. You know and appreciate that passing the bar requires hard work. But you also do not expect to *fail*. You are generally confident about your reasoning and writing skills. You may play the odds, trying hard to figure out how to do just enough to pass, but no more. Why? I sus-pect that many of you feel so insecure about the economy and job market that you put inordinate pressure on yourselves throughout law school to rack up experiences and bolster your resumes with moot court, law review, student bar associations, competi-tions, externships, and the like. But in trying to do so much, you may have unknow-ingly sacrificed the depth of your legal education and bar success training. How many of you 3Ls or 4Ls are thinking, "I will start preparing for the bar in June, after finals. I just don't have any spare time now. I'm exhausted. I am maxed out. And any energy I do have, I need to throw into extracurricular activities. It will look good and I'll be just a bit more competitive if I serve on the board of one more student organization, compete in one more advocacy round, take on one more pro bono project. I can focus on the bar exam in two months. I'll be fine."

If you can handle the extracurricular activities, OK. But you must realize that an additional line or two on your resume will *not* make up for failing the bar exam. So be sure you are on target in the way you spend your time. If you are struggling in school, make the bar a priority. Take the time during law school to read this book cover to cover, and plan ahead so you're not taken by surprise and find you just don't have enough time to do it all in June and July. Take your current classes seriously so you don't have to learn in bar review what you could have mastered in school.

Bottom line: Do the work, slowly and steadily. Do whatever it takes. Make it your *business* to pass.

ALWAYS BEAR IN MIND THAT YOUR OWN RESOLUTION TO SUCCEED IS MORE IMPORTANT THAN ANY OTHER THING.

— ABRAHAM LINCOLN —

WHAT ARE SOME TRAPS TO AVOID?

Some students are too busy with work or family to devote the time necessary for bar studies. Some don't pass because they don't enroll in a reputable bar review (or don't do the work in the course they sign up for). Others find themselves doing too much "bar learning" when it should mostly be review. Students may be told by upperclassmen, professors, or bar review salespeople that they can easily pick up subjects in bar review. Many 3Ls, for example, have taken an impressive array of electives but have not taken courses addressing criminal procedure, remedies, or business organizations. When we discuss bar planning and they realize how much they have to catch up on, they panic. The need to learn a lot of new material often sets in motion a negative cycle: students are reluctant to take practice tests when they don't know the law, so they postpone skills practice, and then end up even further behind the curve. Two full-time months may be sufficient for bar *review*. It may not be enough to learn several new subjects, review every other subject, and develop the skills needed to pass.

"IT'S A FUNNY THING ABOUT LIFE: IF YOU REFUSE TO ACCEPT ANYTHING BUT THE BEST YOU VERY OFTEN GET IT."

— W. SOMERSET MAUGHAM.[5] —

1

SET YOUR GOAL AND COMMIT TO SUCCESS

- Do You Really Want the Esq. or Only the J.D.?

- Why Do You Want to Pass the Bar Exam?

- Believe You Will Pass, and Mirror that Belief with "I Will" Language.

- Watch Your Language: In Law School, in Bar Prep, in Life.

- Bust the Sources of Self-Doubt.

- Eliminate the Threat of Stereotypes.

- Sometimes it Helps to Toughen Up or Let Things Roll Off.

- Celebrate Your Mistakes.

- Know and Exemplify the Ten Common Denominators Among Those Who Pass the Bar Exam.

- Return to Your Goal, in Print.

Declare your commitment to success. Include the date you will *sit* for the exam. Say it out loud; then write or type it: *I **will** pass the* [enter your jurisdiction and administration date] *bar exam!*

"A GOAL IS CREATED THREE TIMES. FIRST AS A MENTAL PICTURE. SECOND, WHEN WRITTEN DOWN TO ADD CLARITY AND DIMENSION. AND THIRD, WHEN YOU TAKE ACTION TOWARDS ITS ACHIEVEMENT."

— GARY RYAN BLAIR[6] —

SITTING FOR THE BAR EXAM

What an expression! It's a sensible one given its Old English origins, but this phrase—which simply means "taking" the exam—may sound a bit silly. Ever wonder, "*What am I gonna do? Stand and write for days?*" Sounds more like a tapas bar than a bar exam. But isn't it fitting that we still insist on using an expression that is so formal, or, some might say, arrogant? Own it. Think of it not as silly or pretentious, but as elevating the process. You're not going in just to *take* a test. This *is* special. Your future rides on it. You are preparing to *be* the lawyer, the top dog, the woman or man in charge, someone potentially responsible for people's lives and livelihoods. On test day, you will be on an interview before your state's bar examiners. So prepare now to "sit for" *and pass* the bar exam!

The first and most critical step is deciding what *you* want. Whether you are contemplating going to law school or are in the middle of your studies, or you have already graduated and just received a heavy stack of bar review books, there is still time to make certain you *really* want this: to be a licensed member of the bar.

Are you thinking: "What the heck does she mean, 'Do I want it?'" Don't take the question as insulting. Too many people fail bar exams because they don't really want to *be* lawyers, or aren't ready to assume such a significant responsibility.

I graduated law school at age 25, and one of my first clients was an engineer in his sixties who had been forced to file for bankruptcy. His wife, children, and grandchildren depended on him, and he was looking to *me* for advice. That was intimidating, and humbling, but it taught me more about "professional responsibility"—what it means to be a lawyer and how daunting that can be—than any reading or study ever had or would. (I often think that professional responsibility training during law school should require all law students to be clients in at least one matter, just as those seeking psychology degrees often have to undergo counseling, to see what being on the "other side" feels like.)

And so I ask, with the utmost respect, *are you ready* to be *responsible* for other people's lives and livelihoods? (Remember, you will not be alone. You will likely work for and with other lawyers who can and will guide you if you ask for help. Even those who start solo practices will find plenty of mentoring resources. But you must seek them out.) This question is not meant to put a damper on anyone's enthusiasm, but simply to get you thinking so that you can acknowledge, and eliminate or at least diffuse, any concerns that may unintentionally and/or unnecessarily become obstacles to bar passage.

Some people went to law school to fulfill a parent's dream. Others opted for law by default. Many are put off by how difficult it is today to find decent law jobs. Some dread the life of a lawyer, perceiving all attorneys as drowning in billable hours. These are reasonable concerns. It is not crazy, even after having invested and succeeded in law school, to have doubts about pursuing law as a career. However: *Do not let career concerns lead to failing the bar exam.* First pass the exam; **then** deal with the doubts.

"THE DESIRE OF REWARD IS ONE OF THE STRONGEST INCENTIVES OF HUMAN CONDUCT; ... THE BEST SECURITY FOR THE FIDELITY OF MANKIND IS TO MAKE THEIR INTEREST COINCIDE WITH THEIR DUTY."

— ALEXANDER HAMILTON[7] —

DO YOU REALLY WANT THE ESQ. OR ONLY THE J.D.?

For certain graduates, the J.D. (juris doctor degree, the law school diploma) *is* the end goal. They have no need or desire to become licensed to practice law. Many second- and third-career students begin law school as successful professionals in their fields. They desire the legal education and degree to enhance their earning capacity and expand their employment opportunities. Many do not take the bar exam and never regret that decision. If you are questioning whether to pursue a law degree alone or also your law license, make that decision *now*, before you begin bar prep. Commit to either taking the bar *and* passing it, or not taking the exam at all.

If you think you will ever want to take and pass the bar exam, you will likely be well served by taking it as soon as possible. But you may have good reasons for never wanting or needing the license and happily decide not to take the exam. That is fine. What is *not* fine is taking the exam without being fully invested in passing it.

Every year students ask, "Why shouldn't I just take the exam for the heck of it and see if I pass? I came to law school only for the J.D., and I'll be satisfied with the J.D., but it would be *nice* if I did pass." No, no, no. I cannot say it enough: do *not* go in and wing it! If you don't really want the license, *do not take* the bar exam. Here is why:

- Even if you think you aren't invested in the process, your ego will be. You will get caught up (at least to some extent) in the bar exam frenzy. You cannot avoid it. Sitting for the exam—just being in those testing facilities with other bar takers—will set in motion a host of expectations. You will be disappointed in yourself if you don't pass. Even if you know you didn't work for it, your confidence will take a hit.

- Others may think less of your capability. People will learn that you took, but did not pass, the exam. They won't know that you weren't really trying to pass. All they will know is the results. It "sounds" better to have not ever taken the exam than to have taken it, failed, and then stopped trying.
- It reflects very poorly on your law school. Law schools are judged by bar passage rates. Even if you desire just the J.D., you still want your law school diploma to be as prestigious as possible, right? You owe it to yourself and your classmates, and to anyone who ever has or will put your school's diploma on the wall, to try your hardest to pass. You may not have ever thought of it this way, but "winging it" on the bar exam is truly an affront to your law school colleagues.
- It is a colossal waste of time and money.
- Lastly, it's just good practice to do your best at everything you undertake. Success will follow.

There are some tests you can and should take just to see how you do and to learn from the experience: a simulated bar exam, practice tests generally, and the PSAT, for example. But once you get into the world of exams that count, including the SAT, LSAT, MCAT, GRE, CPA exam, and the bar exam, do your best. The bar exam especially, for the reasons discussed above, should *not* be treated as a "practice test."

Why Do You Want to Pass the Bar Exam?

Sometimes, you must clarify *why* you want to pass the bar exam in order to sufficiently prepare for it. (If you don't really want it, you are more apt to be lured away from studying.)

Years ago, a student approached me during the lunch break of a daylong bar review seminar and told me this would be the tenth year (and the twentieth time) he was taking the bar exam. We talked at length. (His story was far more riveting than any lunch imaginable; I couldn't even think about eating.) It was readily apparent that he knew a lot about law and was very bright. He was also an incredible overachiever. He had come to the United States with nothing and built a life for his parents and his children. He had built a thriving practice as an interpreter and volunteered in an adult ESL program. "What was the hindrance?" I wondered. "Why wasn't this person passing the exam?" I finally thought to ask him how he envisioned life once he passed the bar. He immediately launched into a tirade about how passing the exam would change his life drastically—and *not* for the better. Every lawyer he knew was overworked and bitterly unhappy. Becoming a lawyer had been his parents' dream, not his own. He was happiest teaching English to folks from his native country and helping them become Americans. He didn't want to give that up. But none of the lawyers he knew had any time for volunteer work. Suddenly everything clicked. I made him promise that he would make no changes whatsoever to his life for at least six months after the next bar results were out, regardless of whether he passed or failed. I immediately saw a weight visibly lift from him. We even talked about waiting for a while to open the results envelope to find out whether he passed or failed. (This was in the days before results were posted online.) It turned out that he passed. Was it because some self-imposed pressure to change had finally been lifted? When we talked again, he told me that he still wasn't sure what he would or wouldn't change or whether he would ever practice law, but he was proud of himself for finally passing the bar. I will never know for certain what made the difference, but I have since talked with a number of students who failed two or three times because they weren't ready for whatever they thought they would *have to* do after passing the exam.

What will passing the bar exam mean for you? The goal is that it will *open* doors and create opportunity, rather than saddling you with obligations you don't want.

Believe You Will Pass, and Mirror that Belief with "I Will" Language

Earlier, I asked you to put your commitment to passing the bar in writing:

"I will pass the [enter your jurisdiction and administration date] bar exam."

The wording is not conditional. You are not saying "I *might* pass the bar exam." You are not promising to go in and give it your best shot, thinking that you can always take it again. No! You are saying that you *will* pass this exam. (Note: *This is not:* "I will because I always succeed" or "I will because I deserve to." *This is:* "I will because I am determined to do what it takes to pass, no matter how difficult and time-consuming.") Think about great trial lawyers who have won dozens of cases. Most will *not* tell you that the more they win, the more they wing it. On the contrary, they are apt to prepare more and more carefully as time goes on (perhaps more efficiently and effectively, but no less carefully.) Watch really successful people. Most work very hard at what they do.

You would not have gone to law school in the first place if you weren't a person who thrived on challenge. So I will tell you what I tell every one of my students, "*Don't you dare* go into that bar exam and merely give it a shot. Invest in success, train for success, and see that you obtain it."

To quote Yoda, "Do or do not ... ***there is no try.***"[8]

WATCH YOUR LANGUAGE: IN LAW SCHOOL, IN BAR PREP, IN LIFE.

The great basketball player Michael Jordan once said, "You have to expect things of yourself before you can do them." How do you think of yourself? How do you talk to yourself?

Ask the right questions to get the right answers. Think of yourself *and speak of yourself* as someone who can *and will* succeed. (And if you feel you can't honestly speak to yourself positively because you truly doubt that you'll succeed, read the next section to "bust the sources of self-doubt" and then return to this passage on reframing and rephrasing self-talk.)

Change the tone and content of your own inner dialogue (something totally within your control) to empower you in the quest to achieve your goals and propel you toward success. Consider the following examples:

- *Thought*: Why **can't I** get a higher score on these practice tests?
- *Rephrase*: How **can I** do better on these practice exams next time?

- *Thought*: This easements and covenants stuff [or whatever subject you find challenging] _____ is so difficult. I'll *never* understand it.
- *Rephrase*: Maybe I need to reread the explanations for these questions a couple of times in order to get this. Or, maybe I need to find a different explanation of the concept, one that makes more sense to me. But, I will get it eventually.

- *Thought*: I'll never be able to sit and focus for three days. I can't go ten minutes without checking my phone before I get antsy.
- *Rephrase*: I have a challenge before me to build the endurance needed to focus on the days of my bar exam. I will have to wean myself from all distractions, including this phone, a little bit each day. In two weeks, I should be able to focus for at least two hours in a row and in four weeks for four hours straight. I will then train in four-hour blocks going forward so that I'm ready to perform when I must be *on* and focused during the bar exam.

- *Thought*: There is no way I can write an answer that is as good or detailed as this model answer. I can barely retype what this person wrote in the time allotted.
- *Rephrase*: I am reading sample and model answers to learn from them. I am not taking the bar exam tomorrow. I have time to absorb this way of thinking and writing. The more I read and retype these answers, and study how someone derived an answer from a particular fact pattern, the more I will be able to mimic the style and the easier it will be for me to write answers that are this

QUIZ

How will you describe your feelings about the bar exam when you are midway through bar review in late June? Choose one of the following:

a. I'm dying here—trying to study for the hardest bar exam in the country!
b. I am taking the bar this July and hoping like hell that I pass.
c. This is the worst summer ever; knowing my luck, I'll probably be taking it again in February.
d. I'm training for success on this July's bar exam. The experience is giving me an opportunity to review and solidify all the learning I have done for years. I'm becoming a stronger and more skilled reader, thinker, and writer. I will do this. I will pass the July bar exam.

organized and lengthy within the allotted time. Whether I feel it or not, I know that I improve, learn something, and increase my speed and accuracy with each practice test I take. I just have to keep going. I can do this.

Your self-talk might not be quite as corny as that in the quiz above, and you may use different phrasing, but you get the point. Beware of slipping into negative language and self-defeating thoughts. Stay vigilant. It will be hard to maintain a positive attitude for all eight weeks. You will get tired. You will get frustrated. You will get sick of it. But this book will talk you through those places where people tend to get stuck. Keep it handy. Reread passages any time you start to feel burned out or doubtful and need extra "juice." Remind yourself constantly that you CAN do this, and that you WILL do it. Keep these thoughts in your psyche every minute of every day until the proctors call "Time" at the end of your exam. Say them out loud and frequently. Post them where you will see and read them several times each day.

BUST THE SOURCES OF SELF-DOUBT.

Why *write* your goals? We are biased to believe what we see in print. And you can talk a good talk. You can *say* you want anything. You may well have chosen law because you were a persuasive speaker! But there is a difference between merely wishing or hoping on the one hand, and doing what it takes to make something happen on the other.

This book is about achieving; it's about winning. It is about how to *do*, not just dream. So if you haven't already written or typed the commitment, get out your pen, laptop, tablet, or phone. Write or type: "I will pass the [enter your jurisdiction and administration date] bar exam." Print the commitment if you did not handwrite it.

Are you thinking, "How can I possibly write or type that I *will* pass when I *don't* believe it?" Fair enough. Let's look at common doubts, and expose them to daylight, so that you can dismantle and let go of any remaining blocks and focus from here forward on *how* to succeed—rather than on *whether* you will succeed.

- *Doubt: "My school's bar pass rate is only 60 percent. What if I'm in the 40 percent that doesn't make it? Isn't it presumptuous for me to say 'I will' when statistically 40 percent of my classmates won't?"*

No, it is not presumptuous at all. *You* are not a statistic. And the reason you are reading this book is because you want to make certain YOU are in the pool that passes. (And if your entire law school class adopts this attitude, all the better! I often point students to the quote, "*A rising tide lifts all boats,*" which was initially a reference to the economy but is wholly applicable for classes of bar takers. Positive peer pressure can help you all.)[9]

If your school generally has lower pass rates, you need to work harder and more efficiently than you ever have before. Step up your game. Throw everything you've got behind this. Use statistics if they provide positive peer pressure, but don't let them dictate your fate. You are in control.

If *you* had a low GPA or ranking within your class (and your chance of passing the first time is therefore statistically lower), ask yourself why you earned the grades you did. Problem-solve now. Did you not understand the material in certain classes? If not, consider getting a tutor for and/or spending extra time on those subjects. You will also likely understand things better the second time around.

I am reminded of a student who approached me in bar review confessing he had not understood anything in his law school evidence class, but that it had all come together in bar review. Had he let his low grade in that class dictate his *ability* to master the material for the bar, he would have failed the exam. Instead, he threw himself in, engaged fully in bar review, found that the rules made much more sense than they had in school, and passed the bar. The key to his success was admitting and facing his weakness. In a way, he was fortunate that his professor gave him a low grade; it was his wake-up call. Law schools do students no favors by inflating grades.

Did you not have enough time to study in law school? Maybe you were working while taking courses. Or maybe you have a family and had to spend time caring for them. Can you devote the next few months to preparing for the bar exam? Take out loans if you must, but figure out how to give yourself more time to study. (One of my students passed on the third try because a family member stepped up and offered her a $5,000 loan if she would stop working for six weeks before the exam and give it her all. She did, and it paid off.)

YOU ARE NOT A STATISTIC UNLESS YOU LET YOURSELF BE.

The buzz at your school may be that anyone with a GPA below 2.5 has only a ___ percent chance of passing. If that blank is anything less than 100, you are rightfully concerned. But concern need not lead to defeatism. After all, since when do important things in life come with 100 percent guarantees? Referring to the outcomes of lawsuits, one of my favorite professors would often say, "Toasters come with guarantees; lawyers do not."[10] Stop focusing on the numbers, and concentrate on learning and improving your skills each and every day. My motto is simple: "Worry less; work more."

- *Doubt:* "I don't think I can pass. I've kept this a pretty good secret and managed to pass all my classes, but there is a ton of law I just do **not** understand. I took real property, but never really got easements and covenants. I took contracts, but I don't understand consideration or promissory estoppel. And don't get me started on civil procedure! I couldn't explain *res judicata* if my life depended on it."

No worries. While I urge you to do as much early work as possible so that bar review is mostly "review" and not new learning, some intensive bar prep will involve learning new information. Even if you took every subject in law school, the bar exam tends to cover a wider breadth of material than did most law classes; you will thus continue to memorize new rules (often even up until the day before the exam). This is fine. Do not stress out. While bar review covers more material than was presented in law school courses, the bar exam tests concepts in less depth than do most law school finals. (You can never "learn it all," but you don't have to for the bar exam. You just have to learn enough to pass.) Master the major concepts and areas as soon as you can. If you can do this in pre-bar early start, it will help a lot. If you cannot, as long as you are intensely focused and enrolled in a reliable bar review (in which you participate fully and actively), you should be able to readily learn what you need to know during two months of full-time study. (Notice I said "readily" and not "easily." It is not easy.) It isn't too late. *Now* is your time. Now you *will* master all those rules and concepts you didn't cover or understand in class. How can I be so confident?

- First, bar review will likely present rules and concepts in a more straightforward manner than you experienced in law school. In class, law professors try to hide the ball, training students to think like lawyers. But bar review conveys the material straight up.
- Second, hearing concepts again will allow them to sink in. They will be easier to understand this time around because they will sound familiar and you already have a greater basis for understanding. You are not starting from "square one."
- Third, much of the "new" material you will learn, especially when answering practice MBE questions, involves refining what you already know, as well as adding an array of narrow exceptions or subparts to your basic understanding of certain concepts. For instance, it is easier to understand when double jeopardy attaches than to comprehend what this right fundamentally protects and why. One of the best ways to learn new rules is by studying explanatory answers to sample questions, which is another reason to take lots of practice tests.
- Fourth, you have a greater incentive to really learn it all now! You will work as hard as you need to in order to "get" everything you didn't understand before. If for some reason your bar review doesn't explain a critical concept in a way that makes sense to you, you will find another resource and make sure you get it. You will go in to the bar exam feeling more confident and knowledgeable than you ever imagined. And it will feel great.

CAN YOU EXPLAIN THE RULES TO A LAYPERSON?

If you are weak in a particular subject or subjects and think you will "get by" and pass the bar anyway despite your lack of understanding, think again. Aim to understand every main concept and rule in your outlines well enough that you could explain it to a layperson. Test yourself: Think quickly. Explain "negligence" to a very smart sixteen-year-old.

To a very smart sixteen-year-old? Yes. Your torts professor likely referred to "the reasonable person." I often refer to the fictitious "very smart sixteen-year-old." Why? It helps students picture someone who has no legal training but is intelligent and eager to learn. Imagine that you are explaining a certain legal concept to a niece or nephew, or to the son or daughter of a friend or neighbor. You have to break points down simply, but you would not want to sound condescending. Can you do it? Go ahead. In the space below, explain "negligence" to a very smart sixteen-year-old:

_____

_____

_____

_____

_____

- *Doubt:* "Where exactly do you expect me to get this confidence from? No one in my family ever graduated from college. I'm supposed to pass the bar exam the first time around? Yeah, right. It takes students like me two or three attempts to pass."

You might fear that passing the bar is a goal that's simply too ambitious. It isn't. Few people who really *think* embark on anything big without at least some fear. The key is not to let the fear stop you. Use it. Turn it into adrenalin. Let it make you more motivated. You are not your family. You went to law school. You got in. You finished One L and may even have graduated by the time you are reading this. You have resources.

You have support. People in your school and in the greater legal community will help you if you reach out.

If your family is not helpful or does not believe in you, find others who do. You would be surprised how many lawyers would want to talk with and help you. I am constantly amazed by the outpouring of generosity from alumni who want to give back.

Let's go back to the stated concern: *It takes students like me two or three attempts to pass.* What exactly do you mean? Whatever your background, there are lawyers who share your challenges. I am thrilled to be writing this book at a time when I doubt any current student would be the "first" of any particular minority group to join the legal profession. (If I'm incorrect, I apologize.) To find support from someone who *gets* you, if you do not have that in your school or family, reach out. Cast a wider net. All you need is one person to believe in you to help you believe in yourself. (And do not be too quick to rule out everyone in your law school. People with different challenges may nonetheless empathize and be supportive.)

ELIMINATE THE THREAT OF STEREOTYPES.

Studies show that negative stereotypes can be self-fulfilling prophecies.[11] Get rid of them. (Many of my nontraditional students express how *old* they feel to be taking the bar exam. They doubt that they can compete with the "kids." But once we talk about this and they hear from alumni who are often older than they are, they are better able to let go of their concerns.) *Do not sit for the bar exam feeling inferior because of your age, ethnicity, gender, disability, or any other stereotypical reason.* Know that many others in the room feel exactly the way you do, for their own reasons. Let go of your doubts. Think of yourself simply as a bar applicant with challenges, like many others, who is doing his or her best. Your best *is* good enough.

Do not for one minute think that my suggesting you let go of stereotypes means that I don't believe they exist, that I don't understand, or that I think it is easy to let go of them. They do exist, and we all internalize them to some extent. But when you are putting yourself on the line as you will be when taking the bar exam, you must put the negatives out of your mind, at least temporarily. I am not suggesting denial; I am proposing a deliberate compartmentalization. You must build a gate around the doubts and shut them out during bar prep and the bar exam.

Take a hard look at those people "like you" who *have* passed. And stop thinking about anything that defeats you or interferes with your confidence until *after you pass.* *Then* fight prejudice, dismantle stereotypes, and make the world a better place. The wonderful thing is that *when you pass*, you will be able to use that positive experience of shattering a stereotype to help you believe that you can do so again and again in the future. (Remember the "lifelong cycle of success" I wished for you in the beginning of this book? Breaking stereotypes and busting doubts are integral steps in the process of achieving your goals.)

SOMETIMES IT HELPS TO TOUGHEN UP OR LET THINGS ROLL OFF.

It is critical that we point out and combat inappropriate bigotry and sexism. But if one professor or classmate does not seem to value your opinion, or if you sense that someone does not believe in your abilities, it might help (especially now) to let it roll off. You control what you let bother you. Work hard to keep the negatives out now. And toughen up. You chose *law*. This is not a profession or training ground that specializes in nurturing. You will find many who are arrogant and treat you as "less than." It does not mean you are. Know who you are and why you are in law school. Work harder in law school and to pass the bar exam than you have ever worked on anything *because you want to be your best*. Let not the ignorance of any one person hinder your pursuit of your own success. And *do not* let stereotypes that you might hold about yourself, or that others might believe about you, get in the way.

- *Doubt: I have crazy test anxiety. While I'm studying, I basically believe I'll pass; but when test day arrives, I freak out. How can I confidently say I will pass this, the biggest test of all?*

Acknowledge legitimate fear without letting it block you. This *is* a tough test. (In some states, it's tougher than others, but it's not easy anywhere.) If you weren't at least concerned, there would be something wrong with you. (And if you aren't concerned at all, take a simulated bar exam.) The key is to turn nerves into adrenalin rather than letting them paralyze you. If you let it, fear can become the most powerful of motivators. It will make you stronger and more prepared for success.

No one is suggesting that you should not be concerned. You can be scared and still pass. You simply cannot say you don't believe in your own ability to pass, and you cannot let yourself freeze up. Find tools to help you stay calm and to work through test anxiety. Look at the strategies suggested in Chapter 7, including reading aloud under your breath (subvocalization). Being prepared and having the right tools will greatly reduce text anxiety.

"WE GAIN STRENGTH, AND COURAGE, AND CONFIDENCE BY EACH EXPERIENCE IN WHICH WE REALLY STOP TO LOOK FEAR IN THE FACE ... WE MUST DO THAT WHICH WE THINK WE CANNOT."

— ELEANOR ROOSEVELT —

CELEBRATE YOUR MISTAKES.

An interesting professional trait, cultivated from the first days of law school and often continuing into law practice, is a fear of risk-taking and an overabundance of caution. For law students, this fear may begin when one is humiliated in class by an arrogant law professor or put down by classmates in a study group of blowhards. The theory behind some of this "training" is to toughen students up so they will not cave when facing a hostile judge or contentious opposing counsel. Sometimes it strengthens students, but sometimes it makes them all the more fearful. For practicing lawyers, it may originate from and be (quite reasonably) perpetuated by the ever-present cloud of malpractice threats. Fear of making mistakes pervades the minds and files of litigators, and can become an oppressive and stressful life theme of the lawyer. Identify this fear as a professional hazard now. Use bar preparation to break the pattern before it becomes ingrained. When you make mistakes on practice tests, be happy. Errors are opportunities to get the concepts right on the actual exam.

In contrast to lawyers, successful business people often "celebrate" mistakes—or at least do not fear them the way lawyers do. In some industries, if a business person isn't making mistakes, the assumption is "he or she must not be trying hard enough, must not be taking enough risks, or must not be very innovative or cutting-edge." In law, however, people tend to avoid mistakes at all costs. We are trained to think through the "parade of horribles" in excruciating detail, to walk the "slippery slopes" up and down until we find and assess every possible ramification of every conceivable outcome—all so that there are no mistakes. We internalize this fear of making mistakes and thereby suffer. Caution may indeed be the mark of a good lawyer; an ounce of prevention (or Preventive Law) can sometimes save your client millions of dollars (and may help ward off malpractice suits).[12] But if you can develop a thick skin and know that *some mistakes are good*, or at least okay, you may ultimately find more solutions and greater success. Again, in bar prep, celebrate your mistakes. From them, you can learn the root causes of your errors and avoid mishaps on the actual exam.

KNOW AND EXEMPLIFY THE TEN COMMON DENOMINATORS AMONG THOSE WHO PASS THE BAR EXAM.

Read each denominator and the notes below it. Find your own way of making these denominators nonnegotiable aspects of your bar prep experience.

1. You decided you want to pass the bar exam.

You are determined to pass it. Think positively as much as possible: "I *will* pass this bar exam." You have not set yourself up to fail. You NEVER say anything like:

- "I'll just try it out and see what the test is like." (NO!)
- "I'm too busy to study now, but I'll knock it out at the last minute. I always do." (No way!)
- "I can always take it again, right?"

You don't torture yourself now thinking about exactly what your job situation will be. You want to pass; you are doing everything you can to pass; and you will figure out the rest in time.

2. Your priorities are in line with your decision to pass.

You are someone who studies when your schedule says to study. Period. You regard every study appointment with yourself as if it were an appointment with a world-renowned specialist whom you've waited six months to see and who has the cure/treatment you desperately need. Your priorities are studying, sleeping, eating right, and exercising. You have put off everything that can wait until after the bar exam. (Chapters 4 and 7 will help you with this process.)

3. You have a plan for bar success that includes enrolling in a reliable bar review program, and you have funds in place to pay for the course.

You have drafted a bar exam business plan. (See Chapter 2.) You have made a commitment to invest in yourself by seeking help from experts and enrolling in a reputable full-service bar review. You have set up a bar fund. If need be, you will take out bar loans or work as a "rep" (someone who helps recruit others to take the course) to finance your own bar review course. Your plan also includes time off from work, child care, household help, and any other assistance you may need.

4. You have a study schedule.

You have calendared exactly how you will *implement* your plan each day. You have calendared what, where, and when you will study. You have done this by fusing the bar review course schedule with your personal calendar. You have a work area where you can focus. And you have posted your schedule somewhere visible so that those you live with know when you are studying and when you will make time for them. Chapter 7 walks you through the process of creating and updating your study schedule.

5. You have eliminated or reduced distractions.

You don't answer e-mails, phone calls, texts, or IMs while studying. You focus. You don't go into chat rooms to read about everyone else's freak-outs. You don't worry about what people predict will or won't be on your exam. You study everything that the examiners say may be tested, concentrating most on what your bar review indicates is most important. (Chapters 4 and 9 will help you battle distractions.)

6. You look things up that you don't understand. You learn before you memorize.

You can explain all the relevant rules simply and clearly to someone who has no legal background. If you can't, you look stuff up until you can. (Chapters 5 and 8 will help you determine what you know well and what you still need to learn.)

7. You avoid negative people.

You recognize the "negative voices" and avoid them. They may come from people you love or total strangers. They may be blunt and belittling ("Why do you think you are smart enough to be a lawyer?"). They may be passively destructive ("Why are you away from your desk? If you keep taking time off like this, you'll never pass.") They may be experienced lawyers reminiscing about their "bar exam horror stories."

Too many people share their negativity. Some do not know how to be positive. Others may be genuinely afraid for you. But you are on the road to success. Don't waste time or energy now trying to understand why someone makes a negative remark; just step away. Chapter 6 will help you clarify who is supportive so that you can surround yourself with positive influences. Put off (or put out) those who are not helpful, at least until after the bar. (This may be one piece of advice you should heed far beyond the bar exam.) Yes, it's good to be mindful of some critique and open to suggestions for improvement. But why do many successful artists avoid critics' reviews? They can be stifling and harmful.

8. You are routinely taking practice tests in all of the areas to be tested, not worrying about scores but working to constantly improve.

Every day, you take practice tests under timed conditions. After completing these tests, you compare and contrast your answers with sample answers. You take away concrete methods to improve after every practice session. (See Chapter 8.)

9. You have handled all of the details concerning exam day.

You have the clock you will bring into the exam. You have read all of the instructions about what you may bring in with you and how it is to be contained (you know about clear plastic bags). You have made all of your hotel reservations ahead of time and have paid all of your bills. You won't be sitting in the bar exam distracted by whether the dog was fed, or feeling cold because you forgot to dress in layers. You have taken care of everything—now all you have to do is pass. (More on this in later chapters, especially Chapter 9, which focuses on the home stretch.)

10. You have planned something FUN after the exam.

You will be taking yourself and perhaps someone you love to Tahiti, or another special place, once the exam is over! Or you will be buying something big that you, your family, or significant other has very much wanted. If you are on a tight budget, plan a laughter-filled potluck at a beautiful local park. Just make sure that you and those who sacrificed with you have something superb to look forward to. (Chapter 10 looks at what happens after you take the exam.)

"THE TEST BEFORE US AS A PEOPLE IS NOT WHETHER OUR COMMITMENTS MATCH OUR WILL AND OUR COURAGE; BUT WHETHER WE HAVE THE WILL AND COURAGE TO MATCH OUR COMMITMENTS."

— LYNDON B. JOHNSON —

RETURN TO YOUR GOAL, IN PRINT.

Have you written or typed your goal yet? Hopefully you now see that the doubts that may have prevented you from expressing your goal with conviction are reasonable, but that you can transform your fears into challenges rather than roadblocks. Once you identify and articulate those challenges, you can problem-solve, find a way to trust yourself, do what is required, and move forward on the path to success.

If you still refuse to write, "*I will pass*," figure out why. A thoughtful person should indeed have a healthy respect for the exam; courage is pushing through fears and moving forward despite them.

Write or type; then print and post:

"I WILL PASS THE _____, 20__ BAR EXAM."

DEVELOP A PLAN FOR SUCCESS: YOUR GPS TO BAR PASSAGE

- Success Time Line:
  From Orientation to Graduation
  - Orientation: Get the Most Out of It.
  - 1L: Plan for Success from Day One: Look Ahead.
    - Become a critical bar reader.
    - Know your strengths and weaknesses.
  - Upper-Division Law Students: Build on Your Foundation and Continue Moving Forward.
    - Think carefully about the coursework you select in law school.
    - Incorporate practice exams into your study schedule.
    - Develop a bar success plan.
    - Logistics
    - Resources
    - MPRE
    - Moral Character
  - Six to Twelve Months Before the Exam
    - Learn about your bar exam.
    - Embrace the eight-week countdown.
- Planning for Bar Exam Success
  - Draft your bar success plan.
- Early Start: A Good Idea for Everyone—and Essential for Nontraditional Students and Those Who Are Not Excelling in Law School
  - What should I work on in early start?
  - Early-start questionnaire for nontraditional students

Imagine driving across the United States without a map or GPS system. Unless you are taking a route you travel regularly, even short journeys require road maps. Intensive bar preparation is a "long, strange trip" (apologies to the Grateful Dead). You need your "GPS"—what I call your success plan. And you don't want to be frantically pulling together in June and July what you will need to execute that plan. Start early.

This chapter gives you a bar exam time line (a snapshot of what is likely to come up in the various planning stages) and then helps you draft your plan. Like a business plan, your success plan should take into account the time, funding, and training required to pass the bar exam. Later chapters refer to study schedules that set out when you will execute the tasks in the study portion of your plan. Both bar exam success plans and study schedules are "living" documents, meant to be revised and updated when you encounter challenges or new ways to maximize your productivity.

Knowing what to expect and seeing it in writing will help you plan ahead so that you can carve out the time and pull together the money necessary to avoid last-minute obstacles. Drafting your bar exam success plan and posting your study schedule also helps secure "buy-in" from family and friends. (More on help from family and friends in Chapter 6.)

DON'T BE BLINDSIDED BY UNEXPECTED COSTS.

Many students don't realize they will have to pay for a bar review course *after* law school. Others budget for a review course, but are caught off guard by bar fees and costs, as well as summer living expenses. (In addition to the costs of a review course, there may be fees to register with your state bar, to sit for the exam itself and to take the MPRE, and to process your moral character application.) Some people end up having to drive long distances on exam days because they did not plan for and cannot afford to stay in a hotel near the exam site. Others try to cut expenses by skipping a reliable bar review course—only to fail the exam and incur far more debt repeating it than they would have had they properly invested the first time.

SUCCESS TIME LINE:
FROM ORIENTATION TO GRADUATION

Some say bar success begins in June. This is not correct: it should begin on day one of law school orientation.

Orientation: Get the Most Out of It.

Faculty members put a lot of thought into orientation. Their advice will help you succeed every step of the way. But because it is all new, you do not always grasp the importance of what is said. And they often present more information than you can absorb in one sitting. Also, most people (you included) are likely nervous. Many wonder:

1. *Are all of these people smarter than me?* The answer to this one is simple: no.
2. *Will I do as well here as I did in college?* Similar thoughts present themselves with every new academic challenge. But, looking back, was high school that much harder than middle school? Was college more trying than some of those tough AP classes in high school?
3. *Will I be humiliated in class?* Maybe. If so, you will live through it. Most lawyers experienced a few rough grilling sessions when they were students. For some, these sessions turned out to be beneficial. (I know of at least one incident in which a person who was grilled for an entire hour in class was later given a job offer in part because of having survived that ordeal.) Do not take it personally, and do not let it bother you. Rarely, if ever, are students *graded* on the quality of in-class responses. And most professors grade anonymously; what happens in class and on exams is entirely separate.
4. *Will I make friends?* You may be checking out your future classmates, wondering whom you will like and who is the nasty competitive type you should avoid. Remember that this is professional school. Consider your classmates as colleagues. They will remember what you said and did. They may refer clients your way for decades to come, or give you leads about coveted jobs. Some may even end up being your law or business partners.

So, despite the nerves and distracting thoughts, pay as close attention as you can during orientation. Record the names and titles of the people who speak. Write down any helpful tips. (If you need something, recalling advice that person gave at orientation can be a great icebreaker to ask someone, as well as an opportunity to begin a positive relationship with that person.) Start an "Orientation/Law School Administration" file. Continue to keep track of people you connect with and services the school offers. Knowing whom to talk to when you have a concern can mean the difference between succeeding or not.

ORIENTATION WORKSHEET

(Note points made and who made them as soon as possible after orientation.)

TITLE	NAME	NOTES
Dean of Students	_____	_____
Director of Academic Support	_____	_____
Director of Financial Aid Services	_____	_____
Career Planning and Placement	_____	_____
[ ]	_____	_____
[ ]	_____	_____

1L: Plan for Success from Day One: Look Ahead.

I will never forget being invited as a guest speaker to talk about bar preparation at a law school orientation. I was simply asked to give a preview of what to expect down the line—and to let the students know that the better they planned, the more likely they would be to pass the bar exam. The dean of the law school also spoke, and, in addition to other brilliant advice, she told these (largely nontraditional) students that one of the most important keys to success in law school and on the bar exam for those with children was to be good to the grandparents! She urged this group of incoming students to build strong networks so that they could free up the time they would need for law school and bar study. She emphasized the importance of thinking ahead and delegating as many responsibilities as possible, including child care.

You can take some of the steps listed below, such as becoming a critical reader, from the very beginning of law school. Other later steps in this section, such as taking the MPRE and working on your moral character application, merit attention in 2L and 3L.

Become a critical bar reader.

The most important factor in bar success is critical reading. (This is likely the most important part of success in law school and law practice as well.) Get into habits such as circling the words *and* and *or*. Underline key terms. Annotate in the margins. Read aloud. Look up words you do not know. And reread passages you don't understand.

(More on critical reading in Chapter 8.) Maintain these habits and improve this skill throughout your years in school.

LAW STUDENT ACTIVE-READER QUIZ

If you are currently in school, consider your habits. Read the statements below and place a **T** for **True** or an **F** for **False** in front of each one.

____ I read the Table of Contents before I read my assigned cases to see where they fit into the course as a whole.

____ I read hornbook passages about assigned cases to help put the case law into context within the subject as a whole.

____ I brief every case myself (rather than relying on "canned briefs").

____ I write my course outlines on an ongoing basis as I progress through the material.

____ I write my own course outlines rather than (or in addition to) studying from commercial outlines.

____ I listen carefully in class.

____ I take notes and combat distractions from others in class.

____ I try to restate case holdings in my own words.

____ I look up words I don't understand.

____ I am in a study group or have a study buddy, and we explain rules and concepts to each other.

____ I have found that I study more effectively alone, so that is what I do.

____ I have tried to explain what I'm learning in law school to friends and family who are laypeople.

____ I read the notes and questions following cases in the casebook.

____ I diagram the scene or relationships of the parties in a case as I am reading the case.

____ I write notes and thoughts in the margins of my casebook; I don't just "highlight."

____ I note points that I do not understand or agree with when I read.

____ I read the dissenting, as well as the majority, opinions.

____ I write flash cards with the holdings of cases on them, as well as definitions of terms I look up.

____ I read in a well-lit area and try to do most of my reading when I'm not too tired.

The more **True** answers you have, the more engaged you likely are in your reading.

LAW SCHOOL TIP: READ CASES MORE THAN ONCE.

Disabuse yourself of the notion that you'll "get it" after reading a case just once. Simple cases that you understand after a first read are gifts. You will have to read and reread most of them. And, you may still not get it after a second read, but only after you think, take notes, read the casebook author's notes and maybe a hornbook passage that relates to the rules regarding this type of case, and then read the case yet again.

Know your Strengths and Weaknesses.

Learn how to identify weak areas and strengthen them. Consider the following:

Do you understand the reasoning in the cases you are reading? Are your reading and writing skills weaker than you would like them to be? Do you know how to take notes? Are you having a hard time concentrating in class?

Be aware of gaps in your legal education, such as areas within subjects you are taking that your professor did not cover or that you don't understand. Plan your class schedule thoughtfully (which courses you should take, and why). Did you get a particularly low grade in any classes? Are there subjects you are uncomfortable with?

Skills. Pay attention during midterms and finals to become aware of skills you need to improve, such as reading or typing faster. You may be able to improve in these areas, especially if you start early.

Physical health. Get in the best shape possible. If you have an exercise routine, continue it. If not, start one. Exercise consistently during school, bar preparation, and beyond. It helps relieve stress, increases your energy and acuity, and often makes you sleep better as well. Get your eyes tested regularly, and schedule a general physical exam if you have not had one recently. And tell your doctor if you have any concerns so that they can be addressed right away. (A student came to office hours toward the end of 3L describing back pain she feared might prevent her from sitting for three-hour blocks during the bar exam. She had been tough and suffered through the pain all through law school. I urged her to seek treatment immediately. Hopefully, that would help relieve the pain, but, if not, she needed to begin documenting the condition as soon as possible in case she needed special accommodations during the exam.)

TESTING ACCOMMODATIONS

Being granted accommodations for a disability in law school does not mean you will receive accommodations on the bar exam. If you have a disability and believe you would benefit from having accommodations on the bar exam, research what your jurisdiction requires and how to make such a request. You may need a well-established paper trail, so consult the appropriate medical experts and keep every bit of information you receive from them. Do not wait until the last minute. Often the documentation requirements are more stringent for the bar exam than in law school, and the process may take a long time.

STILL IN LAW SCHOOL AND PLANNING FOR SUCCESS?

Give yourself one point for every **Yes** answer and two points for every **No** answer.

____ Studying is my number-one priority.
____ I am actively taking steps to improve my lifestyle or maintain an already healthy one (through exercise and nutrition).
____ I usually get a good night's sleep.
____ I see how law school class discussions differ from law school exams.
____ I'm working on improving or maintaining effective time management.
____ I'm actively combating distractions.
____ I sign up for extracurricular activities only if I have time for them.
____ I am selective about extra responsibilities I commit to.
____ I prepare my own outlines.
____ I regularly take practice tests and study model answers.
____ I ask questions when I don't understand rules and concepts in law school.
____ I change my study and reading methods when they are not working for me.
____ **TOTAL**

What was your score? If you scored in the 10–12 range, excellent! You're on the way. If your score falls in the 13–16 range, you have some work to do, but you can turn things around. If you scored in the 17–20 range, you should do some reassessing soon.

Upper-Division Law Students: Build on Your Foundation and Continue Moving Forward.

For full-time students, this refers to 2L and 3L, and for part-time students, this extends through 4L.

Think carefully about the coursework you select in law school.

Consider taking all or most bar subjects offered, even if they aren't required courses. I say *consider* because studies don't indicate a strong correlation between having taken all or most bar courses and bar passage.[13]

It's true that you may learn more and develop stronger legal analysis, reasoning, and writing skills by taking an elective course that you are "into" than by taking another bar course. I am certain that the many clinical courses I took in law school were instrumental in my having passed the bar exam the first time. These courses focused not only on legal analysis but on factual analysis in a way that proved critical on essays, MBEs, and (especially) performance tests. (In fact, if you aren't taking a trial advocacy or other clinical course in law school, I would highly recommend doing some reading about fact analysis. See selected works by Professors Paul Bergman and David Binder in the Bibliography.)

It's also true that some of the best course selections are so because of the particular professor teaching the course. It can be transformative to study with someone who inspires you or with a leading scholar in a particular field. On the other hand, being nervous about a subject or thinking it's too hard is not a good reason to avoid taking a bar class during law school.

So, since I've noted good reasons to take courses other than bar courses and acknowledged that studies don't show a strong correlation between law school curriculum and bar passage, why am I suggesting that some students are well served by taking as many bar subjects as possible during school? Because bar review can be far less stressful when students are *reviewing* material, rather than learning it for the first time. Some people are downright freaked out when they realize how much brand-new material they have to master. (In certain bar review lectures, such as one about community property in California, I have made it a habit to ask how many students took the class in school. The answer used to be nearly everyone, but is now only about half. The terror in the eyes of many who didn't study the subject in school is hard to ignore, even if I know they can learn what they need to know to pass the bar exam.)

So my suggestion here, *to at least consider taking all or most bar subjects offered*, is just as much about your comfort level with having to quickly learn new material as it is about your ability to learn what you need to. If you decide for good reasons not to take certain classes during school, make time to study at least an introduction to those subjects on your own *before* bar review begins. For example, during winter or spring break in 3L, get a reliable hornbook, study guide, or audio or video lecture that gives an overview of the subjects. Begin slowly but steadily taking practice tests in all subjects that will be tested on your exam, including those you haven't studied in school. Take them open book if you need to, but get into the habit of taking them. (More on practice tests below and in Chapter 8.)

IN LAW SCHOOL AND NOT DOING WELL?

How far off are you? If you are close to being on target, you may simply need some fine-tuning or minor adjustments. Obtain practice tests or released exams with sample passing answers, and study them. Start by trying to find your own professors' past exams. Many law libraries and ASP faculty keep them and will give you copies if you simply ask. Professors often will do this, too. (Students frequently share stories of their grades significantly increasing after they have found the courage to talk to their professors and ask them for help.)

If you are further off the mark—for instance, if you are getting Cs, Ds, or Fs or are on or near academic probation—find out why and get help now. Use your school's resources. Beware of commercial entities preying on law students' fears and trying to sell you solutions. There are no quick fixes. You need to figure out for yourself or with the help of a reliable resource what you need to adjust. Are you not devoting enough time to your studies? Are you genuinely not getting it? Have you tried hornbooks to help pull the material together, reading things twice or three times? Do whatever it takes. Seek reliable feedback to learn where you are and why, make a turnaround plan, and get back on track. Talk with your professors and academic support faculty as soon as possible.

Incorporate practice exams into your study schedule.
Practice tests are like exercise: continuing the habit is easier than starting it. Begin with bar subjects you are taking in school. Let's say you are in Constitutional Law. Well in advance of the final, locate copies of any released exams your professor has on file. Ask your professor if you cannot find these on your own. Next, determine how this subject is tested on your bar exam while the principles are fresh in your mind. Get some Constitutional Law essay questions from your state bar's website (or a reliable bar review), and obtain some Constitutional Law MBE questions. *Do not, however,*

study these as a substitute for studying your professor's past exams. Bar exams differ from law school exams. But while you are studying the subject (or shortly thereafter) is a good time to at least familiarize yourself with how it is tested on your bar. You will be well served all through law school by regularly taking practice tests (law school exams, preferably those written by your professors, and occasional past bar exams so that you become comfortable with those testing formats and begin to develop bar-related skills). The more comfortable you are taking practice exams, the better you will likely do on actual exams.

CHALLENGES IN READING OR WRITING ENGLISH.

If you aren't confident that you can produce grammatically correct, well-written answers, work on this far in advance of your bar exam. Again, seek help. Answer as many practice questions as possible, and study sample answers. Retype them in full so that you not only learn the law but become familiar with the proper phrasing of rules. Also, get into the habit of reading popular publications to become familiar with colloquial terminology, expressions, or idioms that may appear in fact patterns. (A criminal law burglary question asked about a defendant breaking into a gazebo. Some students, unfamiliar with the word *gazebo*, missed the issue of whether it was a "protected structure.")

Develop a bar success plan.

Begin drafting your bar success plan (discussed later in this chapter). If you are working during law school, save up vacation days and organize your finances and job responsibilities so you can take as much time off as possible in June and July.

Start a bar fund. Seed it with what I call "a latte a day." Even without interest, about $3 per day will total more than $3,000 by the end of law school—a solid start for bar review. You may need more for living expenses, so try to save more if possible. Put any gifts you get during law school into the fund, and save part of any money you earn during school if possible.

If you know your family won't be supportive of your need to "hibernate" the summer before your bar exam, get them used to this by "disappearing" during law school finals. Lay the groundwork so they will not be shocked when you are suddenly not available very often after graduation. (Chapter 6 provides tools, including letters for family and friends, that describe the stress you are under and how they can help. You can use these letters during school, too, by replacing the words *bar exam* with *final exams*. Or let them read this whole book.)

Logistics

You may have to register with your state bar as early as your first year in law school, usually completing forms and paying fees. Check with your school and your state bar, and be sure you are in compliance.

Resources

Keep lists of useful websites, such as those of the National Conference of Bar Examiners and your state bar. Become familiar with these websites and what they have to offer. Develop a relationship with your school's ASP and bar support faculty.

MPRE

Take and pass the MPRE in 2L or 3L (for full-time students) or in 3L or 4L (for part-time students). Make sure your score meets the licensing requirements in your state. (More on the MPRE in Chapter 3 and at www.ncbex.org.)

Moral character

Find out what your state requires to be considered fit for licensing. Many states require that separate applications be completed to be certified as having the requisite moral character. These may take time to complete and time to process, especially with budget cuts in many state bar offices.

Six to Twelve Months Before the Exam

In addition to the points below, this is a good time to determine who will be supportive of you during intensive bar prep and who won't. You should also begin to prepare family and friends for what is to come, and to line up care for children, elderly relatives, pets, etc. (More in Chapter 6.)

Learn more about your bar exam.

To successfully strategize about how to achieve a goal, begin at the end: know exactly where you are going and what to expect. In bar exam terms, know what will be tested, in what order, and in what form.

The good news is that unlike law professors, bar examiners tend to reveal nearly all their cards. There are few major surprises. The questions will cover the material the examiners say they are testing, and typically in the format used on previous tests. Bar examiners give ample notice when they change the testing format, and often release and post past questions and sample answers or outlines.[14] As a colleague often says, "You are *not* going to walk in and find that Question #1 is written in German."[15]

Know how much each part of the exam is worth. This will likely be in your bar review materials. But why wait? Find out by reading your state bar's website, consulting your ASP faculty, or reviewing the comprehensive guide published by the ABA and the National Conference of Bar Examiners.[16] On the Uniform Bar Exam (UBE), the essays are worth 30 percent, the performance tests are worth 20 percent, and the MBE 50 percent of an applicant's total score. Obviously, a student taking this exam who wrote tons of practice essays and took numerous PTs, but relatively few practice MBEs, would be at a distinct disadvantage. On the California bar exam, the essays are worth 39 percent, the PT 26 percent, and the MBE 35 percent. (PTs are worth only 26 percent of the total, but each PT is worth twice what each essay is worth; a strategy favoring this component may thus compensate for a lower score on certain essays.) In New York, essays are worth 40 percent, NY multiple-choice questions 10 percent, the MBE 40 percent, and the MPT 10 percent.

What subjects are tested, and in how much detail? Your bar review course will help you devise a study plan to learn everything you need to know. But, your memory "disk space" is limited; you will want to know which subjects to emphasize and which to hit more superficially. It may be wise to spend more time on areas that you know either will definitely be tested, or are tested frequently, than on those that are tested less commonly. For example, about thirteen subjects are tested on the California Bar Exam, depending on how you define them. Six of those are also tested on the MBE, so you know they will be covered. They may also be tested in certain essay questions, but because you will have to answer multiple-choice questions about these subjects, it is sensible to give them more time and attention. Further, MBE questions tend to be more detailed and more law oriented than essays. It is therefore helpful to have more finely tuned knowledge of the rules in MBE subjects. Strategizing in advance will help you work efficiently, maximize your time, and not burn out. (More on strategies for different types of bar exam testing in Chapter 8.)

PREDICTIONS AND BETTING THAT A CERTAIN AREA OF LAW WILL NOT BE TESTED.

Giving more attention to frequently tested areas does *not* mean hoping something won't be tested, betting on that, and skipping the area altogether. I have seen students do this largely for two reasons: 1) they feel weak in a particular area and decide to ignore it and hope it won't be on their exam, rather than tackling it until they have gained the requisite competence, or 2) a bar review instructor or law school professor says that area won't be tested on this bar.

I happen to work closely with someone whose ability to predict what will appear on the bar exam is legendary. His success rates are extraordinary. If I could get him to predict the stock market with equal accuracy, he, I, and a number of our friends and colleagues might well be multimillionaires. I nonetheless advise everyone to regard any predictions, even his, with extreme caution.[17] You should make certain you are very comfortable handling questions in those areas. If they are tested, you can smile with secret delight at your "edge." But do *not* bank on anyone's predictions. Do not try to "game" the exam. Prepare for questions on every topic the examiners say may be tested. End of story. (And if you don't believe me, ask a number of lawyers about those bar exam horror stories I mentioned in the introduction. Many will tell you they faced questions on topics that their bar review course instructors assured them would not be on the test.) If the examiners say it is within the scope of tested areas, learn it.

In addition to learning what is tested:

- Gather reliable materials to learn any subjects tested on your bar exam that you didn't, or won't, take in law school. Study those.
- Do a pre-bar-review overview of all subjects, particularly of areas you didn't cover or didn't fully understand in classes you did take. Start a folder on each subject.
- Complete or update your bar success plan.
- Work on the moral character portion of your bar application. As noted above, you may need to start on this even earlier depending on your jurisdiction.
- Enroll in a reputable bar review. (Note: You may enroll in a bar review in 1L, perhaps receiving a substantial discount. Your school may offer a deal with a par-

ticular bar review. Make sure your bar review is right for you. More on choosing a bar review in Chapter 5.)
- Become aware of how you spend your time and what distracts you. (See Chapter 4.)
- Begin doing some open-book testing with all question types that will be on your bar exam: essays, MBEs, or PTs.
- Review your bar fund. Hopefully, you have been stashing away money since orientation and now have enough to pay for the bar review course (in addition to having some time off from work if you are working), but now is the time to research bar loans and scholarships if your fund is low. Figure out a way to obtain the money you need to get the expert help you deserve. Do not opt to skimp on bar review because you don't have the money. If you fail the bar exam, your costs will multiply and it will be even longer before you can begin paying back your student loans.

Embrace the eight-week countdown.

We will look in detail at, and plan for, intensive bar preparation in later chapters, but, as a preview, think about this sequence: 1) finals, 2) graduation, and 3) a pile of bar review materials to master!

Ideally, your bar review will give you a solid schedule, taking you through subject by subject and covering everything tested on your exam in about seven weeks. The schedule will tell you what to do and in what order. Hopefully, your bar review will also provide faculty to answer questions if you are unclear about certain concepts. In bar review, you will also

- go to or listen online to lectures reviewing the law tested on your bar, noting heavily tested areas and distinctions where your exam requires knowledge of state and federal law;
- read outlines that provide summaries of the relevant law you need to know for each subject;
- develop testing skills by attending essay, MBE, and performance-test workshops; and
- answer practice questions, study sample or model answers, and submit your own answers for grading and critique.

Grossly oversimplified, June will be slow and overwhelming; July will fly by and be filled with adrenaline. The most important place to start will be with your bar review schedule. Stay on track. You may need to add extra practice tests to your training routine, but, at a minimum, do everything your bar review schedule calls for. In addition, get on a regimen of daily MBEs, regular essay writing (every day or every other day, writing essays out in full and outlining others, which can be done open-book if you are doing this before July), and weekly or biweekly performance-test drafting. In other words, take the basic bar review calendar and blend it with your own needs (exercise, sleep, work or family obligations) and extra preparation, so you know exactly how to stay on track. (Chapter 7 will discuss study schedules and help you create one suited to you.)

Midway into June, you will want to begin taking a hard look at your skills and substantive knowledge, assessing where you are weak and adjusting your schedule to target any weaknesses. Make every effort to stick to your bar review, avoid distractions, and cement what is hopefully now your regular practice test routine. Don't be overly concerned with scores, but focus on your training by completing the questions under timed conditions, studying answers, and self-assessing to improve. Your goal is to learn and improve each and every day.

By the end of June, you may need to fight burnout. You will have come through what essentially amounts to four to five weeks of finals. (How tired were you in school after any single final exam?) But seeing the calendar turn from June to July will bring a boost of adrenaline. You can finally see light at the end of the tunnel and know that you are in the homestretch. On July 1, you will still be nearly a month away from taking the bar, though, so you must pace yourself. You don't want to peak too early and be exhausted by the time the exam comes.

At least a week, if not two weeks, before the exam, you will likely be finishing the formal bar review schedule, having looked at least briefly at all the subjects covered on your exam. You will want to complete a simulated exam and learn from that experience. And, by a week before the exam, you should have completed one-page "cheat sheets" for every subject on your exam. (I will never forget one of my law school professors, shoving paper in his back pocket to demonstrate, saying, "*Pretend* that you were going to cheat on the exam and you could fit only one page of notes on each subject in your pocket. What would you write on those pages? Get that ready at least a week before the exam." It was a graphic demonstration, and very helpful advice!)

The week before the exam, you will also take care of last-minute test day details, deciding what you will wear, eat, and take into the exam. (Review the rules on what your jurisdiction allows in the exam room!) You'll want to plan your exam day mornings and evenings, as well as your lunch breaks. Chapter 9 provides strategies for how best to structure your bar days and nights, based on what works and what to beware of.

You will walk out of the exam exhausted, most likely not knowing how you did. (Don't worry. My suspicion is that people who are certain they passed may not have seen all the issues. I am always happier when people tell me just after the exam, "Well, I don't know how I did, but I did my best.") You will be enormously relieved that it's finally over. But the next few months of waiting for your results will weigh heavily until the moment of truth arrives (a day that varies between jurisdictions, but is often in November). Either you will have passed and can celebrate, or you will need to dust yourself off and prepare to pass the next exam.

Again, this time line is an overview. All of these stages will be detailed in later chapters. And each person may experience these stages differently. This time line is intended only to give a basic sense of what lies ahead.

Let's turn now to look more closely at advanced planning tools.

DO NOT MAKE RADICAL CHANGES DURING BAR REVIEW.

It's not the time to experiment with a new diet or quit drinking coffee. Do those things if you want to *after* your bar exam! Be careful about what you eat, and try to eat healthfully. You need power meals. You may need to limit caffeine and sugar because you want and need sustained high energy, not short-lived bursts of pep that will subsequently leave you feeling down and sometimes even more tired. But this is not a time to go cold turkey, especially on something you depend on.

PLANNING FOR BAR EXAM SUCCESS

Business plans start with mission statements. Yours is the goal you put in writing in Chapter 1: to pass the [*insert date and jurisdiction*] bar exam. Many or even most of your resources will be directed toward achieving that goal.

Note: For some people, deciding where to sit for the bar exam is easy. They know where they want to work and therefore where they must take and pass the bar. Others must decide where they want to live and work, and sit for the bar exam accordingly. This is a fundamental question. If you need help in determining the best place or places for you (some people want or need to be licensed in multiple jurisdictions), talk to your mentor, trusted faculty, or your school's career services staff.

After clarifying their mission, successful businesspeople typically research what they will need to do and plan ahead before launching their enterprise. Because intensive bar review begins immediately after graduation, your window for this preparation phase is during your last year of law school. Nontraditional students, especially those in four-year part-time programs, need to get their plan together by the beginning of fourth year.

Note: Traditional students need to plan ahead and dedicate two months to full-time study. Nontraditional students need to plan ahead and dedicate six to eight months to part-time study.

Planning ahead will prevent problems, reduce stress, and increase the likelihood of your passing the bar the first time around. It will allow you to focus on your studies and get in shape for peak performance in June and July. You may have pulled all-nighters before finals in college or law school, "learning it all" the week before an exam, but you cannot pass the bar exam that way. (As my colleagues and I often say, "The bar exam is a marathon, not a sprint.")

Among the planning steps to take, do the following during your last year of law school, well before graduation:

- Get a handle on bar subjects you never took or learned in law school. If there are either subjects you never studied in law school or areas you studied but never really understood, take some time in your last year of law school to at least read through a good hornbook or study aid on the subject.

DON'T BLAME YOUR PROFESSORS OR YOUR LAW SCHOOL.

Don't fall into the useless trap of blaming your professors for not teaching everything you need to know. For example, it might be great if every torts class covered every possible area tested on the bar. But many torts professors go into such depth regarding intentional torts and negligence that time runs short when considering defamation and economic torts. But this is not a problem. The depth of study in the areas you did cover taught you how to learn the rules. Would you have wanted a class that zoomed through everything so fast that you covered everything, but did not understand anything? Of course not. You needed the depth to master the analytical skills. It allowed you to learn how to learn. From now on, spend your time doing that instead of complaining. Learning and studying will get you to bar passage; complaining will only compound your frustration. For the rest of your life, there will be things you do not know and need to learn. (Before appearing in court, you will study so the judge doesn't ask questions you cannot answer.) This is your opportunity. Learn what you need to know now, and learn it well. And be thankful that you have learned how to learn.

- Start exercising. You will need this stress release during bar review. If you do not have a daily exercise routine, start one now. I am *not* suggesting you try a new sport or do anything strenuous that you are not used to. You don't want an injury now. But if you are currently not very active, you will be surprised by how much better you will feel and handle stress after adding even a daily walk into your routine.

- Take care of business. Whatever details you think you may have to deal with in June and July, handle them now (or put them off until after August). Examples include arranging for child care or pet care during bar review and the bar exam, buying birthday presents ahead of time, and paying bills in advance if you can. Anything you don't have to concern yourself with during the summer means more time for studying and getting yourself primed for success.

WORKING STUDENTS

Especially if you are working full-time, consider part-time, flextime, or remote work opportunities; and look into vacation time, unpaid leave, and any other ways to free up as much time as possible to study during the months just prior to your bar exam.

- Research (and, if possible, assemble) the resources you will need. Using the business metaphor, if you know you will need administrative assistance to run a company, you will want to secure funding to pay personnel and perhaps even begin interviewing candidates ahead of time to find the best employees. If you have not yet enrolled in a full-service, reputable bar review, you will need to sign up for one. If you start early, you can shop around. Look at the materials different companies produce, check out their websites, chat with their representatives, and talk with recent graduates who passed your bar exam and ask them what they liked and disliked about their bar review.

You will also need time and money, as detailed below. A business needs to operate efficiently and productively to make money. This may require start-up capital, equipment, personnel, and a physical space to operate. To facilitate first-time bar passage, you will need

- a budget and funding to pay for things like test fees, bar review, and lodging;
- time dedicated to study (a lot of time!);
- an efficient calendaring system;
- a good place to study (somewhere you can concentrate);

- reliable resources to learn from; and
- "buy-in" or support from your inner circle (or the tools to distance yourself if they are not supportive, as outlined in Chapter 6).

"BEFORE EVERYTHING ELSE, GETTING READY IS THE SECRET OF SUCCESS."

— HENRY FORD —

Drafting Your Bar Success Plan

Start filling in the information in the worksheet below, and you will have the basics of your bar success plan. You will also see more clearly what you still need to do to prepare to pass.

The Basics: Bar Exam Administration

I am sitting for **and will pass** the
_____
(fill in administration)

bar exam on _____ in _____
(fill in dates)   (fill in location).

Website for my state bar for bar exam rules and filing requirements:

_____

Website for additional information on any multistate tests my bar includes:

_____

The deadline for timely filing of my application to sit for the bar and the date exam fees are due is:

_____

I have completed my state bar's registration requirements. ☐ Yes ☐ Not yet

I have booked travel arrangements and lodging ☐ Yes ☐ Not yet
(or calendared the dates I will do so). _____

I have completed my jurisdiction's moral character requirements. ☐ Yes ☐ Not yet
(Note: these may be quite complicated and take a great deal of time to complete.
Be sure to research the requirements and filing fee information. Also, get reliable
advice before completing your paperwork if you have concerns about anything
in your past or present that might reflect poorly on you, including *but not limited
to* brushes with the law, mental instability, substance abuse, dishonesty, or certain
financial problems such as bankruptcies that suggest evading creditors.)

The Basics: About My Bar Exam

My bar exam lasts for _____ days and tests the following subjects:

_____

_____

_____

_____

_____

_____

The forms of testing (e.g., essay, PT, MBE, other) on my bar exam include
a(n) _____ portion, worth _____ percent;
a(n) _____ portion, worth _____ percent;
a(n) _____ portion, worth _____ percent; and
a(n) _____ portion, worth _____ percent.

Bar Review

I am enrolled in _____ commercial bar review(s).

Dedicated Time

I have dedicated _____ hours per week to bar exam study beginning _____, 20_____.

I will increase that number of hours to _____ as of _____, 20_____.

For working students: I have taken a leave from work to focus on my bar studies.
☐ Yes ☐ No

If I could not take off entirely, I have reduced my work hours from _____ to _____ for my bar studies.

I have cleared my calendar in May, June, and July of anything (professional, social, or otherwise) that can be put off until August, including:

_____.

I am still working to find ways to defer:

_____.

(List events and commitments that you know or predict will require your participation in June and July. Identifying these well ahead of time will help you figure out how to either put off or manage them.)

Managing Distractions (See Chapter 3)

I have identified the following as potentially taking time away from my studies:

_____.

My biggest distractions tend to be:

_____.

I will eliminate/reduce the following distractions and defer the following obligations from May through July:

_____.

Bar Exam Budget
I have already paid for or set aside money in a bar fund for the items below.
☐ Yes ☐ No

If not, I plan on working now to secure loans, gifts, or other funding for the items below:

Registration with my state bar or board of bar examiners: $_____

Sitting for the bar exam (filing fees): $_____

(Be sure to calendar deadlines so you avoid late fees.)

Taking the MPRE: $_____

☐ (If you have not yet passed the MPRE,
    enter the date you are retaking it here)

_____

☐ (If you already took and passed the MPRE, check here)

Submitting the moral character portion of licensing process: $_____

Any incidental costs, such as fingerprinting fees: $_____

Travel to and from the bar exam test site: $_____

Hotel and food at the test site: $_____

(Reserve hotel room well ahead of time, as hotels fill up fast.)

Time off from work for bar studies: $_____

Child care/housekeeping during bar studies: $_____

Trip or something fun for myself or my family or
significant other after the bar exam: $_____

Estimated total of funds needed: $_____

Funds I currently have: $_____

TOTAL FUNDS I STILL NEED TO OBTAIN: $_____

COST-SAVING TIPS

- Calendar deadlines to avoid late fees. These can add up to hundreds of dollars.
- Enroll early in a bar review course (sometimes there are savings for early registration).
- If flying or taking a train to the exam site, book reservations early.
- If there is a choice of location, pick a less-expensive one. (Larger states may have more than one test site. Some may be in cities where hotel and meals are significantly cheaper.) For example, in California, a hotel in Century City may run close to $250 per night, whereas a hotel in Ontario may be $150 or less.) Of course, balance this with extra costs, if any, of traveling to a more remote site.
- Find a hotel with a refrigerator, and bring or buy some of your own food. (Not only will it be cheaper than hotel food, you will also have more options to choose from.)
- An after-bar trip does not have to be costly. If funds are tight, then consider camping weekends, local outdoor day trips, picnics, movie days, and more.

Written Study Schedule (See Chapter 7)

I have a written study schedule ☐ Yes ☐ Not yet
or I will create a written study schedule by _____.

The following are places I know I can study effectively, without interruption (e.g., office, home, law library): _____.

My study schedule includes my "study office hours" that I will post so it is clear to everyone in my world when I will be busy studying and am not to be interrupted.
☐ Yes ☐ Not yet

My study schedule includes hours for specific tasks, such as:
- Listening to bar review lectures   _____
- Reading and studying bar review outlines   _____
- Attending bar review workshops and completing
  all assignments   _____
- Creating my own summary outlines   _____
- Memorizing the law   _____
- Outlining practice essays and reviewing sample answers   _____

- Writing practice essays in full under timed conditions and studying sample answers   _____
- Completing MBEs under timed conditions and studying answer choices   _____
- Writing PTs in full under timed conditions and studying sample answers   _____

Calendaring System

☐ I have a central location (program or book) where I log all my deadlines, appointments, etc.

☐ I have an effective reminder system.

Confidence and Motivation

At this point, my greatest strengths going into bar exam preparation are:

1. _____ .

2. _____ .

3. _____ .

At this point, my biggest concerns going into bar exam preparation are:

1. _____ .

2. _____ .

3. _____ .

Other Bar Planning Issues

Health issues:

I have taken steps to deal with any health issues that might interfere with my ability to do my best on the bar exam. ☐ Yes ☐ No
(If you have received accommodations in law school and expect to receive the same or similar on the bar exam, you must complete the necessary paperwork for that.)

I have had my vision and hearing checked in the past year. ☐ Yes ☐ No

Dependent care:
I have taken steps to arrange for any needed care for children, older or ill relatives, pets, etc. ☐ Yes ☐ No

EARLY START: A GOOD IDEA FOR EVERYONE; ESSENTIAL FOR NONTRADITIONAL AND WEAKER STUDENTS

Nontraditional students generally have less time to study than do traditional students. They typically cannot take off all of June and July and do nothing but study as many traditional students do. To stay competitive (and pass the bar), nontraditional students must start *before* June. Those whose law school GPAs fall below typically passing numbers in their school also must start early.

Chapter 8 details how to tackle performance tests, bar essays, and multiple-choice questions. Here, the focus is simply on how to use each type of test *in early start* to get your feet wet, as well as how to incorporate practice tests into your routine in a low-stress way. Remember, in the introduction, early start was defined as the four- to five-month period before formal bar review courses begin, which thus occurs during your last year of law school.

What should I work on in early start?

One of the best places to start is on performance tests (PTs). (If your jurisdiction's bar exam does not include a PT, move on to the discussions below about multiple-choice and open-book essays.) Each multistate performance test (MPT) is a ninety-minute test; each California PT is a three-hour exam.

PTs test lawyering skills in "real-life" situations. You (the bar applicant) will role-play a lawyer, or other legal professional such as a law clerk or legislator, in a mock situation in which you perform basic tasks within the time allotted. To excel in performance testing, you must demonstrate proficiency in legal analysis, factual analysis, problem solving, awareness of professional-responsibility issues, and resolving ethical questions. You must also organize information well, manage time efficiently, and communicate with clear, effective writing.

Why start with performance tests? PTs are skills-based exams and are essentially open-book. They require little or no memory. The earlier you develop a strong command of PT skills, the more time you will free up in June and July for essay and MBE training. These are exactly the months during which you will need to ramp up, especially on memorization. You must memorize many rules for the essay and multiple-choice portions of the bar exam. Because memory fades, at least some memorization must be done closer to the exam. In contrast, skills that you develop well become part of you. Drafting PT answers is a bit like riding a bike; once you learn how to do it competently, you don't forget. So invest the time early on to master PT skills, and train extensively by taking at least a dozen practice PTs. (I remind my students throughout the third and fourth years, "If you think that it feels like too much in March or April to invest three hours to take one California PT, or ninety minutes to take one MPT, imagine how you will feel in June." Trust me, you will look at the time block required for one PT and calculate how many MBEs you could take in the same time. When you realize you could complete 50 MBEs in the time it takes to take one MPT (and 100 MBEs in the time you must dedicate for a single California PT), you will torture yourself over deciding the best use of your time. You *cannot* ignore PTs. But, you can alleviate some of the stress they cause by simply mastering the PT in early start.

You can also train early by answering practice MBE questions. Answer daily sets of MBEs, beginning several months before intensive bar prep. To ease in, start in familiar areas such as torts or criminal law. You will review and learn rules by answering the questions and studying explanatory answers, but just as important, if not more so, in early start, is getting into the *habit* of reading this sort of question, and getting a handle on how MBEs are phrased and formatted. Eventually, you'll want to take practice sets in all the subjects. Do not worry in early start about getting a high percentage correct. Just get in a routine of taking MBEs daily, always taking advantage of the opportunity after each question set to learn from the careful study of quality explanatory answers.

In addition to getting practice MBEs from your bar review or other commercial sources, you can also obtain them from the National Conference of Bar Examiners at their online bookstore.[18]

When you take practice MBEs in early start, you can afford to spend more time than the 1.8 minutes per question suggested on the actual MBE. In June and July, you *must* train under timed conditions. When you first start taking practice MBEs, though, you might benefit from going through them slowly, one at a time, reading a question and then the explanatory answer right away to lock in the reasoning and understand why the correct answer is best and the wrong answers are not.

It will also help to write bar essays well ahead of June. I know; you are thinking, "There's no way I can write essays on subjects I haven't studied in years. I don't remember any law." Yes, you can. Just write them open-book. Do what you can by issue spotting, organizing, and applying the rules you know; then look up the other rules. Looking up and writing out rules will help you learn and memorize them.

While they are fresh in your mind, be sure to put any rule statements you look up and learn into a memorizable form, such as paper or electronic flash cards, outlines, flowcharts, or checklists. Organizing and assembling memory tools is another great thing to do in early start; it frees up precious time in June and July.

Get in the habit of writing out your essay and PT answers in full so that they reflect the length, depth, and organization required for a passing answer. Study sample answers and self-assess your performance. (See Chapter 8.) Many state-bar websites list past questions and answers that you can download for free. If you aren't motivated on your own to do early-start work, you may want to enroll in an early-start or supplemental program so you can turn in your answers for review and critique.

Early-start questionnaire for nontraditional students

In addition to working ahead, *thinking* ahead will help prepare you for the two months of intensive review. (And even if you start early and will be working in June and July, you still need to raise your level of intensity during the summer.) For nontraditional students, planning ahead is essential. Below is a list of questions to think about as you look ahead to bar success. Fill them out for yourself, and perhaps share them with a mentor or bar support professor.

Can you take off any time from work before the bar exam? How much time can you take off, and exactly when (June? July?)

_____

What will your study schedule look like, and when will it begin?

_____

_____

_____

What bar review courses are you taking, and why? Are you attending a live class? If so, is it flexible if your work and other commitments prevent you from attending classes? What bar review courses are you taking at regular times? Is there an online alternative that may be more convenient for you?

_____

_____

_____

Do you have a mentor or supportive person to help you stay on track?

_____

Can you study effectively at your place of work?

_____

Do the people you work with know that you are studying for the bar exam?

_____

Can you study effectively at home?

_____

What are you doing to get rid of summer distractions so you can focus fully on studying?

_____

Do you have young children? Do you have reliable child care? Do you have grandparents or other relatives who can take care of your children? (Regularly? In an emergency?)

_____

You are more likely to be married than traditional students. Bar season is not the time to pick fights with your spouse or significant other. It is not the time to make major household or family decisions. Ask yourself, what might come up in June and July that you could take care of in March, April, or May? And what can you delay until August?

_____

_____

If any of these questions trigger ideas about issues you can plan for, weave them into your bar success plan above. Remember, it is a living, working document, meant to be adapted so that your onward march to success is as efficient and productive as possible.

CLIMB THE BAR EXAM MOUNTAIN; TRANSITION FROM STUDENT TO PROFESSIONAL

- Hard work is not glamorous, but it is the most important part of success.
- What are the dos and don'ts of hard work?
- Visualize yourself as a lawyer.
- Draw upon your inspiration.
- Ethical Rules and Professionalism
- Fees, Fingerprinting, and Forms
- Professionalism at the micro level: Act in a professional manner every day.
  - Communicate carefully, respectfully, and in a timely manner.
  - Write and send e-mails wisely and professionally.
  - Read the e-mails that are sent to you.
  - Return calls and e-mails promptly.
  - Be careful about what you post on Facebook and other social media.
  - Be organized.
  - Meet deadlines, be on time, and comply with rules.

Some think of the bar exam as a bridge between law school and law practice. I see it more like a mountain. A bridge makes the journey easier. The bar exam is not designed to make your transition easier, but to see that you have what it takes to survive on the other side. The good news? Once you make the climb successfully, you'll never have to do it again. And you are close. (I ask that students call me "professor" while they are in school, but to feel free to use my first name once they pass the bar. The moment they are licensed, we are colleagues. But it is often hard for people to call former professors by their first names. That mountain between the world of law school and law practice is steep. Do you think of yourself as *almost a colleague*?)

HARD WORK IS NOT GLAMOROUS, BUT IT IS THE MOST IMPORTANT PART OF SUCCESS.

Above all (and perhaps the most critical point missed by many who fail the bar), the cornerstone of successful law study, successful law practice, and being a successful professional is and always will be *hard work*. Perhaps it is human nature to seek the easy route. Even bar reviews today have joined the trend of offering apps and games to supplement lectures and reading. I have nothing against fun in studying or in life. I am all for it. But I remain steadfastly convinced that working slowly, steadily, carefully, and *hard* is essential, especially in law. Persistence and attention to detail may not be glamorous, but they are required for success. Succeed slowly, and you will go far. Rush, and you will fail or produce slipshod work. There are no shortcuts.

"THE HARDER I WORK, THE LUCKIER I GET."

— SAM GOLDWYN —

In this chapter, we will look at how to refocus—to turn away from the temptations of our instant-gratification society and toward developing the patience required for a command of the legal knowledge and skills required to pass the bar exam. By doing this, you can look forward to a successful professional future.

I am always hearing complaints from stressed-out students: *I have to work for* how many *months to get ready for the bar? I should take* how many *practice tests? How do they expect me to know all these rules, in all these subjects? This is ridiculous. This is hard!*

Duh! Of course it's hard. It's law school. You are seeking a license that will enable you to be responsible for people's lives and livelihoods. It should be hard! And if you really wanted things to be easy, you would not have enrolled in law school.

We have come to expect easy, *and quick*, solutions. We expect to find every answer in a moment's Internet search. In the past, we might have had to look for hours for the right book and correct passage in that book, not to mention travel time getting to and from the library. But just because some information may be available any time of day or night at the touch of a finger does not mean the information is correct or that you understand it. And even if you understand it, you may not be able to communicate it effectively to someone else.

Law school and the bar exam, although they require a memorized bank of knowledge, are not about regurgitating facts such as those available in an encyclopedia. They are about *reasoning*. They are about seeing how rules and principles you have learned apply to new facts, and *why* a particular outcome should result in each new situation. There is no way you can "learn it all." Learn what you need to, and take the time and effort necessary to develop your ability to reason to logical conclusions.

In the "real world," you will wish that all you had to deal with were facts, rules, and logic. People's lives and legal problems are riddled with emotion and passion. You may work with opposing counsel, colleagues, or even decision makers whose concerns are not about following the rules, fairness, or justice, but about revenge, self-promotion, and climbing the ladder. They may exhibit displaced anger. (Picture the person who is angry at the boss but kicks the dog.) Such issues pose far more difficult challenges than law school or the bar exam because they are irrational.

Do not expect the hard work to get faster, to get easier, or to end. Toss aside the microwave mentality. Think slow cooking in an old-fashioned oven. The future is not going to get simpler. There is not an economist in town who thinks we are heading any time soon back to any sort of 1950s' "Happy Days." Your days will be filled with challenge. To make your future successful, you must find a way to make peace with hard work, to embrace challenge, and, hopefully, to delight in victories that come after the sweat and tears.

When in doubt, in bar review and in life, always and at every turn, get back to work. But do not view hard work as punishment. Seasoned with a bit of luck, hard work is the key ingredient to success. And you will be happier if you see it as worthwhile and rewarding in the end, and realize how fortunate you are to be able to pursue an academic or professional goal.

I will talk about working hard at every phase of your preparing and sitting for the exam: creating a bar plan, actively listening to lectures and taking notes, taking many practice tests under timed conditions, studying sample answers, and looking up rules you don't understand. If you are expecting to find some magic formula in this book, some incantation you can recite to pass the exam, stop reading. There isn't one. And if someone is trying to sell you a bar review or study course so foolproof that the exam will write itself, don't buy it. Don't be the fool.

If you accept the notion that hard work is good, read on. Do not waste one moment feeling bitter or angry or annoyed that you *have to* study. You *get* to study! It truly is a privilege. Change any perspective you may have to the contrary. Consider the daily work struggles of manual laborers or the many people fighting to survive war or hunger. Recognize the gift that it is to be able to spend time studying.

EXERCISE: What are the dos and don'ts of hard work?
Do:
- Stay limber in mind and spirit—keep taking practice tests, exercising, and eating well!
- Sleep, as much as possible!
- Laugh and smile while you work. The exam you are about to take is not torture. It's hard work. And it will be a huge accomplishment when you pass. You are doing this because you *want* to. It is a privilege to be able to dedicate the time and effort to achieve what you desire.

Do not:
- Work to the point of exhaustion.
- Think it's frivolous to take time off from work for exercise (it will, in fact, make you more productive).
- Spend a lot of time studying areas that are not very important.

Your turn. List what you want to remind yourself to do and not to do:

I want to make sure I do:

_____

_____

_____

I want to make sure I do not:

_____

_____

_____

VISUALIZE YOURSELF AS A LAWYER.

When training for bar success, practice introducing yourself as a lawyer. I know that may sound crazy and silly, but somehow just saying the words underscores how close you are to achieving this goal. Go ahead. Stand in front of a mirror and say the following:

"Hello, my name is _____. I am an attorney licensed here in [your state]. I'm pleased to meet you."

Repeat it a few times. Get comfortable saying it. *Being a lawyer is not just what you are doing, but who you are.* To move through this next phase, think of yourself as having *already* succeeded; you are simply complying with a few remaining formalities. (This is so much more powerful than thinking of yourself as someone who will try, but might not make it!)

Join a local bar association as a student member. Attend some meetings. Introduce yourself to the attorneys. Get to know them. Think of yourself as one of them.

Take an hour out of a morning or afternoon, stop by a local courthouse, and walk the corridors. Imagine yourself as one of the "suits" rushing around with your briefcase. Do they look any smarter than you? (This can be helpful if you do not come from a family of lawyers. If your mom or dad is a lawyer, it is easier to see yourself that way. But if you don't have any close role models in the legal profession, get into that courthouse at the beginning of 3L, if not earlier.) Sit and observe a proceeding. Is there anything you have heard that you don't understand or couldn't understand by asking a few questions? And, if you belong to any local organizations, ask a lawyer to take you around for the day and show you the courthouse. Lawyers love to talk about their work. You won't have time to do this in June or July, so do it in 2L or early in 3L when your schedule permits. (I had no lawyers in my immediate family. And, I will forever be grateful to Loyola Law School Professor Laurie Levenson for taking me around the U.S. District Court in Los Angeles when she was a prosecutor and I was a law student.)

Now, look into your immediate future. Imagine yourself in a large room, with clacking keyboards. The air seems to be equal parts oxygen and nervousness. Proctors pace the aisles. You are at a desk. A focused, slightly crazed-looking person sits on your right, another on your left. You are handed a booklet. When you are told to begin, you break open the seal. Fact patterns are revealed. You have no anxiety. You read with curiosity! These are puzzles, and you have the knowledge to solve them. You know what to do. You proceed methodically. You have a plan. You employ the skills you have developed. And you proceed with confidence to write thorough, logical answers and to select the best answers to multiple-choice questions.

Picture yourself standing before a judge raising your right hand and being sworn in as the newest member of the bar in your state. Now try introducing yourself again as a lawyer. Does it feel more real?

EXERCISE: See yourself as a lawyer. Describe yourself.

What if you had a legal problem? What qualities would you want in the lawyer you hire to represent you?

_____

_____

_____ .

Let me tell you how I see my students—people just like you. *You are thoughtful. You listen and reason well. You read carefully. You are detail oriented. You are someone who has earned the respect of colleagues (and will earn the trust of clients). You keep your word and follow through on promises.* Anything you want to add now about yourself?

_____

_____

_____ .

DRAW UPON YOUR INSPIRATION.

Why did you go to law school? Why law? It may feel like a lifetime ago when you sat down to draft law school admissions essays. What did you write? What were you thinking about?

If you entered law school with a passion or dream, what was it? Did you want to help make equality for all a reality? Did you want to give a voice to people who can't or don't know how to defend themselves? Did you want power? Did you seek the ability to earn a good living for yourself and your family? Did you want fame? Were you thinking of a career in politics?

It will help to keep front and center the reasons that drew you in and propelled you to invest the time and energy and money and effort to get your J.D., especially on long study days when you are tired and don't feel like working. Remembering the dreams will keep that fire lit!

In one recent January session, preparing December grads for a February bar exam, a student offered this thought: "Yesterday was Martin Luther King's birthday—a day that reminds me every year why I went to law school. I see this man, between the Washington Monument and Lincoln Memorial, a man who not long before that speech had not even been permitted to sit at a lunch counter with white people, and I hear those words with which he transfixed the world. I want a law license to continue to help make that dream a reality." Do you remember the first time you heard that speech? Did it inspire you?

Take a moment. Why did *you* choose law school? What power will this license give you? Will it enable you to earn a living and support yourself and your family? Will it serve as a tool to effect positive change, help people, and make the world a better place?

I am reminded of a more-recent speech, given by a former student, who passionately described several superheroes and what she admired about them. Though some, such as Superman, Wonder Woman, and Spider-Man, had impressive magical powers, she was most inspired by Batman, a guy who achieved amazing things *without* supernatural powers, a distinctly human individual. What makes Batman so strong? His knowledge and his power tools! She spoke of the power her legal education had given her. She said she wore her law license like a "tool belt" and felt an awesome force each time she rose in court to speak on behalf of clients.[19]

What if you went to law school to fulfill someone else's dream? That may not be a bad reason; you will make that person proud. And you will have a degree and a license that bring opportunity and flexibility.

What if you really had no good reasons? You weren't ready to work full-time, so you came to law school. Look around now. Find at least one lawyer or legal organization you admire. In addition to practicing lawyers, consider those who are entrepreneurs or serve on the board of directors of large corporations or nonprofits. Look at lawyers who speak for people who cannot, and at those who solve problems or give advice. Find at least one lawyer with qualities you respect or who has professional opportunities you seek. Identify your purpose for pursuing a career in law. (Chapter 10 provides more information on legal and nonlegal careers for those trained as lawyers.)

You may scoff at this discussion of dreams. You came to law school to find a job that would pay the bills and feed a family and, hopefully, repay your now-hefty student-loan debt. You don't just want to pass the bar exam; you *need* to. This, too, can be helpful. (Always look for the silver lining in everything.) You have an even greater incentive to work hard than someone who merely wants it. Needing to pass will keep that fire lit. In fact, not needing to pass poses a significant challenge to many nontraditional students, especially those who already have jobs. If you are in the "don't need to pass" boat, find a way to want to pass so badly that you will do whatever it takes.

YOU MAY NEED THE LICENSE LATER EVEN IF YOU DON'T FEEL YOU NEED IT NOW.

One of my nontraditional students didn't think he really needed to take and pass the bar exam. He had a steady, well-paying job for years. Midway through bar review, after working all four years of law school and many years prior at the same job, he was unexpectedly laid off. Suddenly, he *needed* to pass the bar exam. He has since gone from working in a small practice to being a partner in a large firm and is licensed in multiple jurisdictions.

Hard work is easier when you hold onto your dreams. It's a bit like tennis, where your eyes must focus first on where the ball is coming from and then on where you want it to go with your stroke and follow-through. Here, too, you need to first look briefly back to when you began your studies and why you pursued a legal education, so you can then look confidently toward where you are heading.

Finishing law school and the intense challenge of successful bar preparation can feel like moving through a darkened, endless tunnel. Seeing the light of a hopeful future after you are sworn in will help you keep moving, taking the right steps, and doing the necessary follow-through to realize your full potential. It may be more difficult in today's uncertain economic times to muster that confidence when looking toward the future, but it is important to at least have a basic belief that you are pursuing something worthwhile in order to put in the work necessary for success.

ETHICAL RULES AND PROFESSIONALISM

In practice, you will have to follow the rules. Learning these rules will help you in law school, in a professional responsibility course, and in your efforts to pass the MPRE. You must also have a command of these rules to pass a bar exam's professional responsibility essay question and, possibly, to tackle an ethical issue on a performance test.

In addition to following rules, you must develop habits of acting as a conscientious professional, sharpening your organizational skills, and handling other details that will make bar passage easier and lay the groundwork for a lifetime of success.

The rules

When preparing for the MPRE and a professional responsibility essay, your focus will be on ethics. This chapter is about seeing yourself as a lawyer. As a lawyer, you must protect your moral character and build your reputation. Strive to become known not only as smart, but as reliable and hardworking. Think of yourself as the partner in a law firm. Would you be a desirable associate to hire? Make yourself one! (Thinking of yourself as the boss helps to bolster your identity shift.) In terms of ethics, you are always in charge. It is no defense to say, "Well, the senior partner told me to do it. . . ." If you are signing something or appearing in court and stating words on the record, or taking actions with respect to client funds, confidentiality, or other matters, you'd better be ready to stand by what you write, say, and do. And if a senior partner asks you to do something you are not comfortable with, refuse. It would be better to lose a job than to lose your license!

ARE YOU TAKING THE MPRE?
TEST YOURSELF!

The purpose of this exercise is to get you thinking generally about the importance of the MPRE and the many areas it covers. (Time spent preparing for the MPRE will also help you on a professional responsibility essay or performance test that includes ethical issues.) Note: Both of the quizzes below are based on information from the National Conference of Bar Examiners at the time of writing. Verify the most current details about any and all multistate tests (including the MPRE) before you take them. Visit the website for the National Conference of Bar Examiners (www.ncbex.org) for the most current details.[20]

Part A: Check which, if any, of the following will be tested:

___ Admission to the profession
___ Regulation after admission—lawyer discipline
___ Mandatory and permissive reporting of professional misconduct
___ Unauthorized practice of law—by lawyers and nonlawyers
___ Multijurisdictional practice
___ Fee division with a nonlawyer
___ Historical incidents of lawyers committing crimes
___ Law firm and other forms of practice
___ Formation of the client–lawyer relationship
___ Scope, objective, and means of the representation
___ Termination of the client–lawyer relationship
___ Client–lawyer contracts
___ Communications with the client
___ Fees

___ Client confidentiality
___ Conflicts of interest
___ Acquiring an interest in litigation
___ Business transactions with clients
___ Competence necessary to undertake representation
___ Candor to the tribunal
___ Fairness to opposing party and counsel
___ Communications with represented persons
___ Communications with unrepresented persons
___ Establishing and maintaining client trust accounts
___ Advertising and other public communications about legal services
___ Judicial conduct, and assisting judicial misconduct

ANSWER: All of the above (and many more!), with the exception of historical incidents of lawyers committing crimes, will be tested.

Part B: What percentage of the questions will likely be in the selected areas listed below?

Percentage	Topic
_____ percent	Regulation of the legal profession
_____ percent	The client–lawyer relationship
_____ percent	Client confidentiality
_____ percent	Conflicts of interest
_____ percent	Competence, legal malpractice, and other civil liability
_____ percent	Litigation and other forms of advocacy
_____ percent	Transactions and communications with persons other than clients
_____ percent	Different roles of the lawyer
_____ percent	Safekeeping funds and other property
_____ percent	Communications about legal services
_____ percent	Lawyers' duties to the public and the legal system
_____ percent	Judicial conduct

ANSWERS:
Regulation of the legal profession (6 percent–12 percent)
The client–lawyer relationship (10 percent–16 percent)
Client confidentiality (6 percent–12 percent)
Conflicts of interest (12 percent–18 percent)
Competence, legal malpractice, and other civil liability (6 percent–12 percent)

Litigation and other forms of advocacy (10 percent–16 percent)

Transactions and communications with persons other than clients (2 percent–8 percent)

Different roles of the lawyer (4 percent–10 percent)

Safekeeping funds and other property (2 percent–8 percent)

Communications about legal services (4 percent–10 percent)

Lawyers' duties to the public and the legal system (2 percent–4 percent)

Judicial conduct (2 percent–8 percent)

FEES, FINGERPRINTING, AND FORMS

To complete the moral character portion of your state's licensing procedures, study your jurisdiction's specific procedures and requirements. Listed below are some general standards from the ABA regarding character and fitness. They may be similar to your state's requirements. If you believe there is any potential issue about your own fitness, consider obtaining some preventive advice from an attorney who represents lawyers who are sanctioned or disbarred. (In California at the time of this writing, the application for moral character fitness costs $500, and there is an additional $500 fee to appeal a finding that one is not fit. If you have concerns, a one-hour meeting with a lawyer who regularly represents lawyers in disciplinary proceedings may be well worth your while—perhaps preventing you from completing the application in a way that causes a denial in the first place.)

From the 2013 Comprehensive Guide to Bar Admission Requirements[21]

Standard of Character and Fitness. A lawyer should be one whose record of conduct justifies the trust of clients, adversaries, courts, and others with respect to the professional duties owed to them. A record manifesting a significant deficiency in the honesty, trustworthiness, diligence, or reliability of an applicant may constitute a basis for denial of admission.

Relevant Conduct. The revelation or discovery of any of the following should be treated as cause for further inquiry before the bar examining authority decides whether the applicant possesses the character and fitness to practice law:

- unlawful conduct
- academic misconduct
- making of false statements, including omissions

- misconduct in employment
- acts involving dishonesty, fraud, deceit, or misrepresentation
- abuse of legal process
- neglect of financial responsibilities
- neglect of professional obligations
- violation of an order of a court
- evidence of mental or emotional instability
- evidence of drug or alcohol dependency
- denial of admission to the bar in another jurisdiction on character and fitness grounds
- disciplinary action by a lawyer, disciplinary agency, or other professional disciplinary agency of any jurisdiction

EXERCISE:

Complete the worksheet below for your own information. If you have concerns, mark the paper "Privileged and Confidential" and do not show it to or discuss it with anyone other than the lawyer you consult.

Is there anything in my background that might fall under one of the categories listed above?

_____

_____

_____

Are my potential concerns also actionable violations in my jurisdiction?

_____

_____

_____

If so, the following are names of people I might contact to find a trustworthy lawyer who specializes in these matters:

_____

_____

_____

PROFESSIONALISM AT THE MICRO LEVEL: ACT IN A PROFESSIONAL MANNER EVERY DAY.

See yourself in the future as a lawyer, but see yourself now as already a *professional*, someone who takes deadlines seriously, returns calls and e-mails promptly, arrives on time, keeps appointments, and effectively manages his or her calendar. These qualities will help you now to pass the bar, and later to succeed in practice and in life.

To be licensed to practice law, as noted, you must know the applicable ethical rules, but to be *successful* for a lifetime, you must also act in a professional manner. Start now. It will help you on the job, in bar prep, and on the PT portion of the bar exam itself, which often tests ethical or professional issues.

Professionalism is about more than just following written rules. It is about earning and keeping people's trust. Everyone you meet and work with now—your classmates, friends, family, and colleagues—is a potential referral source. Make sure they would want to refer you! (I remember a college classmate cheating on an exam. He later went to law school. If I am ever asked to refer him for some case or job opportunity, I won't.) Think about whom you trust, and whom you don't.

In a PT file, you may read about a lawyer doing something that is not against the rules per se but is not conduct you would condone (for example, not returning a call promptly or failing to thoroughly explain all available options to a client). You may well get points for writing about such a concern.

Being ethical and professional does not mean never making mistakes. Having served on faculty honor-code committees for decades, I have seen students come forth immediately to report themselves after inadvertently committing a violation. Often, these matters were treated as good-faith errors and were quickly resolved. In contrast, the students who tried to hide or cover up alleged violations were often found culpable and ended up facing far more serious consequences than had they initially admitted wrongdoing. The same is often true in practice. Lawyers make mistakes. (Why do you think they call it the *practice* of law?) Most mistakes are correctable. But you have to have your antennae up so that you realize when you or those you work with make mistakes; be willing and have the courage to speak up about such errors; and figure out how to fix them. This topic has been included many times on performance tests.

The following should be habits for life, and, starting now, will help you pass the bar exam.

Communicate carefully, respectfully, and in a timely manner.

We talked about many helpful practices to begin early in law school, including reading critically, taking practice tests, and paying attention to detail. Be sure to also develop good communication habits. The tips below are by no means exhaustive, but are just a few observations about communication that may not be self-evident to today's law students or the faculty and professionals you work with.

- Write and send e-mails wisely and professionally.
- Watch what you write and how you phrase the message.
- Don't be too quick to hit *Send*. If at all possible, put e-mails in a draft folder for at least a few hours (and if you can and still be timely, overnight). Reread them with fresh eyes before sending. You may be under a lot of stress finishing up law school and studying for the bar exam, and you may not catch typos, inappropriate wording or tone, or other issues that might stand out if you reread the message.
- Do not send e-mails you may later regret. Professors are often your best references for first law jobs, so be polite when writing to them. A colleague showed me a student's e-mail. It was rude in tone, used text-message-style abbreviations ("u" instead of "you" and "b4" instead of "before" in an e-mail to a professor is *not* professional), and, to boot, was sent during class! My guess is that this professor will not be giving this student the most glowing of recommendations. Although you may not view texting shorthand in an e-mail as inappropriate, many older lawyers do.
- There is nothing wrong with asking your professor questions, or even challenging him or her, as long as you do so in a professional manner.
- Send law school and work e-mails from a professional-sounding e-mail address, for example, one that includes your first and last names and uses your school or some other standard e-mail service as a provider. Avoid being cute, clever, or "cool" in both e-mails and e-mail addresses. (People will notice, and *not* in a favorable way, if your address is something like beers4me@lawstudentsforwild-fun.com.[22])

Think of e-mail as having more in common with a snail-mail letter than a text or tweet. Err on the side of formality.

GENERATIONAL COMMUNICATION DIVIDE

Experienced lawyers: Take the time to train your new lawyers in e-mail, phone-call, and letter-writing etiquette. You wouldn't think twice about having to train someone to make an effective appearance in court. You may also have to mentor new lawyers (especially younger graduates) in using appropriately formal communication. Discuss this as forthrightly as possible. Do not be condescending, but do not assume anything. Letter writing, something that seemed so fundamental to most people older than 40, is all but dead for younger folks. Explain what you expect and why, and tell them how you communicate with clients, opposing counsel, colleagues, and others. Note why you include certain points and why you exclude others. Mentoring costs money. You lose billable time when you are teaching younger lawyers. But it costs far more to have to redo someone's work, or, worse still, lose a client. And, new lawyers, you share this mentoring responsibility. *You must ask for help.* Some older lawyers may think you want to figure something out on your own, or should, and may not know that you would like help. Do try to figure some things out on your own, but then ask for help.

Read the e-mails that are sent to you.

Texting versus e-mailing is yet another generational divide. Many younger people do not communicate by e-mail. Older professionals do. (In what are now truly ancient times, law schools had actual physical student mailboxes. Hard copies of notices would be placed in students' boxes, and students would be expected to read them.) Most law school administrators and faculty today communicate by e-mail. But today's students often do not always read e-mails, or do not read them carefully enough to calendar dates and note other important information in the messages. The disconnect is troubling. Students often miss a great deal that those sending messages assume has been read and understood.

Many ASP and bar support faculty spend extensive time and energy setting up programs and opportunities to help students succeed; yet they often express how difficult it is to get students to attend events, even when food or prizes are offered. I suspect many do not attend because they did not read the e-mail.

Get in the habit during school of reading your e-mail. You may find that your messages often contain helpful information. And it can be embarrassing and make you look less competent when you repeatedly ask professors or administrators about things that have already been clearly communicated in e-mails. In June and July, you will have to be selective about e-mail. But even then, continue to at least check messages from your school administration, the state bar, and your ASP or bar support faculty.

AN E-MAIL SENT IS NOT ALWAYS AN E-MAIL RECEIVED AND READ.

It is too often assumed that an e-mail sent is an e-mail received and read. But e-mails often end up in spam folders, or, for other reasons, are never read by the intended recipients. Despite this, the sender may believe his or her e-mail was read and understood accurately. We need standardized etiquette for e-mail. In the meantime, we need to do more thinking when communicating. Do your part, beginning now. As a professional, make it your business to answer all e-mails that call for replies. If you do not have time for a thoughtful response, send a brief acknowledgment noting that you received and will reply to the e-mail as soon as possible. Then, calendar a date to follow up so you do get to that e-mail and respond fully. When someone e-mails requesting that you do something, send a reply e-mail when the task is completed. And if you are working on an e-mailed with other people, be sure to date the draft and note the version if you are making edits, additions, or corrections as e-mails may cross or be delayed.

Return calls and e-mails promptly.

This is more geared toward before and after intensive bar review. In June and July, you want to limit time on the phone, e-mailing, and texting as much as possible. But as a professional, make a habit of returning every call, letter, or e-mail as promptly as possible. Don't leave people hanging. If you don't know something, or need more time, indicate that, and then be sure to get back to the person when you say you will.

Be careful about what you post on Facebook and other social media.

Again, let's take as a given that today's readers have a harder time finding jobs than previous generations did. Employers *will* look at what you post. Know that. Act accordingly. (When in doubt, don't post.) You may want to post accomplishments that *do* reflect well on you, such as placing in a moot-court competition or being selected for a school honor. Remember that posting something illegal may affect your moral character application (and possibly worse). Posting something immoral, or even in bad taste, can influence your professional reputation. Be careful.

Be Organized.

Keep lists. Keep important papers. File documents, notes, and paperwork in a logical way so that you can easily retrieve them. You can scan everything and keep electronic copies if you do not want paper ones; just be sure to back up your data and have everything organized in an accessible manner.

Meet Deadlines, Be on Time, and Comply with Rules.

These critical ingredients to becoming a successful professional, especially a lawyer, are habits that you can cement (or begin if you have not already) during bar prep. While it may seem obvious that lawyers must comply with deadlines, students frequently miss them. Law school professors and deans nationwide lament the numbers of students who regularly turn work in late without even requesting extensions. A court will not continue a hearing without your requesting an extension and typically having good cause.

At every turn, you are creating your reputation. You are either enhancing or diminishing it. People remember when you are rude or late. People remember when you meet deadlines and when you do not.

People regularly fail bar exams because they do not upload their answers on time. Some are not even allowed to sit for the exam because they arrive late to the testing site. (You may be required to arrive twenty to thirty minutes before the exam actually starts, and failure to do so may result in your being deemed late.) Other applicants are kicked out during the exam because they bring in forbidden items or wear prohibited clothing. These problems can easily be prevented by simply studying the information and notices from your bar examiners. Be sure to read all relevant rules and guidelines carefully.

HOW DO YOU KEEP YOUR OWN CALENDAR?

Do you keep a calendar? Do you log into one central site all your upcoming appointments, deadlines, and meetings? Do you have a reminder system? You may be able to find easy-to-follow, helpful tutorials for online calendaring systems. There are many dates you will need to calendar, including when forms and fees are due. File on time to avoid late fees, and get into this habit so that you handle client matters in a timely fashion. (Failure to effectively calendar in law practice can have dire results, for both you and your clients.)

REDUCE DISTRACTIONS, INCREASE YOUR FOCUS, AND MANAGE YOUR TIME

- Time Management for Bar Applicants
  - Some basics of time management during bar prep
    - Align your schedule with Bar Standard Time.
    - Engage in active learning.
    - Set up a calendaring system.
    - Protect your time.
    - Keep commitments to yourself firm, but maintain flexibility within your schedule.
    - Track your time.
    - Combat e-distractions.
    - Time-management tips for law students who are parents
- Multitasking, Endurance, and Increasing Focus
  - Strive for consistency.
  - Stay healthy: Reduce stress, eat right, exercise, and sleep.
- Top ten tips that will help everyone, especially nontraditional students

During intensive bar prep, your primary focus should be on passing the bar. This does not mean your entire focus has to be on studying. It means that everything you do must move you toward achieving your goal. Sleeping well, exercising regularly, and eating healthy foods prepare your body and mind to perform effectively. You need to be functioning in high gear while studying and on grueling exam days. You need to be in the best shape possible to stay focused and productive.

For two months, you will live in a bar exam "boot camp" where the test is your highest priority. You must be "on"—in mind, body, and spirit. To do this, you will need to ruthlessly protect your time and learn to manage distractions and demands that steal your study time. This chapter will help you assess where your time goes so you can cut back on and eventually get rid of whatever distracts you or does not move you forward. Charts and worksheets will help you track your time and maximize efficiency. You will develop strategies to resist what pulls you away from study and language to help you say no when offers tempt you. Letters are also provided that you can send to family and friends to help prepare them and let them know how they can help you.

Some of you are working full-time or raising families while studying. You need strategies to juggle your competing responsibilities. Many nontraditional law students are also physicians, pilots, accountants, engineers, architects, nurses, or businesspeople who cannot simply set aside the many demands they face. These "distractions" are obligations. One cannot tell a young child who needs to eat, "Not now—I'm studying," or delay a critical medical procedure for an aging parent. You may not be able to put off a transatlantic flight, especially if you are the pilot! But you are still taking the same intensely challenging exam as are other students. You may need to employ different strategies, but much of your battle will be the same. So, to prepare for that battle, you must carve out and protect as much of your time as possible.

Each student is also unique. You learn and process information in different ways than others do. You may be "on" at different times of the day; what helps you focus may differ greatly from what works for others. To be at your best and most productive, find what works for you. Pave your own path to success.

TIME MANAGEMENT FOR BAR APPLICANTS

Passing the bar exam requires focus and self-discipline. Distractions must be reduced and eventually eliminated. Ease into the high-gear months by tackling time management early.

"IN READING THE LIVES OF GREAT MEN, I FOUND THAT THE FIRST VICTORY THEY WON WAS OVER THEMSELVES . . . SELF-DISCIPLINE WITH ALL OF THEM CAME FIRST."

— HARRY S. TRUMAN —

Some Basics of Time Management During Bar Prep

Effectively managing your time during bar prep is similar to time management generally, but the need for efficiency is greater. You don't have a moment to waste. Intensive bar prep is like two month of finals; it is an extended time crunch. (Litigators go into "trial mode" and face similar pressures.) To fit everything you must do into the most efficient schedule, you must first know how you currently spend your time, then triage and prioritize.

The charts and tips below will help you consider how much time things take and determine the best order in which to accomplish tasks. Pay attention to whether something is better done before or after another task. For example, it may be more productive to listen to the lecture or review the outline before doing a certain practice test. You should also get into the habit of noting the time of day you are most productive so you can schedule things earlier or later accordingly.

Align your schedule with "Bar Standard Time."

By the time you sit for the exam, your internal body clock should be on "Bar Standard Time." In other words, your peak concentration periods should be from approximately 9:00 a.m. to noon and 2:00 to 5:00 p.m. There are two ways to get into that routine: either make the bar schedule your schedule from the outset, or study when you are most alert (even if that's 2:00 a.m.) before July, and then gradually switch to bar exam timing in July.

It is important to know when you are most and least productive in order to efficiently schedule tasks. Do active work at times when you are most alert and passive work when you are less revved up. For example, you need to be "on" to do independent tasks such as taking practice tests and analyzing model answers. Doing those when you are dragging is counterproductive. But you may be able to listen to bar review lectures even when you are not quite as alert; they may help keep you awake and engaged.

Engage in active learning.

I think of active learning as a way of understanding information and mastering skills when you are fully engaged. Passive learning, by contrast, is more a process of simply letting yourself absorb information. Generally speaking, the more you interact with material, the more you will retain. Active learning also saves time because you tend to "get" concepts more readily when you are fully engaged, reducing the time necessary to review. (Ever read the same passage several times and not understand a word? You know what I am talking about. That is a waste of time. Developing good active-reading skills helps your comprehension and retention.)

Bar preparation requires both active and passive learning. Why? You just cannot be "on," in high gear, all day, every day for two months. You need breaks. You also need to make the most of both high-energy and low-energy cycles by balancing active and passive learning. You may be too tired to effectively continue high-gear work, but can push yourself to continue studying for another few hours if you switch to a less-active task. For instance, let's say you have been reading a bar review outline and taking practice tests in a certain subject, and you are tired. You might take a break or call it a day and go to sleep, or you might close your eyes and just listen to either a lecture on that topic or a recording of yourself reading related rule statements. To help you calendar both active and passive learning, you need to determine what sorts of tasks require full engagement and what you can learn more easily, by simply letting information in. Start by completing the exercise below. As you read about different aspects of bar preparation in this book, think about which tasks require more energy than others.

Active/Passive Learning Exercise

List tasks that you need to complete, and note whether they are active or passive. If you can, try to then rank all the tasks below in descending order from most to least active, with 1 being most active.

Task/Activity	Active/Passive	Rank
Read outlines.	_____	_____
Study outlines.	_____	_____
Attend/listen to bar review lectures.	_____	_____
Complete practice tests and analyze answers.	_____	_____
Copy model answers to practice tests.	_____	_____
Make flash cards/charts/checklists.	_____	_____
Memorize rules using flash cards/ charts/checklists.	_____	_____
Look up rules you do not understand.	_____	_____

Make recordings of rule statements.	_____	_____
Listen to recordings of rule statements.	_____	_____
Prepare and eat meals.	_____	_____
Pay bills, do chores, and exercise.	_____	_____

Set up a calendaring system.

The better you are at calendaring, the smoother bar prep (and life!) will likely go. You may log bar study tasks into an online calendaring system or in a hard-copy planner, or both. You may sync your calendars so that what you need to do each day is both on your laptop and your phone or tablet. You can color-code tasks, online or on paper, perhaps highlighting in yellow what still needs to be done and in green what has already been completed. Some people also find it useful to make to-do lists each day and cross off items as they are accomplished.

Protect your time.

Reduce, and then work to eliminate, distractions in the final weeks. (More on this below.) We have an endless supply of distractions, from invasive texts, e-mails, and phone calls to internal distractions such as worry and fear. There are worthwhile distractions and those that can only be called an extraordinary waste of time.

Now your task is to become aware of where your time goes. Armed with this awareness, you will be able to manage your days and make certain you are on—and stay on—the path to success. It will also help you battle the "time thieves" that steal minutes without us even noticing. One sneaky time thief is transition time. You may not be aware of how much time gets wasted when you move between tasks. Unconscious spending of time is like unconscious consumption of calories. (We fail to count the minutes between tasks just like we fail to count snacks between meals. But they add up.)

Another time thief is procrastination. When we avoid doing something, we often fill the gap with something unimportant. To battle this, keep lists of active and passive tasks. When you are too tired to do an active task such as taking a practice test, or find yourself procrastinating, do something less demanding but that nonetheless needs to be done. (Pay bills. Take walks. If it makes you feel like you are wasting less time, you can listen to recorded lectures, or your own voice reading rule statements, while you sweat off the procrastination.)

Above all, keep commitments to yourself. You are important. And your future is worth every ounce of time, energy, money, and commitment you are investing right now. Don't let anyone tell you otherwise. (Chapter 6 provides strategies to deal with people who do not support you and to combat the negative effects of such people.)

QUIZ

You have to study, and you have to pay bills. Does this lead you to waste time?

Do you:

1. Start the day with the bills, then start worrying about money, so you look up something on your bank statement, then realize you haven't balanced your checkbook in a while, only to find you have wasted an hour on paying two bills that could have been paid in ten minutes?
2. Study first and pay those bills at the end of a productive day, when you are too tired to do any more reading or thinking?
3. Study for a four-hour block; then take a break to have a snack and pay the bills while eating something?

There is no right answer. You have to know yourself. Be sure you do what you need to in the order you need to do it, however, to keep your focus on study.

*Keep commitments to yourself firm,
but maintain flexibility within your schedule.*

Think of a study commitment to yourself as you would an appointment with an expert physician you have waited months to see. You would not cancel unless there were an emergency. Don't cancel on yourself.

Have a "Plan B" ready so you can modify your schedule if necessary. Let's say you calendared 7:00 to 8:00 a.m. to work on practice MBEs (and, of course, to review explanatory answers). But you find it's an off day; you are unable to focus. (You catch yourself reading the same fact pattern over and over again.) What should you do? First, try forcing yourself to focus. Get up. Stretch. And try again. If that doesn't work, drink some water. That may wake you up. If need be, splash the water on your face. But if after these steps you still aren't alert enough to work and learn productively, shift to another, less-active (but necessary) task and return to the practice questions later. In other words, stay committed to your schedule, but not rigidly so. Push yourself, but not if it's counterproductive. Do remain accountable, though. If a task must be done today and you do not complete it in the morning, be sure it gets done by evening.

If you are a nontraditional student, depending on your other commitments, you may be more successful with a target goal of accomplishing certain tasks over several days, especially if you have an unpredictable work schedule. A Monday one week may be particularly heavy, but later in the week things lighten up. You may have to finish on Thursday what you'd planned to complete at the beginning of the week. That's fine. Again, just stay accountable. Make sure it gets done at the alternative time you designate. Be sure to read tips and suggestions below on creative ways to capture extra time, such as listening to lectures while commuting or taking practice MBEs during your lunch break.

Track your time.

How do you start reducing distractions and make more time for bar preparation? Begin by identifying what takes up your time. Look at each day for at least a week, preferably two. Start when you wake up and end when you go to sleep. Log what you do in fifteen-minute increments if you can, just as you would bill a client. This is an effective way to see where your time is being used productively and where it is slipping away. You cannot effectively reduce distractions when you do not know what is distracting you! You can list or chart what you do, or use the sample daily time sheet below.

SAMPLE DAILY TIME SHEET:

Print and daily complete the chart below for two weeks to help see where your time is going. This is a sample. You can use a day planner or law office time sheet that specifies your tasks and activities down to the tenth of an hour.

Date & Day of the Week	Activity (List everything you did in each time block)	Initiated by You?	Total Time Spent	Necessity or Distraction?	Notes: Eliminate? Defer? Do at a Different Time? Multitask?
Morning					
Afternoon					
Evening					

Each week, add up your time-sheet entries in the spaces below, noting how much time you spend doing exactly what. Remember that there are only 168 hours in a week!

Hours Task

____ Work (Be aware of how many hours you work at home or in an office, and whether that office is a place that is conducive to bar study.)

____ Non-work-related communication, such as with family and friends. Be sure to include phoning, texting, Skyping, instant messaging (IM), in-person visits, and the like.

____ Extended-family commitments, including dinners, parties, celebrations, and helping relatives with errands or tasks they depend on you for. Only log these once, so if you include these in another category below, leave this one blank.

____ Commute to work, to school, and to bar review in summer if attending a live course.

____ Exercise

____ Religious observances, including holidays, weddings, bar mitzvahs, christenings, Sabbath celebrations, and the like. Be sure to log time for home observance, prayer, and activities at a church, synagogue, or other religious establishment.

____ Community, neighborhood, or other volunteer work

____ Child care, care of elderly or other relatives, pet care (including walking the dog)

____ Sleep

____ Meal preparation (include shopping and cooking)

____ Eating meals (basic sustenance and family meals that extend beyond the time it takes to eat)

____ Personal hygiene (showering, hair care, dressing) and health care (your own, and what you do for young children or others who depend on you)

____ Personal finance and record keeping (paying the bills, sorting through mail, etc.)

____ Personal recreation and relaxation (TV, movies, social media, and whatever else you do to unwind)

____ Other: _____.

____ **Subtotal:** _____.

____ *Study*

Assessment: Does your list total more than 168 hours? Is your study time equal to 168 minus the subtotal of the time for the other items? In other words, are you actually studying for as much time as you think you are? Note that study was listed last because people tend to inflate the time spent studying. Ultimately, you will want to reorder this list, in ink, so that studying comes first. You will then work to fit everything else in, after and around your study time, in pencil. If you run out of time, try to borrow it from areas you can better afford to skimp on. For example, eat for a shorter amount of time, take shorter showers, buy healthy prepared foods instead of cooking, tell family and friends you will see them in August, arrange for child care, etc.

After charting how you spend your time, you should have a better sense of what you do that is productive and what steals or wastes your time. List your preliminary conclusions below, beginning with those activities you can eliminate, reduce the amount of time spent on, or defer until after July. Of the activities that remain, can any be completed in less time or while multitasking? Consider the following examples:

- I have to eat, but I can shave off prep time by shopping, cooking, and freezing meals for the week each Sunday evening—while listening to bar review lectures!
- I have to walk the dog, but I can use that time to get my own exercise in (and, again, listen to bar review lectures while walking or running).
- I have to pay bills, but that doesn't require the same kind of focus that studying does, so I'll do that later, *after* I have put in a good day's work and I'm too tired to study any more.
- I have to acknowledge the birthdays of family and friends, but I will send them all an e-mail or note that says "rain check for a birthday celebration in August."
- I have to get the most out of my practice tests, so I'll take them first thing, when I am most focused.

EXERCISE: Doing what you must do more efficiently

List things you have to do, as well as creative ways to do them faster or while multitasking.

I have to _____, but I can save time by_____.

I have to _____, but I can save time by_____.

I have to _____, but I can save time by_____.

I have to _____, but I can save time by_____.

What about things to defer until after July? Some may be the following:

- Unless they help you, close your Facebook, Twitter, and other online social media accounts, or at least post "Unavailable until August" on them. Some people find support in the online community; they use posts to stay motivated. Others find social media a waste of time. Reading posts about the bar exam freaks them out. The bottom line: unless it helps keep you focused on study and accountable, take a break from social media activity until after the bar.
- Close or deactivate your IM, or set an autoreply that you are out and returning in August. (And tell people you will not reply to texts unless they are about life or death matters until after the bar.)
- Lose the chat groups. These not only waste your time, but they are insidious because they spread rampant misinformation. You don't need "advice" from fools and naysayers. You need to study!
- Stop your own blogging, unless it helps you. (One of my former students posted a tip for every MBE question she got wrong and found that it both reinforced her own learning and helped others. The entries became online flash cards.)
- Record a message on your voice mail saying you are gone until the end of July.
- Put an out of office message on your e mail, and tell close friends and family that unless they put the word *URGENT* in the subject line, you won't read their messages until after July. (Note: If you must stay connected, check e-mail at the end of the day, *after* you are done studying.)

What can I spend less time on, eliminate, or defer?

Activity	Defer until after the bar, or spend less time on in June and July
1._____	_____
2._____	_____
3._____	_____
4. _____	_____
5. _____	_____

One of the greatest interrupters is other people trying to reach you. Do not interrupt yourself or your study flow for phone calls, texts, IMs, or e mail. This is critical. It is so easy to say, "It's just one call," or "It's just one message," or "I would have needed a break anyway sooner or later." Even with a short call, what will break is your concentration.

Will you be answering calls during the exam? No! So don't interrupt yourself now. If you must look at texts and e mails (for work, for example), create "communication office hours." At those times only, once or twice a day, check your messages. Set these hours at a time when you are less efficient, during your least productive time. Whatever e mail, texts, or other correspondence you do not get to during today's office hours, handle tomorrow. Do not cut into your study, sleep, or exercise time. Be vigilant. Protect your time. Focus on the big goal—passing the bar. Nearly everything else can wait.

IT CAN WAIT

It can wait. In a movie-theater preview/public-service announcement requesting quiet during the film, the famous actor Billy Crystal asks that the audience silence their cell phones. The theater darkens, the audience munches popcorn, then everyone turns and stares when Billy Crystal's phone rings. He doesn't realize it is his phone and complains that the phone's owner should turn it off. When he sees the ringing is actually his own phone, he sheepishly sinks into his chair and panics. Should he answer or not? What if it's his doctor telling him he only has a short while to live? He succumbs to temptation and listens to the message. His dry cleaning is ready. The theater screen flashes, "It can wait!"—and his face tells all. When you are studying and your phone rings, tell yourself, "It can wait!"

Combat e-distractions.

Reducing e-distractions is particularly difficult because most of you study online, at least to some extent. Your bar review may be online, but even if it is in person there will likely be a website and online materials you need to review. Thus, the very same tool you learn from also lures you away from studying. Because of that, it may be even more tempting to just check the gossip while you are online. Unless you have positive peer pressure or support online, most social media will not move you toward bar success. They are at best a distraction; more often they are blatantly destructive. (You freak out when hot-air blowhards say they have been studying sixteen hours a day, implying that you're a loser if you are not. Other people share their anxiety. But you likely already have enough of your own! You don't need to hear about everyone else's.) Social media are also a haven for misinformation. If you must surf the net (if it's become an addiction that you cannot break), visit reliable sites that you know are helpful. For example, go to the websites of your state bar, the National Conference of Bar Examiners, your bar review, and sites recommended by your ASP faculty. Print a sheet of trustworthy websites and keep it near your computer.

EXERCISE: Reliable websites I want readily accessible during bar prep:

Name	Website
1. National Conference of Bar Examiners	ncbex.org
2._____	_____
3._____	_____
4._____	_____
5._____	_____

List five e-distractions. Next to each, think of ways to manage or eliminate the distraction.

E-distraction	Manage or Eliminate By:
1._____	_____
2._____	_____
3._____	_____
4._____	_____
5._____	_____

Time-Management Tips for Law Students Who Are Parents

Many nontraditional students say they feel guilty that law school is taking them away from their kids. If your children are in elementary school, middle school, or high school, realize that your studying is positive role modeling. You are teaching them discipline and the value of hard work through your actions. (This is much more effective than preaching!) Don't be surprised if your children do better in school when you are also studying. The following are a few practical pointers:

- If you have dependent children or aging parents who must be able to reach you in an emergency, give them a code or special ringtone for an emergency call or text. You'll know if it's something you need to read or listen to right away or if it can wait until when you decide to take the study break you have earned by completing whatever tasks were on your schedule.

- Keep "office hours" so your family knows when you are studying and not to be interrupted, and when you are available. Even if family time is an hour at dinner every night, keep your commitment. It is even more important when you are gone a lot to be consistent and reliable. If they know when they can depend on you to give them your full attention at one certain time each day, they may be better able to leave you alone the rest of the day.
- Be sure to include your family (children, significant other, parents) in your studying when you can productively do so. When you take breaks, ask them to test you with flash cards. (Just be prepared, your kids may memorize the rules before you do!)
- Play audio versions of your bar review lectures while you are driving, cooking, cleaning, or playing with your kids.
- Bring flash cards (or, better still, have them on your smartphone) to test yourself if you are at the park or waiting in line at the market.
- If you have young children, read your bar review outlines aloud. Infants and toddlers mostly just want to hear your voice and be close to you. Whether you are reading Dr. Seuss, Shakespeare, or *Farnsworth on Contracts* may not matter!
- Plan a fun after-bar trip or activity and let your kids (if age appropriate) decide what that will be.[23] (I work with many students who take the bar in southern California and bring their families to Disneyland for a few days after the exam.)

MOVE OUT. THIS SOUNDS EXTREME, BUT SOME PEOPLE NEED TO LEAVE HOME TO FIND QUIET.

A student recently told me of his significant involvement with a nonprofit organization involved in animal rescues. The work requires him to frequently and with no notice drop everything to help in emergencies with homeless and abused animals. This same student also noted that family and friends often stop by his home. He decided to move out for June and July so that he could have total focus, without interruptions. Another graduate who recently passed the bar told me that with his family's permission he moved out for six weeks prior to the exam, and lived in a summer dorm on a college campus nearby where he was going to take the bar exam. (Some colleges have inexpensive summer housing.) Yet another student whose home was too noisy to concentrate visited all the local libraries and coffee shops in April and May until he found a comfortable place to study.

MULTITASKING, BUILDING ENDURANCE, AND INCREASING FOCUS

Once you know where your time is going, you can use your time and energy to train to perform more effectively. The following charts and exercises will help you see how you are spending your time and better manage it. First, some thoughts on multitasking.

I may not win friends by suggesting that a good place to start looking at critically is how and when you multitask. But to build the physical and mental endurance to focus for long, uninterrupted blocks on the bar exam, you must train. Some multitasking is great. I call it "capturing time." You may be able to effectively listen to law lectures while you drive or commute by public transportation, exercise, or cook. But multitasking has its downsides. We are so used to it that we tend not to give intense focus to anything. We check e-mail and texts at the dinner table, while paying bills, even in the bathroom! How many of you regularly use your phone or laptop for personal matters during class while your professor is talking? (If you do, I can guarantee you are not getting the most of what that person has to offer, and are likely missing key points.)

Most people try to do so much at once that they don't give themselves an opportunity to ever be truly focused. Given the hectic lives of many law students, it may feel like a break to *just* focus on the bar exam. It can be a relief to say no to everything else for a few months, to put aside all the stuff you don't want to do or deal with and give your total concentration to something you really desire.

Give it a try. When you are studying, focus only on studying. If you are taking a practice test and catch yourself pulling out your phone, looking out the window, or contemplating the holes in your jeans, force yourself back into the question, back into the moment. Reread the facts, aloud if you need to.

I challenge you to see how long you can go with this single-minded focus. Try to build up to working productively in four-hour blocks. If you can be "on" for four-hour stretches, three-hour testing blocks (common on bar exams) will seem very doable. (If you are used to lifting ten-pound weights, five-pounders feel easy.)

CAPTURING TIME.

Again, some multitasking is productive. Use commute time in cars, trains, or buses; listen to podcasts or make tapes of yourself reading rules from your outlines. Listen while you exercise. (One of my students managed to purchase a waterproof listening device so she could study while swimming!) Use some family and friend time, when people are willing to test you, on flash cards. (Younger kids love to quiz their parents!) Use mealtimes; form study groups with classmates and talk about and debrief practice questions over lunch or dinner.

"DO A LITTLE MORE EACH DAY THAN YOU THINK YOU POSSIBLY CAN."

— LOWELL THOMAS —

BE SELECTIVE IN THE WORK YOU DO. USE BETTER, NOT JUST MORE, MATERIALS.

Don't buy every supplemental resource you see. Too much information will distract you and waste your time. Worse still, some of that material may not be from reliable sources. When you review law that is wrong, it is not only a waste (a neutral, if you will), but it will undo progress you have made (a severe negative—a time thief.) If you get caught up in contradictory sources, you may find yourself more confused than ever and having to start over. No time for that! Enroll in a reputable bar review and trust their materials. Remember, too, that rule statements are often phrased differently while still conveying the same elements, standard, factors, and the like. Do not be nitpicky about phrasing. Learn the underlying concepts. (Chapter 5 explains the need for, and how to ensure that you get, quality help from qualified experts.)

Strive for consistency.

Whatever time you give each day to study, keep your schedule consistent. Keep the commitment to spend a focused amount of time each day on preparing for the bar exam, preferably in uninterrupted blocks that mirror the length of time you will have to perform on your bar exam. And continue asking what you can give up to make *more* study time. Remember, the sacrifice is temporary!

Bar prep really is a full-time endeavor, even if you are working while studying. A student e-mailed me two weeks into bar review, saying how shocked she was that the study schedule mapped out activities for seven days a week. She thought it would be a five-days-a-week schedule, with time to "catch up on the weekends." No. (Bar reviews usually include lectures and other lessons for at least six days each week and often they include or you will have to include on your own homework on the 7th day.) This is yet another reason I urge you to plan early, get your schedule in place, and work out your time-management issues. I don't care how smart you are—if you don't put in the time, you will regret it.

Stay Healthy: Reduce Stress, Eat Right, Exercise, and Sleep

These are all interconnected; the more you eat right, exercise, and sleep, the less stressed you will be.

You need to sleep. You need to be focused and doing your absolute best when you're studying and taking the exam. You cannot perform well if you don't sleep each night and replenish your energy.

You need to exercise. The more fit you are, the better you will be able to concentrate. Physical activity also helps to both relieve stress and improve sleep. Incorporate some exercise in your daily routine, such as walking, swimming, running, or yoga. Pick something easy that you can do without much preparation, equipment, or fanfare. If you feel guilty spending time on exercise, study while you move. Listen to bar review lectures while you walk or run, or read outlines while on the treadmill or stationary bike. (This is one time when multitasking can be your best friend.)

It's normal to be tired. People often underestimate the physical demands of intellectual work. If you are studying with sufficient intensity, you should be exhausted. And bar studies take even more energy because of the stress. Be sure to pace yourself so you peak at exam time and not weeks earlier.

You may feel like people do not get how much work this is and how much pressure you face. They don't. Don't expect them to understand unless they themselves are lawyers. People may begrudge your taking time out for exercise and sleep and not for them. But let me tell you, you need sleep and exercise in order to study well. (Blame your summer disappearance on me. See the letters in Chapter 6 that you can send to family and friends explaining why you are "gone.")

Another reason for fatigue is sleeping difficulties. Anxiety may rob you of a good night's sleep. You may then become even more anxious because you are sleepy and be less productive than you would be if you had slept well. Many bar applicants find it hard to fall asleep because they are so wound up. Others wake frequently in the middle of the night with nightmares about fact patterns. Nontraditional students who must juggle work and family on top of studying may have an even harder time getting enough sleep. But sleep you must! Figure out ways to combat insomnia—before the exam. Some students find it helpful to read a novel before bed; reading about another world takes them far enough away from the law to relax. Others find that TV, a hot bath, or a glass of wine does the trick. Learn what works to get you to fall asleep and stay asleep. (One former student shared that the only way to take his mind off law and fall asleep each night was to read histories of naval battles. He would think about how and where to move the ships and other military strategy issues and would relax enough to forget about his bar studies. Crazy but true!)

"THE HEIGHTS BY GREAT MEN REACHED AND KEPT WERE NOT OBTAINED BY SUDDEN FLIGHT, BUT THEY, WHILE THEIR COMPANIONS SLEPT WERE TOILING UPWARD IN THE NIGHT."

— HENRY WADSWORTH LONGFELLOW —

Keep the Wadsworth quote in mind if you find you cannot sleep on certain nights. You are toiling. And your hard work will pay off.

TOP TEN TIPS THAT WILL HELP EVERYONE, ESPECIALLY NONTRADITIONAL STUDENTS

1. "Believe you can PASS!"

If law is a second or third career or you came to law school later in life, dispel any doubts that as an older person, you can't pass. Baloney! Some things may be more challenging. It may be a challenge to sit for long periods of time and your fingers may cramp from writing or typing for hours. You can work through these.

You set your goal in Chapter 1. Sticking with that goal sometimes poses particular challenges for nontraditional students. You are tempted to slip into thinking, "Well, I'll give it a shot, but I doubt I can pull it off with all the work and family commitments I am juggling."

Cut that out. Such built-in excuses are a setup for failure. You decided to pass, so continue working toward that end with every ounce of energy you can muster. Stop and slap yourself if you find you are saying things like, "I'd like to pass, and I will eventually, but I do have a job that pays the bills for now so it won't be too big a deal if I don't pass this first time. I can always take it again." No. No. No. Passing *is* that big a deal—for you, for your classmates, for your law school.

I remind my students all the time that they are a class; they rise and fall together. If everyone in your class passes the bar exam, you and all of your colleagues will realize positive ripple effects. Do not sell yourself short, and do not let your classmates down. Put as plainly as possible, you are all responsible for the prestige (or lack thereof) of your diplomas. If you don't *need* the license to find a job to feed yourself or your family, you may not be as "hungry" as some of those you are competing against. Your *wanting* to pass thus has to be as powerful as classmates who *need* to. Find the motivation. The high of passing, the stamp of credibility you gain, and the doors that will open all make the effort worth it. And, on the flipside, the cost of failure is far higher than you might imagine. Read Part II of this book if you think, "I can always take it again." (To paraphrase *Apollo 13*, "Failure is not an option.")

2. Secure "buy-in" from family and significant others.

Help those in your support system to understand what you need while studying. And plan something fun to celebrate and thank them when the exam is done. (Chapter 6 includes advice on how to gain family and community support, and how to handle a lack of support.)

3. Start early: Two months is not enough!

When you cannot study as many hours in the day as other students can, you must start earlier. Eight weeks might be sufficient for full-time bar students who average sixty hours per week of studying. But if you are working a demanding job or have extensive family commitments, plan to study throughout your entire last year in law school. Some bar reviews have early-start programs, or you can create your own pre-bar-review schedule. You will want to slowly and steadily review all the subjects tested on the exam and begin incorporating regular practice exams into your week.

4. Carve out several productive hours each day.

Determine when you study most productively, and dedicate those hours exclusively to bar prep. Post your study schedule so that anyone who wants your time knows when you may not be interrupted. Unless it's a true emergency, keep study time for studying. You cannot afford to waste time. (Staring into space or "glazing over" while forcing study into an unproductive time of day is just as much wasted time as taking the afternoon off and going to the beach. Many working students feel guilty about not doing as much during the week, so they study for sixteen-hour days on weekends. But most people cannot sustain high-level productivity for more than eight to ten hours a day. (Even two or three quality hours would be more beneficial than ten hours of spinning your wheels.)

5. Stay organized, disciplined, and committed to success.

Get systems in place to handle whatever must be done while you are studying. Put off everything that can wait until August. Know where everything is. (You can't afford to spend time looking for your keys when you are heading out the door to bar review!)

If there are occasions you must acknowledge in June and July (birthdays or anniversaries), buy cards and gifts (and wrap them) ahead of time and have them ready to go. Or give IOUs and celebrate in August. (More in Chapter 6 on saying no to important occasions that arise in June and July.)

6. Don't skimp on sleep, exercise, or motivating study breaks.

The bar exam is both a physical and mental challenge. It is especially critical to be in shape and feel well, and to every extent possible be ready to perform at your best. (You will need some fun and relaxation to recharge your batteries.)

7. Protect your time. Protect your work space.

Your study hours are precious. Do you hand over the keys to your home without very good reason to do so? Don't hand away your key to success: your time!

Another thing many people find boosts their concentration and productivity is a clear work space. If you have an office or desk that is all yours, keep it that way. And do not share your computer with anyone during bar prep. Keep your spyware and antivirus protections up to date. The last thing you need is a virus on your computer in the weeks before the bar exam.

8. Reduce, and work to eliminate, distractions.

See above. Don't get sucked into anything unless it helps you study, sleep, or recharge your batteries. This is not the time to buy or sell a house, figure out relationship issues, or go on a diet. In fact, it is not a productive time to worry about anything. If you need to, have a good worry in May about whatever is going on; then put your non-bar cares in a box that you will not open until August.

If you find that you are continually worrying, about the bar and everything else, try designating one hour per week as "worry hour." At the appointed time, you can rant, cry, scream, complain, or write a nasty letter (that you will never send) listing everything that is bugging you, bar related or otherwise. When your worry hour is over, put your concerns away for the week and get back to work.

You should also allow absolutely no stressing over how much material there is to learn. When you find yourself worrying about that, get to work. Take a practice test. Review lecture notes. Memorize rule statements with flash cards. Working will get you much further than worrying.

9. Set realistic expectations.

Do not rush yourself through outlines, lectures, or practice tests. It is better to learn what you're spending time on than to hastily go through the material and not really absorb it. Revise your plans if your time estimates are not working. And, when you are too tired to focus, switch tasks or sleep if you need to.

10. Use every minute effectively.

Study when you study. (For example, don't fall into the trap of feeling guilty that you are not studying when you are with family, and feeling guilty that you are not with family when you are studying.) All that gets you is a lot of guilt and not a lot of effective studying. Be in the moment. Use commute time and exercise time to listen to bar review lectures or recordings of your own voice reading rule statements.

GET AND USE QUALITY EXPERT HELP: RELIABLE BAR REVIEW COURSES, ACADEMIC SUPPORT FACULTY, AND TRUSTED MENTORS

- Investing in Yourself
- The Need for and Benefits of Bar Review
  - Beyond bar review
  - Get the most out of your bar review.
  - Be present and engaged.
  - Concentrate.
  - Personalize your bar-review materials.
  - Make sure you understand what you hear and read.
    - Bar review lectures
    - Bar review outlines
      - Understand what is in the outlines.
- Finding a Mentor
  - Mentor credibility

This book is about achieving. It is about success. It is not about pipe dreams. Nowhere am I saying, "Just be confident, and you will pass." Bar review is like a gym membership. You must do more than simply sign up and pay the fee. If that is all you do, you will lose time *and* money and not pass the bar (or get fit).

To succeed, you must fully engage. For bar review, that means sticking to the schedule, attending and listening carefully to all the lectures (live or online), and completing and turning in all the assignments. You must take many practice tests (including hundreds of essays and thousands of multiple-choice questions) and study reliable sample or model answers. (*Sample answers* are student answers that are passing, but not perfect. *Model answers* are those written by bar reviews or bar support faculty and designed as teaching tools.)

Some goals are easier to achieve with the help of experts. Bar passage is one of those. You must learn, memorize, and be able to clearly articulate many rules and concepts. You must master numerous skills, including critical reading, factual and legal analysis, clear and effective writing, and time management. It helps enormously to train with and learn from a team of experts who know what they are talking about. Conversely, it is an act of sabotage to solicit (and often pay dearly for) misinformation. Going it alone or with an unreliable tutor or bar review versus working with a proven, trustworthy bar review course nearly always means the difference between succeeding or not.

Beware. Reliable experts will tell you there are no shortcuts. Studying for the bar is hard work. If anyone promises you a foolproof system, walk away. Quality bar review instructors, like personal trainers, do *not* make it easy. They keep you on track.

A good teacher can clarify confusion and simplify complex concepts. You may have been lucky enough to have had professors who were able to do that; hopefully, you will find others like them in bar review. But even if you understand every aspect of every rule tested on the bar exam (which virtually no one does), the sheer volume of material and marathon nature of the exam make the exam difficult. Most of us do not have instant-recall brains; there is no *search* button in our memory that readily delivers every answer. So, again, do not fall for any course or tutor who sounds too good to be true. There are many scams in bar review. (This is true for first-timers, and even more so for repeat takers, as scammers prey on people's doubts and fears. More on repeating the exam in Part II.)

INVESTING IN YOURSELF

Keeping these caveats in mind, a reliable bar review is a must. You might have made it through law school without supplemental materials or tutoring. This is different. Those who take bar review courses succeed in geometrically greater numbers than those who study on their own.

If you think you cannot afford a bar review course, think again. You cannot afford *not* to take one. If at all possible, start a bar fund on or before day one of law school. (If you are reading this book and are already in law school, start your fund now with whatever money you can.) If you need more money to live on in June and July, bar loans may be available. (Many have high interest rates and strict qualification restrictions. Check them out carefully. Your law school's financial-aid office may be able to help you.) Family may be more willing than you think to lend you money. Local bar associations may also have scholarships. And sometimes you can earn a free course by serving as a bar review rep.

However much it may appear that you can't add another dime of debt to that mounting pile, you must continue investing in yourself. Would you spend time in Chicago in winter without a warm coat, scarf, and boots? Would you go mountain climbing without proper training and sturdy ropes? Taking the bar exam without a reliable bar review is similarly foolish. (It is unwise to cut corners and take a cheaper course if you don't believe it is the best one for you.) Don't sabotage yourself before you start. Spare yourself the far-greater costs of repeating the exam.

THE GRASS IS NOT ALWAYS GREENER

It may taste like a bitter pill watching wealthier or higher-achieving classmates have what seems like an easy time financially while you struggle to budget every dime. Energy spent on resentment generally does not yield productive dividends. 1) You are you, and you are in the position you are in. Resenting someone else will not change your position; 2) What you must work harder for, you likely appreciate more; and 3) You don't know the full price someone is really paying for whatever funds that they have been given. There may be strings attached that you would never want. So focus all your energy on passing the exam. Let everything else go.

THE NEED FOR AND BENEFITS OF BAR REVIEW

You need a *reliable* bar review to stay on track and to confidently trust the process. Especially toward the end of June, you may start dragging. You may get a couple of low scores on practice tests and, with the exam a month away, you may question your preparation. You want to avoid time spent doubting yourself (or your course), so you continue to focus on increasing your knowledge and improving your skills. So what will a bar review offer? A reliable bar review should do the following:

- Provide lectures that review each of the subjects tested on your bar exam.
- Provide outlines that summarize the relevant law you need to know for each subject.
- Help with skills training by providing essay, MBE, and performance-test workshops (if you have a PT in your jurisdiction).
- Flag heavily tested areas.
- Highlight areas that differ or conflict in jurisdictions where you are expected to apply both state and federal rules.
- Provide practice questions and sample or model answers to those questions.
- Grade or critique practice exams. (Note: Even if your bar review critiques all of your practice exams, you should also do your own self-assessment. The time to learn most from taking a practice exam is just after completing it. Chapter 8 explains how to self-assess practice exams.)
- Answer questions if you don't understand something. (But remember, the bar review cannot do the work for you. Your instructors are not taking your bar; you are. You need to know the rules and be able to apply them. So try hard to understand concepts before jumping to ask questions.)
- Provide a calendar to structure your eight-week countdown.

Bar review also helps identify what you do and do not need to know. The bar exam tests an enormous amount of material. In an ideal world, we would say to master everything before you go in. But a) the world is not ideal, and b) that would be a waste of your time, energy, and brain "disk space." A reputable bar review will flag what is heavily tested and what areas have historically never or rarely been tested. That doesn't mean that a never-before-tested area cannot suddenly appear on your exam, but history repeats itself and so do bar examiners. One of the most helpful parts of being enrolled in a reputable bar review is getting sound advice on what should be covered only superficially, if at all, and what you should know in depth.

You may want or need to supplement your bar review, but you should never cut corners. (As a colleague often says, "Bar review is a floor, not a ceiling." In other words, you can (and often should) do more than is on your bar review calendar, but without a very good reason, do not do less than what your bar review tells you to do.

BAR REVIEW IS NOT A MAGIC PILL

Many bar applicants pay for bar review and expect the knowledge will magically enter their brains, kind of like sleeping with textbooks under your pillow. When they find the concepts are not simple, they look for another course that promises to make it easier. Some people end up enrolling in several bar reviews and still failing the bar exam. There are no quick fixes. As we said above, joining a gym will not get you fit. Buying a bar review course will not make you pass the exam. You must do the work, the learning, and the thinking, and take the practice tests.

We talked about the importance of selecting a reliable bar review. It is also important to select a bar review that works for you, not just one your friends sign up for. There may be a number of trustworthy choices. Be an active consumer. As you learn about different bar review options, list any pros and cons, who recommended it, your own impressions, and any follow-up questions. Note the name and contact information of someone who can answer future questions and how to enroll if you decide upon that course.

Bar Review Selection Worksheet

Available full-service bar reviews					
Name/ Contact Info	Pros	Cons	Recommended By	My Impression	Questions

Available Supplemental Bar Reviews					
Name/ Contact Info	Pros	Cons	Recommended By	My Impression	Questions

Beyond bar review

You may attend bar review lectures with others, but much of the work you must do in June and July is independent. And, you cannot just attend bar review lectures and expect to pass the exam. That's sort of like going to a lecture on tennis and expecting to compete at Wimbledon. You need to complete practice exams, learn and memorize rules, and look up what you do not understand.

Even after listening to the best bar review lecturer, there may still be rules or concepts you do not understand. Figure them out, especially if they fall within areas identified as heavily tested. Start by reviewing the outline or your lecture notes. Read examples out loud. Sometimes just looking at a concept another couple of times will make it click. If you still don't understand it, perhaps someone at your bar review can clarify your question. If not, you may want to consult another resource, but do so with caution. You don't need to know every nuance of every rule to pass the bar exam. But if it's something critical, find a way to understand.

Generally it is *not* recommended to go back into your law school class notes during bar prep. Law classes often have a different emphasis and different objectives from bar review. However, if you happened to have a professor who explained an area of law in a way that makes more sense to you than the bar review lecturer, consult those notes. (I was fortunate enough to have the late Jesse Dukeminier as a professor. I consistently turned back to his materials on property because they made sense to me.)

It can be empowering to realize that your confusion may not be exclusively about *you*. Sometimes you hear or read a different explanation, and a concept that was previously mystifying is suddenly clear. Again, it may be you. You may just need to struggle a bit harder with the resources you have. But if you are really baffled, it may save time to quickly consult another source.

During school, I tell all of my students, "If you don't understand something, look it up!" I suggest reading the notes in their casebook and related passages in a reliable hornbook. Hornbooks are treatises that summarize an area of law. They are great references and have helpful examples. There are endless choices of good hornbooks, especially for standard law school courses. Yet many law students have *never* opened a hornbook. (Have you?) One of my first-year professors assigned the superb civil-procedure hornbook by Friedenthal, Kane, and Miller. We studied with *both* that hornbook and a casebook; from week one of law school, my class understood the value of learning from hornbooks. If you are still in school and don't understand something (or want to put your casebook reading in context), instead of rushing first to a commercial study aid (some of which are also helpful), try reading a good horn-book. (Don't be intimidated if it's heavy!) Hardbound hornbooks may look complex because of their size and weight, but you would be surprised how much they can clarify. Between the index, table of contents, and table of cases, you can easily find whatever area you want to focus on, and there is simply no substitute for looking something up and really *getting* it! (If you need recommendations for reliable horn-books, ask your professors, law librarian, or ASP faculty. Note: To clarify confusion during law school, always check first to see what your professors have written. If your professor wrote a leading treatise in a particular area, start there!)

Bar reviews will tell you it is crazy to look anything up outside a bar review outline after May. I would be the first to say, start early so that June and July are *review*. But few feelings are worse than going in to your bar exam hoping they won't test a particular concept because you don't understand it. A negative ripple effect follows when you feel vulnerable. (You may feel even more "stupid" or "exposed" because you are afraid of it being on the exam.) Do not go there. You want the "power ripple." Knowing that you finally *get* a concept makes you feel like you can reason through anything they throw at you. Again, your best bet is to *start early so you have the time to look up what you do not understand.*

CAVEAT: DON'T BE TOO QUICK TO CONSULT ANYTHING BEYOND BAR REVIEW MATERIALS.

During intensive bar prep, consult outside sources *only* with respect to major concepts that you don't understand after trying hard to understand the bar review materials. Do not go to outside sources just because the review course states some rule differently than you learned it. It cannot be emphasized enough: *don't spend precious time in June and July routinely second-guessing your bar review.* Enroll in a reliable course and trust it. One of the great distractors is time spent doubting and questioning your bar review materials. Different sources often state rules slightly differently. Bar review may vary from how you learned rules in law school. That does not mean your bar review *or* your professor was wrong. As long as the fundamentals are the same (for example, causes of action include the same elements), and as long as you understand the concepts, your time is best spent continuing to review additional rules and concepts, and taking more practice tests. Do not waste time drilling down to catch minor disparities.

Get the most out of your bar review.

One size does not fit all, not in shoes nor in bar preparation. What is right for you might not be best for a friend or classmate. In an earlier chapter, we discussed the need to periodically assess your progress, to look at everything in your schedule—from where and what time of day you study and the tasks you complete, to the kinds of food you eat to stay energized. Your bar review course is the principal component of your schedule; it also can be personalized to fit your lifestyle and learning style. We will look at ways to make bar review more effective: a) Be present and engaged; b) Personalize the materials; c) Make sure you understand what you are doing and learning; and d) Follow the schedule and do the work (keep training).

Be present and engaged.

You can enroll in bar review, pay the money, and show up occasionally. You can also be physically present at every session, but mentally miles away. This applies equally to live and online bar reviews. You can sit in front of your computer and log in, just as you can show up to a lecture hall, without actively listening, taking notes, and reviewing points you do not understand.

Do not tell yourself you are paying attention if you are constantly checking your phone or Facebook. Fooling yourself makes you the fool. The people whose texts you are reading instead of focusing intently on bar review will not pay the price if you fail the bar. You will.

Think of it this way: "The buck stops here." At the end of the day, you and you alone are responsible. As the bar applicant, it's all on you to have done your best work by the time you walk into that exam. As an attorney, it will be all on you if you show up unprepared to represent a client. There is no one else to point to or blame. (Death and major illnesses are good excuses for failing to adequately prepare. Are there any others? You tell me.)

Concentrate.

To develop your concentration, start by observing your level of focus. If you find yourself drifting or zoning out while reading, sit up and subvocalize (say it barely audibly) as you look at and touch the words on the page. If you're still losing focus, stand and stretch and sit back down. Still not alert enough? Go to the bathroom and splash water on your face. Yes, that wastes time, but not nearly as much time as will be lost by spacing out entirely. (Note: If you need to use the bathroom during the actual exam, read a question first so you can work on it in your head on your way to and from the restroom.)

Because time is so valuable during intensive bar prep, it is counterproductive to spend even a minute "reading" material you do not learn from. This is not reading; it's glossing over the words. One of my former students, now an alumni bar mentor, calls this "hanging out with the outlines." Your time is better spent taking an open-book practice test, looking up rules in the outline that you don't know as you write your answers. Learning rules in the context of a fact pattern helps you remember them.

Another trap is taking breaks that we tell ourselves are necessary. When weaning yourself off social media and texting, for example, you may suddenly "need" more bathroom and coffee breaks. Sometimes those are genuine necessities, but other times they are ways of procrastinating. You may be subconsciously avoiding facing up to what you do not understand. It is easy to go through the material superficially. It is far more difficult to really understand, learn, and improve your skills. (But the latter gets you to your goal.)

Mastering the ability to focus and be actively engaged in what you do will serve you well for the rest of your life. More immediately, during bar prep:

- You will learn more material, and learn more effectively and efficiently;
- You will be attentive to detail (required on the bar and in law practice, and rather helpful in much of life);
- You will get ready for exam days, including learning to do without your multi-tasking devices when you won't have them; and
- You will have a much better shot at completing all the questions within the allotted time, something that is hard to do when you haven't built up your endurance and can't concentrate for long, uninterrupted time blocks.

Of course, I know you will not have your phone with you in the exam, but unless you train now to really focus, you will find ways to drift off in that testing room. You'll look at the person next to you, watch the proctors, listen to keyboards clacking, or clean your fingernails. You may find you have read the same paragraph several times before you even realize your mind was wandering. But you will pay a hefty price for "checking out."

Personalize your bar review materials.

One of the best ways to be present and get the most out of your review course is to take good notes that are personal to you. Write in your outlines. Online bar reviews often have electronic note-taking systems.

Add hypos that make sense to you. Translate formal rule statements into colloquial, short phrases. (Perhaps you will remember *inadequacy of the legal remedy*, a required element for certain equitable remedies, as the "money won't cut it rule." You might say to yourself: "Yeah, well, to get a court to order specific performance of a contract, the court must be persuaded that money just won't cut it for this plaintiff; dollars just aren't going to fly, it just doesn't give the plaintiff what he bargained for." Now, you would *never* write that on an exam. You might write something such as, "The legal remedy must be found to be inadequate. Here the plaintiff wanted to buy Blackacre, and because Blackacre is a unique parcel of land, money damages will not suffice to fully compensate the plaintiff for the loss of Blackacre." Writing plain-English versions of legal concepts (translations, if you will), may make the meaning of those rules clearer for you and may help you remember the concepts on exams.

For a handwritten flash card, write the term on the front of the card. On the back of the card, at the top, write the succinct and proper phrasing of the rule (the official definition, or what you would write in an essay). Then, on the bottom of the back side of the card, note those plain-English words, images, or references *that make sense to you* to explain that rule.

Try the following short exercise. Take ten seconds to read the sentence below. Think of any specifics you might have learned about this point. In the spaces that follow, write whatever might help you to remember how this sentence might apply on a bar exam question.

Contracts' fact patterns are generally governed by UCC (goods) or common law (land or services).

_____

_____

_____

_____

_____

_____

Example of personalized notes:

Essay Writing: Start contracts question noting which law applies: UCC or common law. UCC transactions in goods — moveable things like refrigerators or "widgets." Common law — basically land or services. (Remember tricky questions like that example where growing crops were considered land, but when harvested or severed from the land they are goods.) The UCC is influential even when not controlling. Look out for mixed UCC & common law fact patterns — remember the exam with the builder who supplied wood (goods) and with that wood built a fence (services). If mixed, can I divide into two contracts? If not, which predominates, goods or services?

This is an easy-to-understand example. But personalizing the materials will help you with both simple and complex points alike. It will also help you prepare to apply what you have learned to practice tests. Any time a bar review lecture flags a concept as important or heavily tested, annotate your materials. Write commentary that makes sense to you.

Let's try again. What is consideration?

_____

_____

_____

_____

_____

_____

ANNOTATING

One of my favorite law professors told our first-year class to write in our case-books. He suggested we not only take notes in the margins, but also write our opinions and reactions to the decisions. Why would he suggest that, especially when students are nearly always instructed *not* to write their opinions on exams? Some day we would find the notes fascinating, he said, and the books would be valuable if we ever became famous. (He mentioned that an annotated casebook from a former U.S. Supreme Court justice had fetched a large sum of money.) Looking back, I suspect his real motive was simply to keep us actively engaged in the material. It worked.

Make sure you understand what you hear and read.

This is a basic premise. When we don't know what certain terms mean, we can't readily understand explanations of concepts that use those terms. But how often do we stop and look them up? Too often we just move on and hope we will "get it" from context clues.

No more. From now on, plan to learn rules and definitions just as you would learn vocabulary when studying a foreign language. Until you are fluent in legalese, stop and look things up. Not only will familiarity with terminology help you understand reading and lectures, but it is critical for essay writing. (There is good reason that despite the abundance of lawyer jokes, people turn to lawyers when they need help resolving problems or tackling complex concerns. We have proved ourselves as thinkers. Graduating from law school and passing the bar exam provide a stamp of credibility that says you can read and reason.) But recalling the phrasing of a rule and making sense of it are two different animals. Likewise, "knowing" a rule and being able to quickly and readily articulate that rule are also two different things. You need the former ("I know it when I see it," to borrow the famous line from an entirely different context) for multiple-choice questions for which you must know the rules, and know them well, in order to determine which answer choice is best. But once that determination is made, you simply bubble in the *A*, *B*, *C*, or *D* accordingly. On essays, however, you must not only know which law you will apply to analyze the issues you identified, but also state those rules rapidly and accurately. So having a command of the terms (fluency) will help you deliver the information you do know in a more effective manner.

For bar exam essays, all the stockpiles of knowledge in your head won't do any good whatsoever if you cannot deliver that information effectively in your written answers. (After every bar, I talk with a number of students who passed the MBE portion and failed the essays.) So again, by exam time at the latest, be sure you are fully fluent in legalese. Yet another reason to start early!

Bar review lectures

Bar review includes lectures during which professors summarize the most important legal concepts and rules tested on your bar exam. They may be live or recorded, online or in person. However the lecture is delivered, you can improve your understanding of what is said by "book-ending" the process.

Before the lecture, read through the outline's table of contents. Look up terms you can't readily define so you can follow the lecture easily and clearly. This will prime you to get the most out of each lecture.

During the lectures, listen as carefully as possible. Don't try to write down every word, as this will prevent you from hearing the professor. Make shorthand notes about points to look up later or to highlight particularly good examples. You may want to flag concepts the lecturer said were frequently tested. Remember, you will have an outline to look up what you don't understand. You need to "lean forward and listen." (See text box below.)

After the lecture, while the material is still fresh, annotate your outline with your lecture notes, examples, charts, lists, and tips on what the professor said is or is not frequently tested. This will help seal in what you learned. Make flash cards (written or digital) for every major rule, looking up rules or concepts you didn't understand during the lecture in your outline. (When I studied for the bar exam, I set aside time after each lecture to do just this. Often just an extra half-hour looking up or rewriting certain points, even thinking a bit more about some of the concepts, made the learning from that lecture much more useful.)

LEAN FORWARD AND LISTEN

I recently attended an outdoor theater production of George Bernard Shaw's *Heartbreak House*. There were no microphones to amplify the actors' voices. But even if they had been blasted from the most-modern soundstage, there were words and thoughts (written in the early part of the twentieth century) that require more effort to understand than today's TV sound bites. After the performance, chatting with one of the actors who asked how the sound was in the back row, he said, "No matter what seat you are in, you have to sort of lean forward and listen to really get what we're saying." Similarly, you have to lean forward and listen to get this bar stuff.

NOTE TAKING

Some people need to take notes to pay attention. For others, the opposite is true: they can't really focus and absorb concepts while taking notes. (One of the great advantages to online lectures is that you can usually replay them. So you may want to just watch and listen the first time around. If it's a live online class, you might want to actively participate in the discussions, and then review the recording and take notes when you replay the session.) If you are in a traditional, live bar review class and you know you will get more from just listening, do that (while also jotting down isolated words that you will want to look up and review in the outline after the lecture). Most or all of what was said in the lecture will probably be in the outline. Get to know yourself and how note taking helps or hinders your learning.

Bar review outlines

Everyone talks about bar review outlines. What are they? How do they help you? Bar review outlines are essentially mini-hornbooks, treatises, or summaries of discrete subjects. A good outline will not only summarize the area of law, but provide clear, easy-to-memorize rule statements; explain the logic and reasoning behind those rules; and provide examples or hypos showing how they have been tested in fact patterns. The bar review outline may also indicate the frequency with which certain areas have appeared on previous exams in your jurisdiction. To help make bar review outlines work for you, you will want to do the following:

- Annotate them with examples and phrasings that make sense to you. (These can come from a bar review lecturer, a professor in law school, or a case or practice-exam fact pattern that you recall.) Write in the margins or type into the text file if your outline is online. Writing will help you remember. (Many people write out new rules several times on a separate piece of paper to seal them in.)
- Chart key areas if you are a visual learner. Make flowcharts.
- Create mnemonics to memorize lists of elements, if they help you. Some people think of the basics of a contract cause of action as FBPD (Formation, Breach, Performance, Damages). Some people remember the mnemonic with the help of another catchy phrase. For example, DBCD stands for the elements of negligence: Duty, Breach, Causation, Damages. You may recall "DBCD" by reme-

bering the phrase "Desserts Bring Calories and Diabetes," or the more-upbeat "Delicious Brownies, Cake, and Donuts."

- Condense them to usable size as you get closer to exam time. Most bar review outlines are long—some several hundred pages. Before your exam, reduce them to a more user-friendly form. Remember: outlines cannot be brought into the exam! Only what is in your brain comes into the test site. So be sure you are using the outlines as learning tools and that the most critical information gets *and stays* in your head.

Bottom line: outlines are only as useful as you make them. So begin bar review doing the assigned reading in the major outlines. Use them as companions to the lectures, helping you learn the frequently tested rules and concepts. As you get closer to test time, by the end of June or early July, transform them into about ten pages each. You will then move the major outlines from your desk to the bookshelf. Keep them on the shelf as references, and shift your focus to using your own shortened summary outlines along with practice tests. Eventually, by the week before the bar exam at the latest, condense each subject to one page. Include on that one page summary approaches, checklists, or a shorthand outline—whatever you would want to take into the exam *if you could* to help you answer a question in that area.

Understand what is in the outlines. You can chart all you want and memorize with clever mnemonics, but if you don't understand the concepts you probably won't be able to apply them correctly. Recalling the phrasing of a rule and making sense of it are two different things. Can you explain a concept to a layperson? If so, you probably understand at least the basics fairly well.

Quick test:
Explain felony murder to a very smart 16-year-old. (See Chapter 1 for more on the fictitious "very smart 16-year-old" standard, and why trying to explain heavily tested concepts to such a person is helpful.)

_____

_____

_____

_____

_____

UNDERSTAND WHAT YOU MEMORIZE

Students often memorize the elements of injunctive relief as IPFBD (Inadequacy of the legal remedy, Property right, Feasibility, Balancing of equities, and Defenses). You must know what those terms mean, though, rather than merely memorizing them. A colleague frequently refers to students who have memorized the term *feasibility*, but are confused about its meaning. They mistakenly assume it refers to whether it is feasible for the *parties* to carry out the order, rather than the accurate meaning, which is whether it is feasible for the *court* to supervise implementation of the order. Do you recall discussions in remedies about whether it would be easier for a court to supervise the tearing down of a second-story house or the building of a new one-story home? This would have been a discussion regarding the element of feasibility.

FINDING A MENTOR

DICTIONARY DEFINITION OF MENTOR: A TRUSTED FRIEND, COUNSELOR OR TEACHER, USUALLY A MORE EXPERIENCED PERSON WHO ADVISES AND SERVES AS BY EXAMPLE.

I will suggest mentors for at least two purposes: a bar mentor discussed below, and a career mentor described in Chapter 10. A bar mentor can:

- Serve as proof that the exam is passable. (You want to look at your mentor, feel encouraged that he or she passed, and believe *unequivocally* that you can, too!);
- Review your study plan or study schedule, remind you of things you may have forgotten, and give you tips (perhaps something simple like reserving your hotel room for an extra night so you don't have to worry about packing up or checking out as you head into your last day of the exam);
- Check in with you weekly in June and July to see that you are staying on your study schedule (this is sort of the "mentor as coach or trainer" function);
- Give you moral support to stay focused and not be bothered by those who don't understand when you say no to social invitations and hibernate to study;
- Help you think through adjusting your study plan or schedule if something is not working for you;
- Encourage and reassure you if you feel guilty or irresponsible when you need extra funds for bar studies, offering the justification that you must not skimp in your preparation if you want to pass the bar the first time; and
- Be a friendly face who "gets it," someone who just pats you on the back and says, "Stick with this. You can do it!"

Mentor Credibility

A key trait of a good bar mentor is his or her ability to convince you that you can pass the bar. A mentor must be someone you find credible. Credibility is one reason I started an alumni bar-mentoring program. Recent graduates are more believable than professors, who likely went to different (perhaps more prestigious) schools and took the bar exam decades earlier. Students are (rightfully) skeptical about the relevance of certain professors' experience. But hearing from someone who has just recently been in your shoes, someone who studied the same books and with the same professors, took the same bar review, and faced the same challenges is extremely persuasive. It carries weight when a recent graduate tells you, "I did it, and you can, too." (If you have a unique situation, you may want a mentor who has been through the same or similar circumstances. Alice, a working mother of two young children, did not find her twenty-seven-year-old, single mentor helpful. "*His* passing the bar doesn't say anything about whether I can. He didn't have a care in the world other than studying." Alice needed a mentor whose life situation was similar to hers when he or she took the bar. You may, too. If so, find one.)

An effective bar mentor must know and appreciate what you are going through. Your family and friends, even if they are supportive, are typically *not* great bar mentors unless they themselves took and passed the bar exam. A supportive professor can be a fine mentor, as can a lawyer in the community, but if you can find an alum (someone from your school who graduated recently and passed the bar) with whom you feel comfortable, he or she may be best suited to help you.

Note: Do not rely on your bar mentor to help you learn the law. Do that work with your bar review and independently, and perhaps with your school's bar support program. Your mentor is a coach, someone who will keep you on target. You are training for the Bar Exam Olympics. The PT, MBE, and essays, as well as any other state-specific portions of your exam, are the individual events you are competing in. You must train to do well, every day, under simulated conditions. A mentor can help hold you accountable for completing all your practice sessions and improving at every turn.

Good mentors will help their protégés to believe in themselves. In the words of a former student to his mentor, "Thank you for everything! Thank you for being there for us, for keeping us in your thoughts, and for having confidence in us even when we did not believe in ourselves. I don't know if you recall, but one time I happened to mention that the PT was going to be my Achilles' heel. You immediately shot back that you would not let me fail the PT. That was the turning point. I knew then that I would blow them away, and I am certain now that of all parts of the exam, I actually did the best on those PTs."

Potential Mentors:

List names of people who might make good mentors. If your school does not have a mentor program that will pair you with someone, reach out to one of the people on your list and see if he or she will agree to mentor you.

_____

_____

_____

_____

_____

ENLIST YOUR TROOPS AND LOSE THE NAYSAYERS: IT TAKES A VILLAGE OF POSITIVE PEOPLE

- Admitting that Some People Will Not "Get It" and Are Not Helpful to You Now
- Helping Those Who Are Supportive Help You
  - Think of analogies to explain your struggles to family or friends
- Saying No to Supportive People Who Still Want Your Time During Bar Study
- Watching Out for Saboteurs
  - Be wary of competitive classmates.
  - Be wary of negative people: friends and strangers.
  - Keep doubters at a distance: build a protective wall around your confidence.
    - Relatives and others who make destructive comments
    - Special problem in law school: professors who doubt you
    - Naysayers

"DO WHAT YOU FEEL IN YOUR HEART TO BE RIGHT, FOR YOU'LL BE CRITICIZED ANYWAY. YOU'LL BE DAMNED IF YOU DO AND DAMNED IF YOU DON'T."

— ELEANOR ROOSEVELT —

We talked in previous chapters about believing in yourself and your ability to pass, and investing in yourself so you have the resources to succeed. This is easier said than done, especially if you do not have a great support system. It is harder still if you must battle people who seek to undermine you.

Some of you contend with cultural, racial, or gender stereotypes that can be psychological barriers to success, or perhaps even a parent, grandparent, or other important person in your life who does not approve of your becoming a lawyer. Others battle financial pressures that cause you to doubt the long-term investment in a professional career when you are obligated (or feel obligated) to help by supplying needed short-term funds. Some face explicit or implicit comments suggesting you are not smart enough to pass the bar exam and become a lawyer. You may find yourself in a relationship with someone who resents the time and energy that bar success requires; he or she may either intentionally or inadvertently sabotage your bar-passage goals. (Some students, when they step back, recognize a pattern. Somehow they got into fights with their partner, spouse, or significant other before *each* set of final exams. If this is you, be careful. Plan to avoid this when you are getting ready for the bar.)

TAKE AN HONEST LOOK AT YOURSELF

Recently one of my 3L students e-mailed me, saying how helpful it had been to plan ahead to battle distractions and surround herself with positive influences. She discussed with her significant other the commitment bar studies would entail and realized they had to break up. He was not willing to support her in the way she would need to pass. She was grateful to have realized this before, rather than during, intensive bar preparation. In her words, "I am glad that you prompted us to take an honest look at how our lives were organized. I feel like I am allowing myself to have a true chance at achieving my goals. I want to truly be able to say I put everything I could into passing the bar."

You may not realize how helpful it can be to avoid those who are not supportive (at least in June and July). For readers who come from professional or academic backgrounds, it is hard to imagine that one's family could prove to be more of an obstacle than an asset. But this is all too real an issue for many. Facing it now will help you not only to pass the bar exam, but to more confidently reach for and achieve all of your professional goals.

Not only do those facing family challenges need a boost, so too do those in the bottom half of their law school class. If you are in this group, the tools in this chapter will help you gain the confidence to rise above statistics and claim the success you desire. The strategies will help you build resistance to those who prey on your own doubts (low pass rates, fewer law jobs, etc.). It will be critical to get rid of or at least dilute negative influences, seek support that is truly useful, avoid "help" that hurts more than supports, and ask directly and explicitly for what you need during this stressful period.

Who makes up your supportive troops? Who is in your inner circle? How can you get them on board? The first part of this analysis involves some triage. Sort people into three categories:

- People who are supportive and "get it" right away
- People who need help learning how to be supportive
- People who are simply not helpful or are downright destructive

Learn to rely primarily on those who are already supportive and "get it": your mentor, other recent graduates who passed the bar exam, ASP faculty and other trusted professors, and lawyers or law clerks you work with. The following sections will teach you how to handle both people who aren't currently supportive but can become so and those you should avoid until after the bar exam.

ADMITTING THAT SOME PEOPLE WILL NOT "GET IT" AND ARE NOT HELPFUL TO YOU NOW

There may be people you cannot enlist for support in studying for the bar exam. These people may come around and even be huge supporters later in your life and career, but right now they don't get it and will not help you pass your exam.

You may have a parent who really didn't want you to go to law school in the first place and now doesn't support your becoming a lawyer. Even if you're financing this goal yourself, and not asking for a dime from that parent, he or she may disapprove of your career choice. Among the parents of students I have worked with over the years, these stand out:

- Jorge's dad, who repeatedly told his law student son to be a "real man," get a "real job," and "stop with the schooling already."
- Wanda's mom, who often wondered aloud why being a secretary "like Mom" was not "good enough" for her daughter.
- Tom's overachieving lawyer dad, who told his slightly laid-back son how much harder he had worked than his son in law school, and that all of his "lazy" friends in school didn't pass the bar exam.

At a recent gathering of students who had just finished taking the bar exam, they shared stories of the many friends who had "broken up with them" during law school and written them off completely during bar prep. These friends just did not understand why there was no time at all to hang out in June or July.[24]

Your best strategy may simply be not to seek help or support from such persons. You may be able to approach them again later, when you are closer to meeting your goal. But in the meantime, find at least one person who *is* supportive and reach out.

Once you triage and have identified a solid group of people or even one truly supportive person, unless those people went to law school and have taken the bar themselves, you will still have to help them understand the kind of support you need.

HELPING THOSE WHO ARE SUPPORTIVE HELP YOU

Some people mean well and want to help you, but don't know how. It can be beneficial to enlist the support of your immediate circle of family and friends, but sometimes you need to guide them. Unless they are lawyers, they will likely have a hard time understanding the intensity of your studies. Even other professionals, such as doctors and engineers, often don't get it.

Still another level of challenge may arise if you are living with someone who doesn't get it. Let's say it's your parent or partner. If you are not able to help that person under-stand what you need, your best strategy may be to study at a library, an empty room in your law school, or any place conducive to focus that is outside your home. Find a place that will allow you to stay and comfortably spread out your books from 8:00 a.m. to 11:00 p.m. every day. The less you are around home, the less likely you will be to succumb to distractions, frustration, or defeatism.

To help people understand your situation, take a look at the letters to family and friends below. There is a version directed toward traditional students and one geared toward nontraditional students. Find the version that seems more relevant and either adapt and personalize it or send it as is. Sign it as being from yourself, or feel free to say it came from a law professor! (They might find it more persuasive.)

If it's easier to talk with someone in person or by phone instead of writing, or if you have to explain this to someone who doesn't read or speak English, borrow whatever language or ideas are useful to explain how they can best help you. (There are suggestions for nonlaw analogies below that may help you in talking with those who have little familiarity with law.)

Note: These letters are intended for the people you expect to be supportive. Do not bother sending such a letter to naysayers. Stay away from those people until August (or March if you're taking the February exam). It is not worth the energy and time it will take to bring them on board before the exam, and you risk their toxic influence permeating your confidence should you try. Again, if this is someone very close to you, the best approach may be something like this:

"I know it's hard to understand. It may seem to you like I'm just taking another test. But to pass this bar exam, I cannot spend any time with you in June or July." And every time you are asked, simply say, "Let's plan something in August. Preparing for the bar will take all of my time in June and July."

LETTER FOR NONTRADITIONAL LAW STUDENTS

Dear Friend, Family, or Significant Other:

Someone close to you is taking an upcoming bar exam; we'll call him or her your B.A. or bar applicant (the "name" s/he will use on the exam). What does that mean for you? Obviously, each person and each family facing this experience differs, but there are often parallels. Here are just some of the challenges your B.A. faces and what has worked for people just like you who want to understand and be supportive. Think of this as both a success and survival note—you want your B.A. to pass the exam, and you want to survive this long haul!

Start with that last point: the bar exam is a long haul, a huge challenge. It represents each graduate's "Mount Everest" climb. One does not reach the summit without proper gear and training. Your B.A. cannot give the bar exam short shrift. It requires total commitment, 100 percent focus, and a great deal of time!

- Expect your B.A. to be "gone" for the two months prior to his/her exam. If your B.A. is also working and has other demands, he or she may need to start early; the "distance" may thus be felt four or five months before the exam. Note: Your B.A. may be present physically, but if he or she is doing what needs to be done to pass, your B.A. will be "gone."
- Your B.A. will be thinking about exam fact patterns while eating, showering, and sleeping—dreaming (or having nightmares) about the exam.
- The person you knew as perhaps a slightly crazed law student will be taken over totally by "bar exam-itis." The good news is that this disease is temporary!
- Your B.A. is in a fierce and exhausting competition. Many of the students your B.A. must compete against come from generations of professionals who support them fully in their effort, pay for their bar studies, bring them food, and even do their laundry!
- Most people studying for the bar exam do not work at anything other than bar study in June and July. They quit, or take leaves from, their jobs to focus exclusively on the bar.
- People hibernate socially and make that clear either by calling everyone they regularly talk with to say, "Goodbye until August," or by leaving outgoing voice-mail and e-mail messages in May saying, "Gone until the end of July. Will return all calls in August." One former student added to her outgoing message, "If anyone wants to know what to do to help me pass the bar, please feel free to contribute to my bar fund. I am taking off two months from work, so I will accept any and all gifts and loans; no contribution is too small. Thank you for your support!" The message of another student, a religious person, asked callers to pray for him.
- Plan a fun after-bar trip, something your B.A. and you (and your family if you have one) can look forward to. After the bar, your B.A. will return mentally as well as physically; it will be a time for you to reconnect.
- Say no in advance to all social commitments for your B.A. (One student told me about an event he reluctantly agreed to attend where, lo and behold, he was seated next to a hotheaded, cocky lawyer who berated him the entire evening for being out rather than studying.)
- Be flexible and willing as much as possible to play every day and evening by ear. If at the last minute your B.A. has put in a productive enough study day that he or she is able to join in a social event, be welcoming. But understand that even if your B.A. has finished studying for the day, he or she may need to sleep, exercise, or just unwind.
- Preparing for success on the bar exam involves much more than just studying; it requires being ready in mind, body, and spirit. Think of your B.A. as a

warrior preparing to go off to battle. Help your warrior prepare to win this battle!

- Delay any important decisions, significant changes, major purchases, and arguments until after the bar. (June and July are not the time to buy a new house, refinance a home, or remodel.) Anything that can wait, let it wait.
- Make life during bar review as easy as possible. Some B.A.s who are parents of young children ship their kids off to grandparents for the summer. Many use paper plates for every meal. And, unfortunately, some choose to save time by eliminating showers. (Kidding there! But you get the point!)
- Help your B.A. get on and stay on a routine study schedule. If you have a family, it will often be helpful for your B.A. to be available on a consistent and predictable basis, even if his or her free time is limited. Encourage your B.A. to set and keep "office hours." Knowing that "Mom or Dad is studying but will be there for me at 7:00 p.m. every night" will help kids immensely. Some B.A.s arrange to be at dinner or breakfast for at least one hour daily. For people who need your B.A. (children, spouses, significant others), it is usually much easier to know you can check in at a certain time rather than have that person unpredictably disappear.
- Study schedules also help your B.A. to make time for practice tests, simulated exams, and downtime when he or she can afford it.
- If there is any interactive studying that would help your B.A., participate. Be willing to test your B.A. with flash cards, if he or she wants that. Agree to play bar review lectures whenever you're in the car together. And be open to listening if your B.A. needs to vent.
- Accommodate your B.A.'s needs during the week of the bar exam. If he or she needs to be alone, respect that. If he or she needs you there, try to be there.
- Note: If your B.A. is not clear about what will make him or her the most well prepared, well rested, and confident going in to the exam, ask. Remind your B.A. that family and friends may love him or her, but you are not mind readers. Especially if you have never taken a bar exam yourself, your B.A. must be clear in articulating how you can best help.
- Last but not least, do not take personally any of your B.A.'s moodiness and tension. Stress comes with bar exam territory. This too shall pass.

Sincerely,

LETTER FOR TRADITIONAL LAW STUDENTS

Dear _____,

As you know, I am taking the bar exam this July. What does that mean? Well, it means I need or at least would very much like your support, and I want to let you know how you can best help me.

Studying for this exam will be a huge challenge. My professor calls it "the law student's Mount Everest." I don't know yet how hard the actual test will be, but I know that to walk in the door prepared I must totally focus in June and July. Total commitment. 100 percent focus. There is no way I can allow myself to go in knowing I have not done my best to get ready, and I know you would not want that for me, either.

So here's what I'm thinking:

- Expect me to be gone for at least two months, June and July. Even when you see me, if you see me, I may not really be present. (If you ask me something, I may not hear you. Even if I respond, I may not know or remember what I said.) I've been told that students become consumed with thinking about exam questions while eating, showering, and even dreaming. The person you have known these past few years as a slightly crazed law student will come down with a disease: bar exam-itis. The good news is that it's temporary!

- I'm preparing for a fierce, exhausting competition. Some compare the exam to a war. Pre-battle preparation is key. If you want to help me win, first and foremost understand that is why I'm gone. Not because I don't care about or want to spend time with you, but because this is what it takes to win. I have to be "all in" for at least two full months.

- If you want to see me just to say hello, you can drop off meals so I don't have to cook or get takeout. But unless you can stomach the idea of bringing food over and testing me with flash cards while we eat, we'll have to put off spending time together until August.

- I will return, physically and mentally, after the exam and we'll plan something fun.

- I'm officially RSVP'ing "No" in advance to all social commitments this summer. You can feel free to tell me when you are planning get-togethers, but don't expect me to come. If at the last minute I feel I've put in a productive enough study day and can get away and it's OK to show up, great. I know that I will miss things. And, I realize this may sound flaky, but it has to be this way.

- If there is anything you need me to help you with—even an important decision—please wait to even ask me about it until after the bar unless it is truly a life-or-death matter.
- FYI, I likely won't even look at, let alone respond to, Facebook messages, tweets, or e-mails. Apologies in advance if you think I'm ignoring you. I'm not. And I am not trying to be rude. If I can, I may check in once a week for messages labeled urgent, but consider me offline until August.
- If I happen to see or speak with you, please do not take personally any sort of moodiness or tension you sense. It's the exam. It's study stress. It has nothing to do with you.

I know you respect how tough this is and how much stress I'm under, but I hope this letter makes it a bit more concrete just how much preparing for this exam will take. I will be gone during June and July, but I promise to resurface in August! And, above all, I want to thank you so much for your unequivocal support.

[signed]

As weird as these letters may sound, they work. Countless relatives of bar takers have approached me at alumni functions to say how much they appreciated these, how the letters helped explain what was going on and how they could assist. Especially for those who have never done this or something similar, it's hard to grasp just how challenging this preparation is. It is more than just time-consuming, it is *all*-consuming.

Using these letters or your own words, take the time to explain the situation to those you want to support you. Let them know what you are facing and what you need.

Think of analogies to explain your struggles to family or friends.

A student recently told me that she had been working hard (putting in many hours), but not yet getting it right. (She was missing lots of MBEs in practice and was stressed. She was also not stating the rules precisely enough on practice essays.) What you already know well, but your family may not, is that hard work alone is not enough; the work must produce results. The bar exam is not an "A for effort" kind of test. For that matter, the legal profession generally is not a holistic, feel-good world. It is logical and detail oriented. I shared this cooking analogy with the student, who took it right back to her family. She later told me it helped enormously in getting the nonlawyers in her family to help understand what she was going through.

Ever try baking a cake without measuring the ingredients? A lot of cooking, great cooking, can be done by eyeballing, estimating, truly winging it. Desserts typically are not that way, especially baked goods. Pastry chefs are more like chemists in their kitchens than Grandma, whose cooking thrived on a pinch of this and a dab of that. Performing well on the bar exam is more like baking a fancy, seven-tiered cake than simmering a forgiving soup or stew where you can throw a mess of vegetables and meats into some water, cook it long enough on slow heat, and something fabulously tasty will usually emerge. For a cake (and bar success), you must put in all the right ingredients (reliable study materials from a trustworthy bar review). You must measure them precisely, add them in the right order, and bake the mixture at the right temperature for the correct amount of time (study actively, take daily practice tests, and learn from every mistake; honing and refining, doing them over and over again) until you get just the right passing recipe!

If you or the person you are trying to explain this to is not into cooking, you might ask the person to imagine working at a high-pressure job that requires logging in to hundreds of different websites each day. Concerned with computer privacy and security, the boss uses passwords that are complex and insists they all be committed to memory. Imagine how alert one would need to be and remain all day long. One digit off, and access is denied. Lawyers are detail oriented. It takes an extraordinary amount of time, focus, and energy to learn the quantity of information tested on bar exams, memorize and get it all right every time, and to tirelessly develop the skills of using and applying those rules in thousands of different factual scenarios.

GOOD LAWYERS ARE ATTENTIVE TO DETAIL.

Betty was meeting with her lawyer, getting ready to prepare for settlement negotiations (and a costly trial if the parties cannot agree). Betty's lawyer proposed meeting over lunch and offered to order in sandwiches. Betty requested turkey, and, when asked what she liked on her sandwich, she replied, "everything except cheese." Betty arrived at the appointed time. Her lawyer rushed in a half-hour late carrying a briefcase and a bag of sandwiches. The lawyer sat down, turned on her computer, and handed Betty a sandwich saying, "OK, here's your turkey and cheese sandwich with nothing else on it." Would you want to hire Betty's lawyer?

Another student told me it was the Mount Everest analogy that finally got his family to understand and stop saying, "You always do well, son. You'll do fine on this, too! Don't worry." Climbing Everest is challenging, to say the least; finally, his parents got why he needed to disappear for two months. Bottom line, whatever the words or analogies you use to explain what you are facing, acknowledge your own needs and try to help those who support you so that they fully understand both the extent of the challenge and how they can help you.

SAYING NO TO SUPPORTIVE PEOPLE WHO STILL WANT YOUR TIME DURING BAR STUDY

You may have the most supportive friends and family in the world, but they may simply not get how intense bar exam preparation must be to succeed. Even if you tell them clearly or send them a letter like those above, they still may not leave you alone. So keep "in your pocket" some ready responses should you be faced with having to say no to some request. Consider the following sample dialogues.

Can't you come to just this one birthday party?

- Mom: "You studied all day! Now, you'll just take off tonight. It's your uncle's eightieth birthday, you know. You can't miss that! "

- Bar applicant, in your head: "But then next week is someone else's birthday, and before you know it, the exam is here. My uncle is not taking the bar for me. Neither are you, Mom. I have to go in there and do it myself. Can't you just give me a break?!"

- Bar applicant's actual reply: "I would love to come, if I could. But this June and July are full-time bar review. I thank you in advance for supporting me in that. After I pass the bar, I'll go to family events. But I cannot take time away from my studies now."

HEAVY GUILT VARIATION OF "Can't you come to just this one birthday party?"

- Mom: "You have always been such a good student. Please just take off tonight. It's Uncle Joe's eightieth birthday. You know he's not doing well. It could be our last chance to see him. And, Aunt Bessie, she'll be there with all the cousins. They will all ask where you are. Besides, you study every day. I am sure you will pass that test. What are you worried about? You are so smart. You've always done well at everything. You'll be fine. This is family."

- Bar applicant, in your head: "If Uncle Joe were dying, I would go visit him in the hospital. But he's having a party! He can't be that sick. I know what all those people will say if I don't pass this bar exam. I just cannot break this commitment to myself. I've got that John Wooden quote on the fridge. I can't go into the bar knowing that I took off for family parties and didn't work as hard as I could have!"

"SUCCESS IS THAT PEACE OF MIND THAT COMES FROM KNOWING YOU'VE DONE EVERYTHING IN YOUR POWER TO BECOME THE VERY BEST YOU'RE CAPABLE OF BECOMING."

— JOHN WOODEN —

- Bar applicant's actual reply: "I want to come, Mom. I love you, and I know it's important to you. Family is important to me, too, Mom. But this is different. Whether I've succeeded before or not, I'm playing in the big leagues now. People who don't step up now get left behind. You know how hard I worked to get into law school, how much you and everyone else have sacrificed to see me get here. I have to step up now. I have to study tonight, and basically every waking minute until the end of July. It just has to be that way. That's how I have to do it.
- *[You might add, if you need to:* "Imagine if you had to go see a lawyer, Mom. Let's say, God forbid, you were wrongly accused of a crime. Your lawyer came to court and didn't know what to say to defend you. She comes up to you as you are being taken off in handcuffs and says, "I'm so sorry, but I had a family birthday party last night, and I just couldn't get to researching your case. I'm really sorry."]

Family expectations can be particularly demanding in certain cultures. Many parents expect their grown children to attend long weekly dinners and other family events, regardless of how much studying they have or whether they are still living at home. If this is your situation, work on it ahead of time. You must find a strategy.

I need you to take me to the doctor.
- Mom: "I have an appointment with the doctor on Friday. I'm counting on you to take me. You know I can't take the bus anymore."
- Bar applicant, in your head: "We talked about this. I asked you to make as many non-urgent appointments as possible before June or after July. I know you're not going to like it, but you will have to make other arrangements."
- Bar applicant's actual reply: "If this is something that can wait until August, please reschedule the appointment. If you have to go now, let's try to think of someone else in the family who could take you. [Even if this is your role in the family—you are the one who always takes your parent to the doctor—speak up and ask someone else to help out this time. You owe this to yourself. If no one else is available, perhaps you can pay for your parent to take a cab to the doctor for any appointments that must be in June or July. The price of cab fare may be far lower in the long run than the price of missing bar review lectures or valuable study time.]

Note: If you must go to doctor or other appointments (for yourself or others) in June or July, bring notes and work to do so that you do not get annoyed or frustrated with having to wait.

It is amazing that even lawyers sometimes forget how much time and energy the bar exam really takes. If you are clerking for an attorney, stop for the summer unless working just a couple of hours in a law office will help keep you motivated. Make sure your colleagues and boss understand your commitment, though. If the lawyer begs you to come in and research something when you know you must be studying for the bar, stick to your studying. (If there is a pro bono case you have your heart in and just don't feel like you can let go for the summer, let go anyway. Say no.) That extra work done now won't matter if you don't pass the bar exam. Pass first; then go the extra mile in helping out.

The Happy-Hour Dilemma
- Friend: "Happy Hour Friday. Be there!"
- Bar Applicant: "Dude, you know I can't. Studying for the bar."
- Friend: "Chill, dude. You study all the time. You're gonna lose your friends. Pretty soon we're not going to invite you any more. You say no all the time."
- Bar applicant, in your head: "Just because you're there drinking your weekend away doesn't mean I should. In ten years, when I'm a successful lawyer and a member of the real bar, you may still be sitting here drinking at this bar. Yeah, but who am I kidding? I so wish I could go! Maybe just this one

night? I could take off just tonight? But I shouldn't. I really have to focus. Do I want to take this damn test again? No way!"

- Bar applicant's actual reply: "Keep inviting me! I'll try to stop by Friday if I can, but this thing is over in July, and Fridays in August I am all over it. (Pause.) Thanks for supporting me through this! You might need a close friend who's a lawyer some day—ha ha! Kidding, dude! But seriously, I'll be back after July."

Remember that friends later become referrals. Don't be shy or embarrassed about your priorities. Whom will all these friends come to when they need legal advice?

The unhelpful study "buddy"
- Friend: "Want to come study with me at the library today?"
- Bar applicant: "No, I think I'm better off studying alone today."
- Friend: "Come on. A bunch of us are going. We'll all help each other. Then we'll go out for some beers after we work."
- Bar applicant, in your head: "Your idea of studying is 80 percent chitchat and 20 percent study. Working with you is not productive for me, and I know it. I end up helping you. I explain things to you, but all you really do is distract me."
- Bar applicant's actual reply: "Thanks for asking. Maybe another time. Today I need to study on my own. If I get enough done, I'll text you and see where you guys went and maybe meet up with you. Otherwise, I'll see you at bar review tomorrow."

Sometimes you slip. You know it would be best to say no and get back to work (or sleep, for that matter), but you think, "Well, just this once." Try not to succumb. Imagine if your lawyer came to court unable to represent you because he or she flaked on prep time. Understand that commitments you make to yourself are as important as those you make to others. As I said in an earlier chapter, think of it this way: would you flake if you were going to an appointment with a doctor or specialist you had waited months to see? No. Of course not. You wouldn't even think of canceling. Your studies must be as important to you as any appointment with anyone on the planet. Follow through. No excuses. Don't be a "no-show" on yourself!

And enlist your troops to help you stay on track. (Post your study schedule so they don't distract you during your "office hours.") If you do slip and end up doing something unproductive, get back on track ASAP. Don't waste any more time feeling guilty. Just get back to work.

Remember, some breaks are helpful. You may return to work able to be more productive. Allow yourself that possibility. Although the warnings about people and activities eating your time should typically be heeded, you may find that sometimes distractions replenish the well and boost your energy. It can be good to take a couple of hours off here and there. Limit the number of these breaks, but don't feel guilty for taking a little time off if the diversion will ultimately help you.

Father's Day hits right in the middle of bar review; so does the Fourth of July. If you are a dad or have a dad, stop for a moment to acknowledge Father's Day. And go to a barbeque or fireworks on the Fourth of July. Some people feel comfortable taking that whole day off. Others feel better putting in a good study day and then enjoying the evening out. Whatever time you do take off, enjoy it! You are doing a good thing in recharging your batteries and preventing burnout.

BEWARE OF SABOTEURS

We discussed people who mean well and don't know how to be supportive. There will be others who are not supportive at all, some intentionally and others inadvertently. You must cut these people loose for the summer.

To better deal with people who may try to sabotage you, it can be helpful to divide them into competitive classmates and others who are generally negative (acquaintances or strangers).

Competitive Classmates

These are the people I call the "blowhards." They are full of themselves. Some may just be so self-absorbed that they make comments they don't even realize are insulting. Ignore them.

Other classmates may try to intimidate you. They may casually claim that they're writing twelve practice essays or doing hundreds of MBE questions each day. Or they may claim to consistently be getting top scores on every practice test. Don't listen to them, and don't let them get to you. First, they're probably not telling the truth. It's tough to write twelve essays a day, in any meaningful way, and still get the rest of your work done—especially if you're also spending any time at night sleeping. Next and most important, stay focused on your own work. Stick to your schedule. Trust your bar review and your mentor. Also, don't let yourself get psyched out if, for example, classmates say they got a higher percentage correct on an MBE practice test than you did. What will move you forward is understanding why you missed the questions you did. Every mistake made now, every missed concept, is an opportunity to get it right on the actual exam. The only score that counts is at the end of the game. So don't let a competitive classmate throw you by claiming he or she got thirty out of thirty-three questions correct when you missed more than twenty. The important thing is to learn by continuing to take practice tests.

Use positive peer pressure if it helps motivate you! But negative peer pressure is usually a complete and total waste of your time, a drain of your precious energy. Learn to rise above it. Success is not just about quantity; it's also about quality. And it's not about what or how someone else does; it's all about you. It's *your* bar exam.

STUDENTS REGULARLY ADMIT (AFTER THE BAR) THAT THEY EMBELLISHED THEIR STUDY RECORD.

If someone is bragging that he or she was up until 2:00 or 3:00 a.m. studying every night and taking hundreds more MBEs and essays and PTs than you, ask yourself:

1. Is that person telling the truth, or just trying to psyche me out?
2. If this is true, is that person so tired or speeding through the material so fast that he or she isn't really learning or improving on the skills necessary to pass?
3. Is that person spending critical time studying the answers after each practice essay and each set of MBE questions? Or has he or she opted to merely answer the questions mechanically without doing the hard work of diagnosing why an answer choice was right or wrong?

Negative People—Friends or Strangers

When faced with a negative person, the best advice is to get away. If they are phoning you or texting you and you have not yet answered, don't. Post an automatic "Away until August" on outgoing e-mail messages. If they speak with you face-to-face or you inadvertently answer a call, use a polite excuse to cut off the conversation immediately. One that works every time is "Excuse me; I have to go to the bathroom."

There will be people who are just dying to tell you about everyone they know—from their neighbor's son to famous people—who failed a bar exam. They are similar to people who simply *must* walk up to pregnant women to share unhelpful stories of horrifying birth experiences. (Stay away from them if you are expecting.) Other people may want to tell you about the dismal legal employment statistics. You do not want a lecture on how tough it may be to find a good job while you are studying for the bar. That may be appropriate before law school or after you pass the bar exam, but not now. It's best to walk away and not listen.

Note: Sometimes it can be even more stressful when people make seemingly positive comments, such as, "Oh, I know you'll pass." To many bar applicants, that just piles on more stress by adding expectations you must live up to. How should you respond? One of my students shared that she would simply reply, "I'm doing my best," and either walk away or change the subject.

Whatever the comments, have a response ready so you don't feel cornered into talking about the exam with anyone who does not have a positive effect on you.

Keep doubters at a distance; build a protective wall around your self-confidence.

How should you deal with people you intuitively know are seeking to undermine your self-confidence or steal your study time? Take steps to keep your self-confidence strong. Remember, passing the bar exam is in some ways like climbing a mountain (an analogy I used earlier). Because it's such a challenge, there may be days when you ask yourself, "Can I do it?" If you need convincing, remember that graduating from law school is credible evidence that you *can* pass. It doesn't mean you will without a great deal of hard work, but it's a good indicator that you have the capability. If you were not the kind of person who thrived when challenged, it's doubtful that you would have started, let alone finished, law school. Some of your classmates flunked out after their first year. You did not. Now look at alumni from your law school who passed the bar exam. Are they *all* smarter than you? Not likely!

Relatives and others making destructive comments

If you need a boost, or a pep talk, ask your mentor, a trusted academic support advisor, or a professor you felt comfortable with. Notice I did not say to ask your mom or dad or Aunt Betty. Why? You must protect yourself, as mentioned earlier. If your parents and other relatives are supportive, they *may* be a great resource. But those who didn't go to professional school themselves sometimes don't get it and sometimes aren't helpful. A mentor who recently passed the bar exam, someone you can rely on, may be more supportive and really understand what you are going through.

And far worse than simply "not getting it" is when people share destructive stereotypes or biases that undermine you. *Warning: The following may appear to some as politically incorrect.* Did you grow up in a family where your mom (or grandma or another relative you love and care about) believed that "girls like you" should "find a good man, get married, and raise a family," and not "waste time" in school? Does Mom really think *her* son should be in business and making *real money*, not spending all his time in school racking up debt? Does Dad think that college and graduate schools are only for rich white folks? Do you have family members who think that all women who want to become lawyers are aggressive and overbearing? Does your family believe that all lawyers are corrupt liars?

Some families do not express (or embrace) these negative stereotypes and will give you their full support, as long as family commitments come first. This mentality might not explicitly undermine your focus on studying, but it may have a similar effect; therefore, it is a big problem. Bar applicants need to focus solely on bar preparation and cannot be there for others while studying for this exam. To compete effectively, you need to be able to give the same intensity to your studies as everyone else is.

Still other family members may make comments that are less direct, but equally destructive. For example, the student whose parent says, "Honey, I love you and you know I'll be proud of you whatever you do. Becoming a lawyer is a great goal, but it's just that you have never been the best student and I don't want to see you get hurt." Ouch! That hurts already. Steel yourself. And find your support elsewhere.

It may not be politically correct, but people *do* think this way. Such thinking can deeply hurt someone studying for the bar. If people in your family or community think along these or similarly negative lines, *do not* look to them for support now. And, do not "buy in" to their negativity. You have every right to be proud of earning a law degree and seeking to obtain a law license.

A note for women whose families do not support your becoming a lawyer: law school will not make you aggressive in any sort of negative way. The rigors of law school should help all law students (men and women alike) learn to write and speak persuasively, as well as think critically—both of which are essential to being an effective professional. And passing the bar exam provides credible evidence that you can perform effectively under extreme pressure. These skills will help you manage, lead, and be responsible for the lives and livelihoods of others, if you so choose. That is a good thing, and there is nothing unfeminine about it.[24]

If you do have negative folks in your life, don't try to change their minds right now. First pass the bar exam, with the help of supportive people, and *then* try to bring them around.

Special problem in law school: professors who doubt you

If you believe a professor thinks that you aren't smart or capable of passing the bar exam, this will likely hurt your confidence. If you have a negative encounter with such a professor, especially in class, first try to shrug it off. There is a good chance he or she doesn't really think less of you, but is either busy or deliberately trying to scare you to prepare you for tough judges. If it's still bothering you, though, you might want to try talking with the person during office hours. You might have an altogether different impression after meeting with him or her. At the very least, be sure to talk with other professors with whom you do feel comfortable, and let yourself feel respected by the way they treat you. Don't let the judgment or perceived judgment of one person sink in or dictate how you view yourself.

The naysayers are out of line.

There are plenty of people who weren't "the best student" who passed the bar exam and are now thriving as lawyers. Just because someone did not *AmJur* all their classes or make law review does not make them stupid or incapable of passing the bar exam. The practicing bar is not made up entirely of those who made law review in law school. Many were C students.

The bar tests basic competencies; it is not a test of genius or scholarship. With 1) basic knowledge of the law (remember that you have two full months of bar review to learn or relearn the rules); 2) basic analytical and writing skills (which you will train intensively to develop every day); and 3) the will to succeed, you *can* pass the bar exam—even if you're not headed for the Supreme Court.

Passing the bar exam involves mastering a set of skills; it requires learning rules of law and how to apply them in a host of factual scenarios under significant time constraints. It does not require exceptional talent. There are tricky parts, sure. It's tough, yes. There is a lot to learn. But it is something most dedicated people who graduate from law school and then prepare and apply themselves can do. You can, too! (As I tell my students, passing the bar exam is more like repairing a car or fixing a sink than painting a Picasso. It may take time and effort to learn how to do it, you must master many skills, but you can learn to do it; it is not something that requires you to have been born with an extraordinary talent.)

Supporters and Saboteurs Worksheets

Complete this triage by filling in the worksheet below. You don't have to show anyone (and it may be best not to). You can even rip this up after you write it if you are concerned about someone seeing it who might be offended. But clarifying for yourself who will help you and who won't during these two months will increase your productivity and save you a lot of stress, as well as prevent wasted time and energy.

Part A: List your supportive troops (Write the names of and contact info for people you know "get it," whom you can call or reach out to when you need a boost.):

1. _____

2. _____

3. _____

4. _____

5. _____

Part B: List people who are supportive, but don't yet "get it":

1. _____

2. _____

3. _____

4. _____

5. _____

Part C: List potential saboteurs (You can name individuals or classes of people; for example, friends on SBA who you know will distract you, or worse):

1. _____

2. _____

3. _____

4. _____

5. _____

Part D: List people to avoid, or, at the very least, whose messages need to be diluted (name individuals who have intentionally or inadvertently made destructive comments or engaged in undermining actions):

1. _____

2. _____

3. _____

4. _____

5. _____

WRITE AND POST YOUR SCHEDULE; THEN ADAPT IT TO MAXIMIZE PRODUCTIVITY

- Sample schedules for traditional and nontraditional students
  - Some people doubt the efficacy of online classes; these doubts are unfounded.
  - Days when you do not have bar-review lectures
  - Daily schedules versus weekly schedules
- The ingredients of a successful schedule
  - Law study: bar review, lectures, and outlines
  - Self-care (including good nutrition, exercise, and sleep)
  - As you plan your schedule, think about when and how you learn best.
  - Variety
- The daily grind: stick to your schedule of daily disciplined and focused work
  - Dealing with anxiety (it's normal to be nervous)
  - Anxiety while taking practice tests
  - Worry while reading a sample answer
  - Anxiety-reducing tools to use any time nerves hit

- Work hard, but work efficiently: reassess your schedule
  - Is my schedule maximizing efficiency?
  - Adapt your schedule as the bar approaches, and make more time for memorizing
  - How to memorize? Break out the flashcards, write it out 50 times, whatever works for you!
  - Preventing burnout: add incentives and levity
  - Reward yourself
  - Bar-exam burnout
  - Humor: you gotta laugh a little
  - Motivate with music
- Finalizing your schedule

"PATIENCE AND PERSEVERANCE HAVE A MAGICAL EFFECT BEFORE WHICH DIFFICULTIES DISAPPEAR AND OBSTACLES VANISH."

— JOHN QUINCY ADAMS[25] —

This chapter will help you concretize and implement the study-schedule portion of your bar success plan. How hard is putting together a study schedule? That depends. For some very organized people, it's easy. Sticking to the schedule may be hard, but creating the timetables is simple. Many others are not used to having to fit so much into such a short amount of time, or it's not intuitive how to determine the most-efficient order of accomplishing tasks.

One might think that calendaring is something basic that *everyone* knows how to do. Not true. Do you keep a regular calendar? Do you have a system to enter in every obligation you have? If not, you need to begin. Learning to calendar and manage your time well will not only help you pass the bar, but provide you with vital skills you will need to be a successful professional. Clients and colleagues alike will need you to be prepared and on time. If you are working and have a family, your ability to juggle time effectively will become especially indispensable.

Let's get started with some sample schedules so you can get an idea of what people do and how they fit it in to their day or week. Then, we'll break down the various ingredients of a successful schedule so you can see the pieces and create your own.

SAMPLE SCHEDULES FOR TRADITIONAL AND NONTRADITIONAL STUDENTS

Below are sample daily schedules. Use these, along with your bar review schedule or calendar, as a starting place. Then begin drafting your own schedule, one that works for you.

You may be asking, "Why should I reinvent the wheel if bar review will give me a schedule?" Your course will likely include a schedule of when each lecture takes place, and it might tell you which assignments to do each day. But you need a personalized schedule that specifies the exact times when you will complete those assignments and take extra practice tests if you can, as well as when you will eat, sleep, work if you are still working, commute, and do everything else that must be done.

The more you stick to a routine, the more likely every minute of your day will be productive. Preferably well in advance of starting bar review, sketch at least a tentative daily schedule and post it prominently in your home (for example, on the fridge, above your computer, or some other place where you will see it every day). If you live with a significant other or your family, make sure your schedule is posted where they will see it.

Before studying the sample schedules, it will be helpful to consider some thoughts on prioritizing. To be certain that specific tasks are accomplished, build your schedule around whatever you *must* get done. Then, do as much as you can of what remains. Your schedule is in many ways the embodiment of your priorities. Schedule around your "musts," taking into account the most-efficient times of day to complete each task.

SAMPLE DAILY STUDY SCHEDULE FOR THE TRADITIONAL STUDENT

- 6:30 a.m. — Wake up, drink coffee, take a shower, eat breakfast. (Wake up at 6:00 a.m. if you want to exercise before breakfast.)
- 7:00–7:30 a.m. — Complete daily MBE set of seventeen in thirty minutes. (Complete more if you are a very early riser.)
- 7:30–8:00 a.m. — Review answers to MBE questions.
- 9:00 a.m.–1:00 p.m. — Attend bar review lectures.*
- 1:00–2:00 p.m. — Lunch. While eating, identify and review any rules you didn't know or understand in morning lecture. (If you can't write and eat at the same time, take twenty minutes after the lecture to type or handwrite all the key points you do not want to forget, examples that made sense, areas your instructor said would likely be heavily tested, etc. Then, eat for twenty to thirty minutes. After that, get back to work!)
- 2:00–6:00 p.m. — Complete any bar review reading or writing assignments. Write extra essays and study sample answers, or complete a PT. Look up any rules you do not understand.
- 6:00–8:00 p.m. — Take a break to exercise and eat dinner.
- 8:00–10:00 p.m. — Do passive work. Review lecture notes and flashcards, or answer a few practice questions lying down. (Many of my students have all of this information on their smartphones and do certain tasks in bed each night while they are resting and winding down.)
- 10:00 p.m. — Relax and go to sleep.

*If you are taking a traditional, in-person bar review course, the classes will be scheduled at certain times, in certain places, and on certain days. You may have flexibility if the course offers more than one lecture per day, but most often the times will be fixed. This is fine as long as the times and locations work for you. But sometimes the commute is too far. Or you will find yourself in a class that meets in the mornings—a time when you could more effectively complete practice tests on your own. You will have to adapt. So meet with a mentor about how to make the situation work for you. (If you are a morning person, get up at 5:00 a.m. and take two hours of practice tests before bar review. Get recordings to listen to while commuting. Think creatively about how best to plot your time.)

Online classes may be more adaptable to your schedule. You may have live online classes that you want to attend synchronously, presenting you with timing issues. However, a key advantage to online study is the flexibility it offers. Courses may be recorded and thus available asynchronously as well, so you can listen whenever (and as many times) as you like.

Some doubt the efficacy of online classes, but these doubts are unfounded

If a quality course is offered and students are committed to learning, they can and will achieve, whether they are sitting in a physical building or a virtual classroom. It is true that some people lack the discipline to turn on their computers and follow the course schedule in a dedicated manner. Some people prefer and benefit from a live bar review course, and that's fine. Others need the accountability that comes from having to show up somewhere each day. But the method of the content delivery should not make or break your paying attention and getting the most out of the program. That is on you. My motto, having taught in an online law school for more than a decade, is "*Distance* learning does not mean *distant* learning."

Online lectures can be live online and synchronous, or prerecorded and asynchronous. The same is true with many bar review courses offering "live" locations. Often students go to a physical classroom, sit together, and watch a video lecture; the professor is not always there lecturing in person. They are synchronous, but by no means live.

Some would say that students are more apt to go to a class every day when they have to be at a physical location than to have the self-motivation to independently follow an online curriculum. Even if it were true that students physically attend lectures more regularly in live locations, it is just as easy to tune out a video in a live location as it is at home. In fact, on your own computer, you can rewind and listen again to what you missed. So you may end up getting more out of an online lecture.

In addition, lectures are only one part of most bar review courses. There are also outlines, practice tests, writing workshops, and more. Students enrolled in live locations often have access to much of this material online, and students who are enrolled in online classes are often shipped paper books (in addition to having electronic copies of materials.) So, the *learning* is often done in a hybrid fashion (part live, part online) whether you are in a so-called online bar review or a so-called live-location bar review. Bottom line: however you study, you *must* be actively engaged, committed to doing the work, and accountable (to yourself if you are self-motivated, or to a mentor or faculty supporter if you need an extra kick in the pants).

Beyond studying, live courses may be good places to find camaraderie and support. On the other hand, some students find fellow applicants competitive and unsupportive. These students attend class and then leave as quickly as possible.

If you are either studying independently or do not have helpful people in your live classes, reach out proactively for support. Connect by phone or e-mail with a mentor, meet a reliable study partner over coffee or a meal, or attend a bar mentoring group. Just be sure that whomever you reach out to is truly supportive. (Review Chapter 6 for how to enlist positive support.)

Days when you do not have bar review lectures

Plan these days carefully so you don't waste time. Make sure to include practice tests and time to learn rules and concepts you don't understand well or at all. Schedule time to work on memorizing rules and plan to increase that time as the exam approaches.

Most important are the practice tests; they will help you to both learn and memorize the law. Learning in the context of fact patterns helps you recall the rules. Have you found yourself saying when you approach a new problem, "Oh yeah, that's like the one I did before in which the only ten acres of land with access to water were not included in the deed"?

Select the practice exams you will complete ahead of time. Avoid spending time deciding which exams to complete on a given day. Knowing what you will do each day leaves no open window for procrastination. If a schedule of practice exams to do on weekends is listed in your bar review calendar, follow that. If not, or if you are doing more than what is assigned, either mark the pages of the exams you plan to complete (noting the date and time you will complete each one), print copies of the exams ahead of time, and put them in a dated folder. Each night, put the next day's folder on your desk. Before you call it quits for the week, choose the practice exams you will write out in full or outline each day of the following week.

Eventually, in July, you'll switch to adding more outlining of essays and less writing them out in full, but not until July. And, even in July, you will still need to write out several essays each week.

SAMPLE STUDY SCHEDULE FOR NONTRADITIONAL STUDENTS

From twelve to three months *before* the exam (that is, during your last year of law school), devote three to six hours per week studying. Each week do at least the following:

- Fifty MBEs—reviewing explanatory answers, writing flashcards for difficult-to-remember rules, and updating your outlines.
- Three essay questions—writing outlines for your answers, reviewing the explanatory answers, writing flashcards for difficult-to-remember rules, and updating your outlines.
- Study a bar review outline (and draft your own condensed version of that outline) for one of the testable essay subjects.
- Take one PT.

Starting three months before the exam (that is, after or near the completion of classes) each weekday do the following:

- One hour before work: do seventeen MBEs in thirty minutes. Review the explanatory answers for thirty minutes, writing flashcards for rules you missed.
- One hour at lunch: read and outline one essay, and study the model answer. Do compare-and-contrast "self-critique" to find ways to improve your analysis and writing.
- One and a half hours immediately after work: write out one full essay and review and study the model answer. (It can be very helpful, especially if being home is distracting, to stay at or near work and get an hour or two of studying in before you head home.)
- Use commute time to listen to bar review lectures or review and memorize rules.
- Dinner
- Listen to bar review lectures or review notes from bar review lectures.

While some people can work a full day, eat dinner, and then study productively for four to five hours straight, many working students find it easier to spread tasks throughout the day, putting in at least some time before, during, and after work. Try both approaches and see which one is more effective for you. (But don't think that because you have to work, you can't also study. People work and pass the bar in great numbers all the time. You can, too. Remember that every hour adds up.)

On weekends during the three months before the exam:

- study full days, from 9:00 a.m. to 6:00 p.m. or longer if you can still focus, with at least one hour for lunch. Combine bar review lectures and looking up rules with additional practice exams.
- Take off evenings for rest and relaxation so you don't burn out and so you will have just as much energy the next day.

Daily Schedules Versus Weekly Schedules

Most people prefer daily schedules. For those studying full-time, daily schedules leave no time to waste deciding what to do. You get up, do your work at the same time each day, and fall in to a productive routine. Even if you are working, write a daily schedule for yourself if your schedule is consistent each day. If you have to adapt it, write down any changes so that they also become tasks that must be completed. But for working students whose commitments vary from day to day, a weekly schedule may be most effective. Let's say you plan to complete seventeen MBEs in a half-hour each morning during breakfast and thirty-three questions in an hour on weekend days, plus allow time following each practice session to review. If you can't always commit to this because some days you have more work than others, consider a weekly schedule with at least 200 MBEs per week plus review time. (Note: these numbers may be *minimums*! You can always do more. But it is more effective to do a consistent number on a regular basis than a marathon session once a week.)

One former student whose work schedule interfered with accomplishing everything on a daily basis felt like a failure because he wasn't getting everything done each day. (The person had multiple engineering degrees and decades of experience in demanding jobs.) He decided to switch to a weekly schedule. He completed more on lighter work days and less on busier ones, and got everything on his list done by week's end. This allowed him to once again think of himself as the success he was, and still is.

Simply changing *when* you do things may make you think of yourself in a different light. Try out scheduling variations as early as you can before or in the beginning of intensive bar review so that you can hit the ground running in June and July.

THE INGREDIENTS OF A SUCCESSFUL SCHEDULE

What goes into an effective bar schedule? Ideally, you should build in law study, skills training, self-care (including exercise, sleep, and good nutrition), and a little bit of relaxation and fun to "replenish the well."

Bar review courses will likely send you a calendar with a class and homework schedule for June and July. Numerous tasks should be detailed in your bar review course. If they are, excellent! Just follow this schedule. But if your course schedule is not sufficiently comprehensive, modify it to include all the required tasks and the specific times you will complete them. You may want to add the following:

- When you will exercise, sleep, and relax
- When you will complete a simulated bar exam if your course does not include one

- Time after each lecture to review rules you did not understand and make flash-cards (or other memory tools) for heavily tested areas

Law study: Bar review lectures and outlines

Attend all bar review lectures and workshops. Listen attentively. Make sure you are awake and alert. If you are attending lectures at a time of day when you are exhausted, consider switching to attend online or via video at a time when you are more energized. (For some students, lectures keep them awake. If you are one of them, schedule those when you are tired and do active independent work when you have more energy. Many of my students find they are most alert in the mornings, so choose to listen to bar review lectures at night when they are too tired to take practice tests, for example.)

To get the most out of the lectures, review the table of contents for the outline *before each lecture* and look up any terms you are not familiar with. (Review the discussion of bar review lectures in Chapter 5.) For some students, taking notes while listening to a lecture helps them learn the material. Others get more out of a lecture by listening intently and then going back and creating notes by either condensing the main outline or expanding the table of contents. Determine which approach is most effective for you.

Self-care (including good nutrition, exercise, and sleep)

Are you running? Jogging? Lifting weights? Punching a punching bag? Playing tennis? You may think it's nuts to suggest that your schedule allows you to take time off for such leisure. But exercise is critical, especially as you prepare for this final stretch. You must let off physical steam (release stress) and keep your body in shape. Exercise is not time off. It is a key piece of your ultimate study effort. (If you feel guilty any time you are not studying, listen to bar review lectures or recordings of rule statements while you exercise.)

If you have a sport you love and do regularly, play a bit of it daily if you can. If you are not "an exercise person," add a half-hour walk to your study day. Do this now. And if you can push it to an occasional jog, or swim, or carry weights with you, all the better.

During each session of your bar exam, your mind will be *on*. And it will work better if oxygen is flowing efficiently through your body. Some nervousness—that which keeps you sharp and alert—is good. But you must shake off the excess nerves that can send you into panic or paralysis. Exercise helps you lose the bad stress while keeping the good energy.

As you plan your schedule, think about when and how you learn best.

You can take one of the many learning-style assessments available online, or your ASP faculty may offer learning-style questionnaires. In the meantime, take the following short quiz to begin thinking about how you learn best. Remember, though, that you don't have to be pigeonholed—or pigeonhole yourself—into one style of learning. Chances are you learn in many different ways, and you may learn best when you are working with more than one sense or modality at the same time. (Hence my continued recommendation to read aloud, under your breath, while pointing at each word so that you are using your senses of sight, touch, and hearing simultaneously.)

Think back on other situations when you had to learn and memorize a great deal of material (perhaps a math class with many formulas or a language class with extensive vocabulary). What helped you the most? Studying is more effective when you do it in ways that fit your personality, your time constraints, and your learning styles.

Take the quiz below to start thinking about how you learn best.

QUIZ

Q: When studying for class, you learn best by:

A:

1) Silently reading your notes, rereading hornbooks and casebooks, looking at flowcharts, etc.
2) Listening to a taped lecture, reading your notes aloud, having someone test you aloud.
3) Drawing diagrams to track issues and rules, writing notes, and outlining material on your computer.

Q: When you go on an interview, what stands out most in your mind afterward?

A:

1) How people looked.
2) The names and qualifications of people you spoke with.
3) What rooms you were in, what you said and did, what you ate, etc.

Q: When you are studying in a library, coffee shop, or bookstore, you are most distracted by:

A:
1) Looking at things on the walls, the people nearby, etc.
2) Listening to the conversations of people nearby, music playing, other sounds.
3) Your feelings, whether you are thirsty or tired, how comfortable your clothes are, etc.

Q: When you are trying to figure out some concept you don't understand, you:
A:
1) Read until you get it.
2) Ask someone to explain it to you.
3) Review the problem in your mind, and diagram it out.

Did you answer with mostly *1* responses? If so, you might tend toward the visual. If you chose mostly *2* answers, you might be more of an auditory learner. Primarily *3* responses might suggest that you lean toward kinesthetic learning styles. Those who wanted to answer with all three responses may like variety, and might learn in different ways in different situations. Some people also learn some concepts better by listening or talking and others by reading or diagramming, depending on the subject or area of law. Again, there is no need to pigeonhole yourself into a specific learning style. Simply being aware and knowing that the way you receive and process information may vary can be empowering.

You can't change the way a bar review lecture is conducted, but you can adapt your own independent study according to how you learn best. Think about this as you plan your study schedule. If you tend to be a visual learner, make more time for drawing charts and diagrams, using flashcards, and color-coding material. Build in more listening or talking time if you learn best through hearing. If you are more of a kinesthetic learner, get up and move around, take breaks at regular intervals, study standing up sometimes, diagram things in vivid colors, and consider joining a study group. Allow your studying time to work for you by knowing how you learn best. You are fighting the bar. Don't fight yourself. (A song I like to play in bar mentoring goes, "I fought the law and the law won." Of course, I change the ending to ". . . and *I* won.")[26]

Draft Schedule

Drawing upon what you now know, try to sketch out an effective schedule. Further scheduling variations will then be discussed, and you will update your draft.

6 a.m. _____

7 a.m. _____

8 a.m. _____

9 a.m. _____

10 a.m. _____

11 a.m. _____

Noon _____

1 p.m. _____

2 p.m. _____

3 p.m. _____

4 p.m. _____

5 p.m. _____

6 p.m. _____

7 p.m. _____

8 p.m. _____

9 p.m. _____

10 p.m. _____

11 p.m. _____

Variety

As noted, studying in different ways can help appeal to the diverse ways you learn. Shaking things up can also prevent burnout and get you through the long, tough days.

Change locations once or twice a week. As a reward for studying well in your regular study spot, take a stack of practice exams outdoors (somewhere with a great view). Or bring work to a favorite coffee shop or bookstore and sit in a comfy chair. (Make sure it's a place where you can focus.)

Vary your studying techniques. As we said, variety alone may help you stay on course, but making your studies fun is even better. (Do you still think preparing for the bar exam has to be torture? Come on. Really? Try to make it as enjoyable as possible.) Working in a different manner may enhance your learning. If you're tired of the same old listening to lectures and reading outlines:

- Talk through concepts or rules you don't understand with a friend, study buddy, or mentor (perhaps over coffee). If it is someone who will stay focused and not distract you, the person doesn't have to have a legal background. (As noted previously, if you can explain something clearly to a layperson, you are ready to use that concept in an essay on the bar exam.)
- Set some of your mnemonics, checklists, or summary outlines to music. Memorize rules by singing them to the melody of a popular tune. (One of my professors set all of civil procedure to music and had my section do a singing review for all of the other first-years.)
- If you're a visual learner, make charts and diagrams.
- Include some funny images (perhaps a cartoon that makes you laugh) in your study materials, or maybe place a picture of James Bond with his gun pointed near the portion of your crimes outline that mentions the deadly-weapon doctrine.
- Make a recording of yourself reading key rules out loud. Hearing your own voice confidently stating rules may have an empowering effect, even if you were reading the rules when you made the recording. (A student recently shared a unique study strategy: recording her own voice reading rule statements, but in a thick and funny stage accent. Somehow adding the accent triggered her memory such that it helped her retain all the rules. It also made her laugh a bit along the way.)

What are your ideas for making bar study an enjoyable experience? Yes, you must take this time seriously and be fully committed to success, but that doesn't mean that it has to be painful or you must feel sorry for yourself. Find ways to see the light at the end of each day, and each week; add some light and levity of your own to the process!

THE DAILY GRIND: STICK TO YOUR SCHEDULE OF DAILY, DISCIPLINED, FOCUSED WORK.

If the sample schedules above look doable, that's great! Often people follow them fairly easily the first few days, but fall behind within a couple of weeks and get discouraged. (Others stay on pace, but get exhausted.) "Keep at it," I tell my students so often and so loudly they hate it. But they thank me later. *After* their exam, they say, "I needed those reminders to keep on going." When they pass, they say, "I heard your voice in those dark moments when I was tired and drained. When I was ready to give up, I just kept moving forward."

You may also hate me for this chapter, perhaps for the entire book. But if any of it helps to keep you studying and taking practice tests, you, too, may find that the anger subsides amidst the great celebrations of bar passage. (And please take a moment if you can to drop me a note and share your success stories.)

"RARELY DO WE FIND MEN WHO WILLINGLY ENGAGE IN HARD, SOLID THINKING. THERE IS AN ALMOST UNIVERSAL QUEST FOR EASY ANSWERS AND HALF-BAKED SOLUTIONS. NOTHING PAINS SOME PEOPLE MORE THAN HAVING TO THINK."

— DR. MARTIN LUTHER KING JR. —

Don't expect each day to be miraculous. Expect it to be hard work. A lot of your preparation may seem like drudgery, but every bit of effort is worth the spectacular payoff down the road. Expect to be tired. Keep pushing forward anyway.

Be determined. Keep your goal, your "endgame," in mind. You are in training. It's not supposed to be easy. Learn as you go, one day at a time. Trust that if you put in what it takes, you will get where you need to go. Use every good moment you have to study, sleep, or otherwise prepare. Don't waste anyone's time fooling yourself; if you aren't effectively using your time, get on the ball. Don't spin your wheels. When you hit a wall (and you will!), change gears or stop and take a break.

Don't quit or get discouraged at the first signs of losing focus. You need to build your stamina. Push yourself. It's not easy. But when you find yourself reading the same thing over and over, looking out the window and not "hearing" yourself, take a break. Maybe take a nap. Sometimes after just twenty minutes of shut-eye, you can get back in gear and be more productive. Above all, remain patient. Keep moving forward.

Work hard. Work steadily. Work smart. Work when others are goofing off. (And do not waste one moment feeling sorry for yourself that you *have to* work while others play. You *get to* work. And you will get to reap the future rewards of that hard work.)

Pace yourself and don't burn out. Do what it takes to keep moving forward, slowly but steadily, on this road to success. The following suggestions are offered to help you press on when you are dragging.

Dealing with anxiety (it's normal to be nervous)

When I describe study schedules to students who are further away from the bar exam, they are usually fine and able to calmly think through things. When I have the same discussion with people about one week into bar review, they panic: "There is too much material to learn. I can't do it. I will never learn all of this."

Of course you can! And you will. How? One day at a time, improving slowly but surely.[27]

Put your nerves in a box.[28] And get to work. Instead of spending time and energy on worrying, put it into studying. It's too early in the first weeks of June to stress out. That is the time to focus on getting into a study routine. Don't expect to get practice questions right! Just keep answering them and studying the sample answers. Walk away from every study session having learned something. Keep improving. Keep moving forward. And you will be fine.

I understand that it's easy for me to say, "Just don't worry." I tell myself that every day, and I still worry! But there are tools to help you "put the worry in boxes" and keep it contained when it does surface. Ultimately, if you can actually learn to channel your nerves into adrenaline, they can become powerful tools rather than paralyzing traps. That's the goal!

COURAGE IS A SPECIAL KIND OF KNOWLEDGE: THE KNOWLEDGE OF HOW TO FEAR WHAT OUGHT TO BE FEARED AND HOW NOT TO FEAR WHAT OUGHT NOT TO BE FEARED.

— DAVID BEN-GURION —

What should you do when you're blocked by anxiety? That depends on when the nerves hit. Let's consider different strategies for different times you find yourself getting nervous.

Anxiety while taking practice tests

If paralyzing anxiety prevents forward movement while you are taking a practice test, the immediate mission is to get the intellectual flow going again—take the edge off. Try simply reading and outlining if answering the question in full right now feels too stressful. Read the sample answer.

Many states release sample passing answers; your bar review may offer model answers. After trying to analyze a question (and preferably writing out your own answer, unless you are too panicked to do so), read the sample answer. See how your answer compares. (See "Self-Assessment Tools" in Chapter 8). Now take this one step further. *Copy the sample answer.* (Write it out longhand or retype it, word for word.)

Copying good sample or model answers can be especially helpful when even looking at those answers stresses you out (when you fall into "I could never write something like this" thinking), or when you are too tired to fully analyze a question and answer by reading alone. It is easy. It is simple and low-stress. You can tell yourself that *all* you are doing is copying. But as you write or type, your mind will sync with your hands, and your brain will register what a "complete" and passing answer sounds *and feels* like. What often happens is that you begin typing and you see that this answer adds one more sentence where you might have stopped, helping you correct a problem of writing in too conclusory a manner. Or, you may find the opposite; you see that the answer stops after making a point when you would have gone on and on—writing in a too-verbose or disorganized manner, sometimes even undermining your own logic that would have scored points had you written more clearly and succinctly.

When you are nervous or overtired, copying answers is one of the best tools. It is not stressful; it just involves retyping. It calms students down because it's not demanding, but it often works wonders to bolster their understanding.

Worry while reading a sample answer.

You might find yourself overwhelmed or intimidated when self-assessing a completed practice question by studying a model or sample answer. It may feel like you will never be able to write that thorough of an answer. You must lift yourself out of that thinking immediately. Copying the answer, as noted above, is one way to begin to believe that you *could* write something like that, and get yourself acclimated. Another effective way to unblock these sorts of nerves is by "reverse engineering" the question.

Many educators suggest this sort of "looking backward" approach, which involves deconstructing your thinking, and there are different ways of doing this. My approach is to start by simply reading an essay-question fact pattern and model answer aloud. Then, *looking at the answer*, write an outline. Outline the answer, asking yourself as you do, "What would I have needed in an outline to write this kind of an answer?" Then, look back at the facts. "Where in the facts do I see words that trigger the points in my outline?" Sometimes, studying the answer and working backward helps you see what was important in the question. Outlining sample or model answers in this way will not only usually help you relax and see how certain facts were significant, but should also help you recognize logical ways to organize your analysis of the key issues.

Copying answers, outlining, and reverse engineering are all tools that will help you get the juices flowing again when you feel stalled. They seem easy because you are working from answers, so they tend to reduce anxiety. But somehow they often empower people. The very act of retyping and understanding the words coming from your own hands will build skills you need to learn to write similar answers on your own. Likewise, seeing both how an answer flows from a question and how pieces of the question trigger components of the answer helps build your test-taking skills. And, this process works effectively to deconstruct MBEs and performance tests as well as essays.

As you work, tell yourself, "I can do this. I see the organization. It makes sense. When I'm in the exam, this is how my analysis will flow." Smile, and force yourself to take a deep breath. Keep yourself in as positive a frame of mind as possible to keep your brain energized.

Anxiety-reducing tools to use any time nerves hit

As we explored previously, some techniques work particularly well during an exam or at other specific times. Other strategies are helpful any time you feel anxious. (You may feel nervous when you go to your bar review class and find yourself confused, and you may feel overwhelmed reading the outline and seeing concepts you do not know or understand. Go back and review the sections in Chapter 5 on getting the most out of bar review; you will see tools that will not only help you learn, but help calm you during the process.)

Intensive bar preparation lasts for two tense, crazy months. These simple steps will help when nerves hit:

- Breathe deeply and slowly. Slow, steady, deep breaths will often release the nerves and "paralysis" that comes from them. We tend to tense up when we are nervous, and often forget to breathe properly. You will read more clearly and think more clearly when the oxygen is flowing freely.

- Visualize yourself in the exam setting. Picture yourself thinking and your words flowing. As you take practice tests, imagine taking them in a room full of palpable stress (perhaps picture the place you took the LSAT, SAT, FYLSE, or any other standardized test). Recall the nervous energy and how you prevailed in spite of it. (Maybe part of you thrived on the challenge!) Envision yourself now and on your upcoming exams reading questions; bubbling in multiple-choice answers; writing essay and performance-test responses; and feeling calm, confident, and in control.

- Talk to yourself, calmly and positively. Positive thinking is critical! Tell yourself every day that you *can* do this. Say it aloud several times each day. Banish from your mind any past test-taking experiences that were not positive. Replace them with empowering images of you conquering challenges. Ban phrases such as, "I'm not good at standardized tests." That is hogwash, and you know it! You got into law school, and may even have successfully completed law school by the time you have read this chapter. You are not only good—you are excellent at taking these tests. Rid your speech (and mind) of all that is not positive and strong. Ultimately, remember that you will be alone on the exam. So figure out how to talk yourself down from the ledge. (One former student said she got through several mini panic attacks during the bar exam by telling herself that it was "just another practice test." When she felt the pressure mount, she whispered to herself, "This is just another practice test. You've been doing these all summer. No big deal. You know what to do. Just keep reading and thinking. It's a puzzle. It all fits together. You'll see.")

Notice that the strategies above can be employed without "props." There are many things you can do to de-stress in June and July, *before the exam*, such as drink a cup of tea, take a walk, go to a yoga class, meditate, take a hot bath, or talk with someone who loves and supports you. But none of those can be done *during* the exam. It is important to develop some effective calming habits that you can employ during practice tests that will also be useable if you find yourself panicking *on the actual exam*. These techniques *will* help.

But by far *the most effective tool to combat nerves is adequate preparation*. The better your training, the more prepared you are, the less your nerves will hinder you. If you do feel nervous, which is normal no matter how hard you have studied, you will be much more able to turn the nervousness into adrenaline so it serves, rather than defeats, you.

CONTAGIOUS ANXIETY.

If anyone tells you "don't be nervous" or suggests that it is stupid to be nervous, he or she is either ignorant, needs a "reality check," or is just plain full of garbage. It is *normal* to be nervous. If you are not a little nervous, you likely do not appreciate the seriousness of what you are doing. You might find it helpful when others share that they too are nervous. (And whether they tell you so or not, they are.) It makes you feel you are not alone. That's great, unless their nerves are contagious and cause you to stress out further. (If that's the case, do not talk about being nervous with classmates or others who share their own anxiety.)

Similarly, sometimes you can talk yourself out of panic, but other times talking about it just gets you worked up further. If that sort of nervousness hits, it may be better to switch gears or take a break (or go to sleep). Figure out now if you are someone who lets go when you talk, or someone who obsesses further and gets more stressed out. And protect yourself as you prepare.

WORK HARD, BUT WORK EFFICIENTLY.
REASSESS YOUR SCHEDULE.

After a week or two of intensive bar preparation, ask yourself whether the location and timing of your studying are maximizing your productivity. Where you study can mean the difference between focusing well and not. Are you studying in your home? Is it quiet? Do you have a dedicated study space? Some people simply cannot focus at a cluttered desk. Some determine their homes are not conducive to study, so they find a good spot elsewhere. You don't have to move out or rent an office to focus effectively (though those things work for some people). Just find a place that works for you. It may be a coffee shop or public library. Many find their law school libraries distracting because classmates stop to chat.

"ADAPT OR PERISH, NOW AS EVER, IS NATURE'S INEXORABLE IMPERATIVE."

— H. G. WELLS —

Your goal is to find a place where, and discover the times when, you are most focused. It is excellent training, though, to take at least a few practice tests or try to study at least a few days in *the most distracting place imaginable*. I urge all of my students to do this so that they don't get so used to the quiet of their home or a library that they are unable to concentrate during the actual exam, when keyboards will be clacking and other applicants will be coughing, sneezing, sighing, groaning, or making other noises. One former student who passed the bar the first time around was determined to overcome his concern about being distracted on the actual exam. How did he do this? He decided to train by completing practice tests each week at the noisiest place he could think of—the top of the stairs in one of the most crowded shopping malls in Los Angeles. He figured (correctly) that if he could focus there, he could focus anywhere. And he did! (By the way, the exam he took and passed the first time around had a rule against perpetuities issue!)

Is my schedule maximizing my efficiency?

Not getting done each day what you need to? Look critically at your schedule. What is, and what is not, working? When are you getting distracted? Are you a working student whose daily schedule varies? If so, try a weekly schedule so you can fit more into days when you have more time, do less on busier days, and still keep up.

Think about when and what you are eating on study days, and whether you are exercising. Those are factors that can help you work more efficiently or slow you down.

Are people interrupting you? When are you working? Are you too tired to focus? Maybe shifting the time of day can help you focus. Or consider changing locations.

Every challenge can be surmounted if you see where the hang-ups are.

Adapt your schedule as the bar approaches, and make more time for memorizing.

Much of early start and bar review may be about learning. Practice exams help you learn the law in context, and help you recall rules when you encounter analogous fact patterns. The best way to retain everything you need to know for exam day is to continuously build on your foundation; learn, refine, and practice throughout the summer; and increase your focus on memorization the closer you get to the exam. (If you had all the rules you needed to know memorized in May, you would likely forget them by the end of July. And you will likely be stunned at how little you remember in August!)

Your goal when you walk into that test is to know each element of each important rule as well as you know your most frequently used password. Your schedule must include adequate time for memorization. The more simply rules are phrased, the easier they will be to memorize and use on the exam. So a main goal throughout early bar review and intensive bar review is to assemble and organize all key rules into memorizable form.

How to memorize? Break out the flashcards, write it out fifty times, do whatever works for you!

Read and reread rule statements aloud. Look at them, listen to them, write them out repeatedly, test yourself, and have others test you. Engage fully in the memorization process. In the age of speed dial, our memories often take the backseat. We don't need them as much as we used to when we walked around with critical numbers in our heads. But by the end of July, your mind needs to act as a sort of Wikipedia for legal rules. When you need the definition of homicide and forms of malice, or a statement of Rules 10b-5 or 16b or UCC Section 2-207, you need them right away. You need instant recall.

Sometimes we need a kick (or trick) to help us recall rules for an exam. Mnemonics are memory-aid techniques that have likely been helping people since ancient times. They can be verbal—perhaps a short rhyme or a key word that helps you remember something. They can be in song. (How many people sing the alphabet song when they need to alphabetize?) They can be based on lists. People often choose the first letter of each word in a list; for example, *IRAC* is a common mnemonic for *Issue, Rule, Analysis, Conclusion*. They can also be visual, such as associating arrows to recall how one concept stems from or links to another.

EXERCISE: How do you memorize best?

You are a student. This is not the first time you have had to memorize. Think back to science (memorizing the periodic table), math (memorizing formulas), history (memorizing dates and names), and foreign languages (memorizing vocabulary). What worked best for you? What made things stick? Did you: 1) Write out, maybe even 50 times, whatever you needed to memorize? 2) Write a flashcard and test yourself, or have others test you? 3) Say it out loud? 4) Put it to song or rhyme, or create a mnemonic? What are your favorite memory tools? (A number of the books and resources on surviving and thriving in law school listed in the Bibliography have helpful suggestions about how to effectively memorize.[29])

1. _____

2. _____

3. _____

4. _____

Preventing burnout: Add incentives and levity.

Studying for the bar exam is a test of endurance. You have to put in many high-gear days and pack into your brain more learning than you ever thought you could absorb, and you have to do this day in and day out for a minimum of about sixty days. This section provides suggestions to help stay on course.

Reward yourself.

During intensive bar prep, give yourself a small but consistent reward each day for doing your best, and a slightly bigger one each week. What is your secret pleasure? What is your not-so-secret pleasure? What makes you smile, feel happy, or comforted? What works for you?

If it's music, buy yourself one new song each evening after you have honestly put in a good, solid day's work. Once a week, give yourself an hour or two off to listen to live music somewhere—maybe on a weekend evening, after having put in a productive study week. Is it movies or TV? Allow yourself a half hour of mindless TV each evening, and go out to a movie theater or watch a movie at home once a week, with popcorn! Is it food or wine? Give yourself some special treat once a day, something at the end of a hard day's learning—chocolate, ice cream, sautéed mushrooms in truffle oil? (Well, I said whatever works for you!) And, once a week, go out to a special restaurant or cook, or have someone else cook, a special meal at home.

The point here is to positively mark each day and each week. You need to stay in the game and not get worn out too early. Expect these months to involve hard work. Do that work with as much energy and focus as is humanly possible. Then, acknowledge and give yourself credit for what you have done. This also helps you count down the weeks and pace yourself. Studying for the bar exam is a long haul. (Note: It is a long haul for your family or significant other, too. If you are a person who uses good food as an incentive, think about possibly taking your family or significant other out for a great meal once per week—a reward for you and them!).

EXERCISE

List how you might reward yourself for a job well done. Some suggestions: watch a mindless TV show; have a great meal with a glass of wine; go out for a movie and popcorn; take a walk outdoors (chant motivational sayings as you walk); drive to a place where you can see the ocean, a beautiful mountain, or some other scenery that takes you out of your day-to-day routine; laugh with a friend who is supportive; eat some Belgian chocolate. (Chocolate won't add brain cells, I know, but it may lift your mood and put a smile on your face.)

What works for you?

_____

_____

_____

_____

After enjoying your reward, get a good night's sleep so you can get back to work the next morning. Slow and steady wins the race.

Above all, be kind to yourself all the way through bar review. This is one of the hardest times in your life, one of the steepest mountains you will have to climb. The good news is, once you pass the bar, you'll have a lifetime license. You'll never have to take the exam again. Just pay your annual dues, complete your jurisdiction's continuing-education requirements, and remain ethical, and you'll keep your license for life.

GIVE YOURSELF A SPECIAL REWARD OR INCENTIVE ON JULY 1

One nice thing about seeing June become July is that adrenaline will kick in. But the last week of June can be particularly rough. People are normally drained, and sometimes a little depressed or discouraged, as June ends. Prepare for a jolt when you see June become July. It can freak you out if you are not ready for it. (You have been saying the date of your bar exam for years. It felt so far off, but suddenly it's nearly here.) You must make that July 1 rush one of adrenaline, not panic.

Bar exam burnout

We talked earlier about anxiety and how to combat nerves. What about fatigue and burnout? Do you know the difference? It is one of degree. If you are just tired, sleeping more may help. For anxiety, try the tips discussed earlier. (And note that you are apt to be more nervous and less able to conquer anxiety when you are tired.) If you are suffering from burnout, recharging your batteries may be a bit more difficult.

Are you burned out? Some people *start* bar review burned out. Others are really dragging by the end of June. What can you do about burnout? First, admit it. Face it so you can correct it. Allowing yourself to be so "done" that you are blocked from putting in further effort will not result in success.

Next, assess whether it's a major burnout. Do you need a half day or full day off? Some people need an entire weekend away. If you know that you are too fried to focus, take time off. Get some fresh air. Change the scenery. Clear your mind.

For minor burnout, the best solution is giving yourself consistent small rewards and breaks that you know you can look forward to after every productive study day. It can also be helpful to break up the day. Put in a focused four-hour block in the morning; then take a good, long lunch break. (Most bar exams actually have long lunch breaks.) You can eat and maybe get in some exercise or even a nap if you need it. (I've known people who napped during the lunch break at the actual bar exam! They set two alarm clocks and arranged for a wake-up call, of course.)

Take a similar break following afternoon and evening study sessions. Spend time with someone supportive, if you have someone in your life who is helpful. If not, spend any downtime with a good book or movie! (Do not spend time with anyone who saps your energy or keeps you from meeting your goal.)

Humor: You gotta laugh a little.

Some people like to watch a comedy every so often, or listen to silly jokes. I came up with the following "Top Ten List" for *how you know you are taking a bar exam*. (Apologies to David Letterman.)

How you know you are taking a bar exam:

10. Your desk and bookshelves are filled with software and books about bars, but none of them tell you where to get a drink.
9. You care how many multiple-choice practice questions other people answer.
8. You study flashcards at red lights.
7. Your iPod or phone has a playlist called something like "Get that Study Groove On."
6. You dream about real property fact patterns.
5. You wake from those dreams wondering what the answer is.
4. You know the differences between Notice, Race-Notice, and Race Statutes, and you care about those differences.
3. You have spent more money in the past few months on bar prep than most of your nonlaw friends spend on car payments.
2. Whenever you have to wait for something, you find yourself calculating how many multiple-choice questions you could have done in the time spent waiting.
1. You spend time thinking about whether you will be able to make it through days of three-hour, anxiety-filled testing blocks without interrupting any of those blocks to go to the bathroom.

Motivate with music

Every time you feel overwhelmed, overloaded, tired, fearful, or discouraged, play music that makes your spirit sing. Music will lift you right out of whatever you are feeling (those feelings, by the way, are totally normal just prior to taking the bar exam).

Sure, there are a few folks who one week into July are saying, "Just bring it on. I am tired of studying, tired of waiting, and as ready as I'll ever be." But they are few and far between. Most people feel overwhelmed and overloaded just before the exam, and want every extra minute possible to prepare.

It's a long haul, the bar exam. If you're tired or feel yourself slowing down, play some inspiring music. And sing along! Find the artists that move you. Even on the actual exam, should you find yourself in an afternoon lull or a moment of panic, humming an uplifting tune in your head may be just the secret weapon to pull you through.

WHAT IS ON YOUR BAR EXAM PLAYLIST?

My favorite bar study song is Jimmy Cliff's "You Can Get It If You Really Want." I also play at the beginning of every motivational session Queen's "We Will Rock You," changing the word "rock" to "pass." (Only when celebrating bar passage do we play the second half of that tune, "We Are the Champions.") What is on your bar exam playlist?

FINALIZING YOUR SCHEDULE

You have all the pieces now to create a very effective study schedule. Take a look back at the draft you wrote earlier and update it, or start fresh. Be sure your schedule includes regular disciplined study *and* regular breaks to recharge your batteries.

6 a.m.

7 a.m.

8 a.m.

9 a.m.

10 a.m.

11 a.m.

Noon

1 p.m.

2 p.m.

3 p.m.

4 p.m.

5 p.m. _____

6 p.m. _____

7 p.m. _____

8 p.m. _____

9 p.m. _____

10 p.m. _____

PRACTICE TESTS:
THE HEAVY LIFTING

- Passing the bar exam requires knowledge, skill, and training
  - I wish I had started earlier
  - Overview of bar exam testing
  - Active reading equals bar reading
  - Where to get practice tests
- The MBE
  - MBE Preparation
  - Practice by completing a consistent number of MBEs every day, under timed conditions
  - How to self-assess MBEs
  - MBE Tips and Strategies
- The Essays
  - Essay-Test Tips and Strategies
  - Crossover questions
  - Practice-essay writing
  - Essays: A closer look at how to read and write them
  - Bar writing is logical writing, and it differs in key ways from law school exam writing.
  - Bar reading and its relationship to bar writing

- Writing examples
- Do not assume: Prove it, and say "why."
- Conclusions
- How to self-assess your practice-essay writing
- Persistence
- Getting your exams graded by someone else
- Self-assessment through reverse engineering
- Performance Tests
  - About performance tests
  - How do performance tests differ from essays
  - How to complete performance tests
  - Overview of this system: Why it works and why it makes sense
  - Adjust the timing to fit your strengths and weaknesses
  - A closer look at each step in the PT approach
  - Practice performance tests and how to self-assess them
  - Remaining steps in the approach
  - PT strategy tips
- Practice Test Scores for all types of bar testing

Previous chapters discussed many success factors, including planning, preparing, knowing what to expect, protecting your time, and learning the law. In this chapter, I will present strategies for effectively completing your bar review course work and, specifically, for tackling practice exams. (The information in this chapter will help you know what to expect and get ready for intensive bar prep; it gives you a head start. The information in this chapter complements but is not a substitute for bar review.) This is the hardest chapter of all. It contains the toughest advice to give regarding the most difficult stage of bar prep. Why? You have done your planning and mapped out your study schedule. From here on, it is just plain hard work—the "heavy lifting" phase. Consider the words of John Quincy Adams: "Patience and perseverance have a magical effect before which difficulties disappear and obstacles vanish."

Think of this training as you would preparation for sports. You must correctly and completely assess what you are doing now and understand where you need to improve. (Picture an athlete watching replays of recent matches, assessing where she can improve her game.) Self-assessment is critical. And after you self-assess, you must take affirmative steps to implement any changes that are necessary.

Completing practice questions without assessing your performance is what I call "Doing the Ostrich." It's like the person who thinks bad news will go away if he or she just ignores it. Not true. Recognize your strengths, and directly face your weaknesses. Do not put your head in the sand. Seize these precious opportunities (after completing practice exams) to improve.

The road to success is yours, but only if you drive. Don't be the passive passenger. Take control. Get to work. After you read this chapter, review your study plan. Make sure it includes sufficient uninterrupted time blocks for taking *and self-assessing* practice tests on top of the time you will need for bar review lectures. And protect that time. Don't be seduced into thinking that passively attending bar review is enough. It isn't.

The months of bar prep will fly by. You will be entering the exam room before you know it. How you choose to spend the months prior to the bar will determine how you go in—confidently, knowing you have done everything in your power to achieve success, or sheepishly, knowing you could have done more. It's your choice.

PASSING THE BAR EXAM REQUIRES KNOWLEDGE, SKILL, *AND* TRAINING.

- You must know and understand the legal rules and principles tested on the exam.
- You must be skilled in what I call active "bar reading" (described in the following sections), clear and effective writing, analytical and logical reasoning, and time management. Bar reading is the first and most critical of these skills, for obvious reasons: If you are not reading correctly and understanding everything you read,

your analysis will be off, usually leading to incorrect or incomplete conclusions. When you fail to read critically, you miss or misinterpret key words, assume information that isn't provided in the question, and make other egregious (yet wholly preventable) errors, *errors you would not have made* had you read carefully enough.

- You must prepare, taking practice tests under timed conditions, self-assessing your performance, and following specific steps to steadily and continuously improve your results.

"I wish I had started earlier!"

I would be quite wealthy if I had a dollar for every student who has told me, "I wish I had started bar prep during my last year of law school." Often, this is expressed simply because bar review takes more time and energy than people think. Expect to work seven days per week for at least eight weeks straight. This can be especially tough for nontraditional, working students. Debbie, a student of mine who was able to reduce her work to part-time in June and July, still found she spent far too much time catching up in bar review. Every day she worked, she lost a day of bar studies. She wished she'd gotten a head start so she wouldn't constantly feel behind. Another of my nontraditional students, Tony, worked all through law school and quite successfully managed his time to do well in both school and on the job. In early June, however, Tony unexpectedly got a promotion that was too good to pass up. Suddenly, the time he had available for bar studies shriveled. Tony was left trying to pack the entire bar review course *and his practice testing* into just two to three hours a day. His new job responsibilities were greater than those of his previous position, and Tony scrambled to make up the difference on weekends by studying fourteen to sixteen hours each day. That didn't work, either, as he was too tired and stressed to really focus and learn well. What was most difficult, Tony found, was freeing up enough time to listen to all of the bar review lectures. Tony was taking an online bar review with an early start, so if he had begun in early March, as I urge all of my nontraditional students to do, he would have had the time to go through nearly all the lectures once *before* June.

You may not get a promotion. You may not even be working during law school. But unanticipated events come up all the time. You might get sick. A family member or your significant other might get sick. Your personal relationships may hit crises. (Unfortunately, too many law students find themselves facing breakups or divorce during or toward the end of law school.) Even a joyous event, such as you or your significant other's getting pregnant, might throw your otherwise meticulously planned schedule into chaos. Some of these challenges make the bar exam (which already seemed ridiculously difficult) seem impossible. Planning ahead can help you buffer the detrimental effects of such curveballs. And, although you can't protect against every scenario by starting early, you can do yourself an enormous favor that may make the difference between passing and failing.

If an unexpected crisis arises, talk to someone who can help you through it. Right away. An empathetic faculty member or mentor may have concrete suggestions to help you tackle the situation. I think of another student whose father passed away shortly before the exam; instead of causing him to postpone the bar, the loss bolstered his determination. He redoubled his efforts. Knowing how proud his father would have been to see him pass the bar exam helped propel him forward. And I have had many students successfully manage pregnancies and caring for infants while studying for the exam. Get good advice from someone who has been there.

Note: In the wake of some tragedies, of course, it makes sense to delay taking the exam. If you have a good reason to postpone it until February, put yourself on an extended study plan rather than waiting and gearing up anew in January.

Overview of bar exam testing

Bar exams typically include some combination of essays, multiple-choice questions, and performance tests. A snapshot of each will first be provided, followed by a consideration of

- what the test is,
- how to practice for this type of test,
- how to self-assess your practice tests, and
- exam-taking tips and strategies.

Just as you will need to become fluent in each substantive area of law tested on the bar, so, too, will you need to become skilled at taking each type of test on your exam. Don't go into the bar hoping they won't test civil procedure, for example. And don't go in saying, "MBEs are my strong point. I'm not good at those PTs." Get good at everything.

THE POWER TRIO OF MBES, ESSAYS, AND PTS

On a recent visit to New Orleans, I sampled dishes reflecting Southern chefs' penchant for flavoring with onions, peppers, and celery. The key is the combination. That flavor would not result from a preparation with boatloads of peppers, but no onions. (Not a foodie? Think of your body's need for diet, exercise, *and* rest. All the exercise in the world won't help if you feed your body poorly or are too tired to function.) Likewise, on bar exams, all of the pieces are critical. Resist the temptation to favor one form of practice testing over another. Slap yourself if you are tempted to fill every hour with practice MBEs because "I can do thirty-three of them in the time it takes to write just one essay." Students tell me all the time, "I can't afford the time to do practice performance tests." I assure you: you cannot afford to *skip* them.

Let's now consider bar essays, MBEs, and PTs. Bar exam essay questions are similar in some respects to law school essay exams. They typically tell a factual story about two or more parties who have some conflict or problem. Your job is to apply the law you know (and have memorized) to these facts, and reason through to logical conclusions that answer whatever questions are asked. The ultimate question may be who prevails, why, and what damages may be awarded; with what crimes may a defendant be convicted; how provisions in a will should be interpreted to determine how property will be distributed; or who will be awarded which assets or incur which debts following a divorce proceeding. Note: Many subissues (additional questions) may need to be resolved in order to reach the ultimate conclusion. (Think about it: to decide whether Paula may prevail against Derek in a cause of action for negligence, you must resolve any issues relating to duty, breach, actual and proximate cause, and damages, and then discuss possible defense theories.)

Bar exams differ from law school essays in that they typically test more issues and areas of law than law school exams, but in less depth. Bar essays may also have shorter fact patterns than law school essay exams.

Bar exams also include multiple-choice testing in the form of the multistate bar exam (MBE) and sometimes also state-specific questions. (Both New York and Florida, for example, test state law with multiple-choice questions in addition to the MBE.) You may not have had any multiple-choice tests in law school. If you did, they were probably fewer in number and may not have been constructed with the complexity (trickiness) of MBE questions.

Like essays, multiple-choice questions are based on a factual story. This similar structure is why we will develop a similar strategy for approaching MBE questions (read the question first; then read the facts). Also like essays, you must read every word carefully. Unlike essays, though, you will be asked to select the *best* answer from a number of choices. MBEs are challenging for many applicants because the questions tend to focus on narrow points of law, and students are given only a short time to reason to that best answer. (Completing each set of 100 questions in three hours allows only 1.8 minutes per question.) MBE success requires detailed knowledge of many legal rules, but does not demand the skill that essays do of articulating those rules in your own words.

Performance tests (PTs) are practical exams during which applicants are placed in legal role-play scenarios. Simulating a lawyer with a client file, you are given papers and source documents to read and law to review, and asked to draft one or more real-world documents based on facts and legal rules you cull from those materials. You may be asked to draft briefs in support of motions, memos, client letters, settlement offers, affidavits, closing arguments, discovery plans, or other documents. PTs are "open book" in that the legal principles are provided in a "library." You, of course, have to extract the rules from primary or secondary sources (for example, by pulling holdings from cases; analyzing statutes; and reading jury instructions, law review articles, or treatises). PTs would be relatively easy for most law graduates *if* they were given more time. But to provide a complete enough answer to pass within the allotted time is *not* easy; it requires mastering an approach and extensively developing the requisite PT skills.

THE PERFORMANCE TEST
PRACTICALLY WRITES ITSELF!

I cannot even begin discussing PTs without being transported back to the voice of a most-charismatic professor who lectured nationwide for decades. In bar review, he practically danced with enthusiasm as he pounded the podium declaring that because it was open book, the PT was the easy part of the exam, joyously concluding, "Why, it practically writes itself!" Having taken PTs myself since my first year of law school, I knew they were tough. (They were also fair in my view, but in no way easy.) Though I appreciated his desire to calm and reassure the crowd, I knew better. And, given his age, I knew this professor hadn't taken a performance test on *his* bar exam. PTs are fairly new additions to bar exams. If anyone tells you they are easy, find out when he or she took the exam!

Active reading equals bar reading

Before considering specifics about how to tackle these exams and improve your skills (and, ultimately, your scores), let's first focus on *the most critical habit you can develop*: becoming an effective bar reader. Active bar reading is the single most important key to bar passage; it is the success thread that runs through all types of bar testing. While there are unique aspects to and strategies for tackling the different forms of testing, all of them require this highly focused form of active reading that I refer to as "bar reading."[30]

What is bar reading?

Bar reading certainly includes careful reading, but it also involves being deeply engaged with the material, *analyzing* as you read. You superimpose a mental template (rules and issues in a logical structure) on top of the words so that you immediately see their significance, and begin reasoning them into order. You will need to have law organized and memorized—and then read facts to assess whether they prove or disprove elements of identifiable causes of action or other legal theories.

Unless you have a photographic memory, bar reading also involves note taking. Sometimes you will jot notes in the margins or on top of words on the exam itself; other times you will type thoughts separately. You will want to note any word or words that appear to trigger a discussion or analysis of some particular area of law. (This is sometimes called *issue spotting*, as we'll discuss in detail below.) For example, suppose you are reading a criminal law fact pattern and see that the defendant was diagnosed with schizophrenia. You would immediately underline the word *schizophrenia* and jot something like "Insanity defense?" on top of it or in the margin. All of the tests for insanity require that the defendant suffer from a mental disease or defect. So, although this one word does not necessarily mean that insanity is a discussable issue, it may be, and you need to be alert to the possibility. Consider another example: if a criminal law fact pattern indicated a defendant was engaged in some other crime at the time a death resulted, what might that suggest? Yes, that's right: it's a tip-off that felony murder might be a discussable issue. Again, you might ultimately conclude that the felony murder rule does not apply. Perhaps it's not a dangerous felony, or the rule is inapplicable for some other reason. But it still may be a relevant and discussable issue. Remember, it is often just as important to recognize that the rule is implicated though not satisfied, and discuss why the moving party will *not* win, as it is to prove when the moving party prevails. The main point of bar essay testing is not to demonstrate that you know the best answer. That is for MBEs. Rather, the essay allows you to demonstrate that you know what questions the facts give rise to and how (given the law you know and articulate), and why these facts tend to prove or disprove relative claims or defenses.

While every essay will be different in some respects, there are often parallels in essay exams. Writing many practice exams will help you see which issues tend to arise in similar fact patterns, and will help you easily spot words that suggest particular issues.

When bar reading, you will also want to circle or put a box around certain words, such as party names, the first time they are introduced.[31] Circle the connecting words *and* and *or* when reading MBE interrogatories and answer choices, as well as documents such as contractual provisions in a PT file and statutes in a PT library. You cannot afford to miss even one *and* or *or*. It may change the entire meaning. Underline, highlight, or otherwise clearly mark the holdings in cases in the PT library.

Most importantly, though, bar reading involves *thinking* while you read. It requires asking yourself *why* each word in the fact pattern is there and whether it triggers some discussable issue. It involves recalling previous fact patterns, and discerning how the new facts are analogous to or distinguishable from other scenarios or examples you recall, so that you can readily determine if a legal theory is relevant or not.

To ensure that you read in this fully engaged manner, lean forward and sit up straight when you read, and develop the habit of simultaneously reading with three senses: touch, sight, and hearing. *Point* to each word with your finger or pencil, as you *read* with your eyes, and softly *say* the words aloud. (Don't read loudly enough to disturb others or be kicked out of the exam room, but just loudly enough so that the words enter your consciousness, a sort of mumbling process called *subvocalization*.)[32]

Bar reading also involves reading certain parts of these exams several times, especially essay interrogatories, fact patterns, and the instructions to performance tests. (We will talk later about how to read a PT file and library.) Multiple-choice testing requires such fast responses that time may not allow for repeated readings, so you must develop a strategy to read those initially with the utmost attention to detail. (Even on the MBE, time permitting, a second read can help a lot.)

Where to get practice tests?

Much of the rest of this chapter is directly or indirectly related to taking practice tests: why to take them, how to take them, and how to self-assess and improve the quality of your answers. (And as much as this may feel like extra busy work you don't have time for, you will be thankful if you develop this habit early on.) So where are these practice tests located, and how do you get ahold of them?

Practice law school exams: Go first to your professor (who may have old exams on file). A professor's past exams are often the best indicator of how he or she will test in the future. Next, go to your school's ASP faculty, law librarian (exams may be on reserve in the library), and possibly upperclassmen who have taken the course before. Last, cautiously employ commercial study aids and outlines. Be sure these are reputable resources that will be helpful to *you*. (Check them out carefully before using them; a book or video that worked for a friend may not help you, or vice versa.)

Practice bar exam questions: In intensive bar prep, a reputable bar review will typically provide all the practice questions you need. You may also be able to get the materials before June to dig in early, if you have already enrolled in (and especially if you have already paid for) your bar review. To find materials to review on your own, you might start with any past exams that are posted on your state bar's website (especially if there are also sample passing answers or issue outlines). You may also be able to purchase updated materials from reputable commercial publications. Note: You can buy practice MBE, MPT, and MEE questions directly from the NCBE (look on their website at www.ncbex.org). You can also find older, used materials from bookstores, law libraries, or online sites. Two caveats: first, the material may be dated and some of the law may have changed. Second, the exam formats may have changed. That said, as long as you are aware of these possible deficiencies, certain old bar review materials can be very useful, especially for early start, when much of your goal is more general exposure than the intensive training that will come in June and July. (Yet another good reason to invest in a reputable bar review for your intensive work, though, is that they will tell you about relevant changes and updates.)

SAMPLE VERSUS MODEL ANSWERS

Some states release passing student answers. Caveat: sample answers may contain errors and still be passing. (Bar exams are pass/fail tests; bar examiners do not expect perfection!) By *model answers*, I mean those written by professors in a reliable bar review or ASP program. Model answers should not contain substantive law errors. Additionally, sample answers are written under timed conditions, whereas model answers may have been crafted and edited for days or weeks. Both can serve as learning tools, but beware of the limitations of each. (Simply put, a sample answer can tell you what you will need to do to pass; a model answer can show you what to strive for.)

THE MBE

The National Conference of Bar Examiners (NCBE) describes the Multistate Bar Examination (MBE) as a "six-hour, 200-question multiple-choice examination covering Constitutional Law, Contracts, Criminal Law and Procedure, Evidence, Real

PRACTICE TESTS: THE HEAVY LIFTING **177**

Property, and Torts." (Soon this list will also include Civil Procedure.) Become familiar with the useful information on the NCBE's website, www.ncbex.org.

MBE questions, like essays, begin with a short fact pattern. The facts are followed by an interrogatory and four answer choices. Applicants are to respond by bubbling in (in number 2 pencil) the best of the four choices on a Scantron answer sheet. (As we will discuss below, the "best" answer is not always the "correct" answer choice!) MBEs require fast-paced reading and thinking. They include 200 questions to be answered in 6 hours: 100 in 3 hours in the morning, and 100 in 3 hours in the afternoon. MBEs tend to test fine distinctions in points of law.

As noted, some jurisdictions also include state-specific multiple-choice questions. These vary a great deal, so be sure you are taking a bar review that is dedicated to helping students in your jurisdiction. Here we will focus on multiple-choice questions as tested on the MBE.

To understand MBE questions, you must have mastered a great many detailed legal rules. You will need to choose the best answer for each question. Therefore, *a* most accurate answer choice must necessarily be included for each question. To make that possible, questions are often crafted such that the answer turns on a rule of law rather than a factual analysis. Essays, by contrast, as we will discuss, often focus more on facts from which differing inferences may be drawn. Taking the same essay facts, applicants may reason through them differently or draw varying conclusions from them. Thus, applicants may write essay answers with different outcomes and still be correct and pass the exam. Because you are writing your own answers, you can present arguments from different points of view (for example, using "Defendant would argue" or "Plaintiff would argue" language). However, there is no room to argue the facts when answering an MBE question.

Mastering the skill of factual analysis is as critical to success on the bar exam as is legal analysis. You must be able to organize relevant facts and establish why they are or are not relevant to particular elements of rules of law. Often the relevance is established only by making certain inferences. In bar exam writing, you must be certain the inferences you make are explicit.[33]

To illustrate, let's take a simple hypothetical criminal law scenario:

> Defendant Dan is approached by Vicious Victor, who is wielding a knife. Dan does not know for certain that Victor intends to kill him, but Dan responds nonetheless by pulling out a gun and shooting Victor, aiming at Victor's toe. Victor dies as a result of the injury.

Assume an MBE posed a question that asked applicants to give the best defense theory presented by this scenario, with the following as answer choices: a) deadly weapon, b) insanity, c) self-defense, or d) intoxication. There are no facts to help Dan establish either an insanity or intoxication defense, and although it isn't certain that Dan would prevail in asserting self-defense as a justification, it is the *best* of the choices given. Why? The focus of the question is on defenses, and Victor's use of a deadly weapon does not in and of itself provide a defense theory. In fact, it might help the prosecutor to convict Dan of a more serious offense, as discussed below. (Note: This is tricky, as MBEs often are, because Victor's use of a knife, a deadly weapon, is necessary to justify Dan having responded with deadly force. But because the question asks what Dan's best defense theory will be, the best response appears to be *c*.)

The best answer would be less certain, however, if this same fact pattern were an essay question asking, "Of what crimes, if any, might Dan be convicted—and why?" You would certainly strive to analyze the issues as clearly as possible, but you might point out how drawing different inferences from the facts in this case could lead to different results. Let's look at this more closely. The prosecutor would assert that Dan committed murder, and unless Dan successfully argued a defense or mitigation theory, he would be convicted of either first- or second-degree murder. A murder is a homicide committed with malice aforethought. Dan killed Victor; therefore, Dan committed the homicide element of murder—that is, the killing of one human being by another. Dan's use of a deadly weapon allows for an *inference* that Dan possessed the intent to kill, which would satisfy the mental state element of murder. (This means the judge or jury deciding the case *could* find that Dan intended to kill Victor just because Dan used a deadly weapon in a deadly manner, without other evidence of Dan's actual intent. This does not have to be the conclusion, but it is permissible.)

Law students will correctly recognize that for a first-degree murder conviction, the prosecution would also have to establish that Dan's shooting was premeditated and deliberate. Both premeditation and deliberation would likely be more difficult to prove under these facts, as Dan's actions appear to have been unplanned. But before we even address these concerns, is it crystal clear that Dan had the required mental state? Not at all.

The prosecution *might* be able to show by virtue of using a deadly weapon that Dan possessed the intent to kill, but that inference would not be mandatory. The judge or jury would not have to come to the same conclusion. The defense could, for example, provide additional facts to counter (or rebut) the inference that Dan intended to kill Victor. For example, the defense might stress that Dan aimed at Victor's toe. (What inference would be drawn from the fact that Dan shot at Victor's toe? Well, one who intends to kill typically aims for the head or a vital organ, rather than the smallest of extremities, right? So having shot at Victor's toe might tend to prove that Dan did not intend to kill.) But the prosecution might in turn contend that aiming to shoot at any part of a victim's body evidences an intent to kill, or, at the very least, an intent to seriously injure, a mental state that would suffice for second-degree murder.

The defense might go on to argue that Dan's actions were justified, that he was acting in self-defense. After all, Victor was the first to draw a weapon, his knife. But in order to prevail in a complete self-defense justification, the defendant has to prove that at the time of action, he or she reasonably and in good faith feared being attacked with imminent deadly force. This could pose a problem for Dan. Why? Well, although it's true that Victor was wielding a deadly weapon himself, the facts specifically state that Dan was uncertain as to whether Victor was intending to kill him. (Maybe Victor wanted to show Dan his knife to prove how vicious he was, without intending to use it on Dan at all.) Unless Dan could establish that he himself believed, and that a reasonable person in his shoes would have believed, that he was about to be attacked by Victor with deadly force, it is doubtful Dan would prevail in claiming self-defense.

Therefore, a logical conclusion to the analysis might be that Dan would *likely* be convicted of second-degree murder because he shot Victor with what can be established was the intent to seriously injure him. (But it's *possible* to have logically concluded that despite aiming at Victor's toe, Dan still likely possessed the intent to kill, especially given his use of a deadly weapon.)

From this short scenario and the fact that we were able to reason to more than one plausible conclusion, you can see how much more room there is for gray areas in essay questions than in MBEs. Learning the differences between the two (along with practicing each) will help you gain a command of effective test-taking strategies. You will likely come to appreciate that you only have to find the best answer on MBEs, and, at the same time, that you will not be trapped into coming up with one right answer to essay questions.

MBE preparation

How should you approach MBEs? When you sit down to complete an MBE question:

- Cover the answer choices so you don't get suckered into selecting a seductive-looking answer before you even know the facts or become biased while reading the facts.
- Next, read the interrogatory (the question at the end of the facts, usually between the facts and the answer choices), which is sometimes referred to as the *call of the question*.
- Then, read the fact pattern and reread the interrogatory. Remember to use bar reading tools, as described previously: read with pencil in hand, touching and subvocalizing each word as you read.
- Now, based upon the law you have memorized, reason through the facts to draw a conclusion that you believe best answers the precise question asked. (Read and analyze this part of the MBE in the same manner you read a bar essay question.)

- Only after completing these steps should you then take your hand off the answer choices and read through the first choice carefully, asking yourself: "Is this choice plausible?" "Is it responsive to the question?" "Does it mirror the answer I reasoned to?" "Is it even a correct statement in and of itself?" If the choice contains an incorrect rule statement, does not answer the question asked, or answers it incorrectly (applies the law incorrectly to these specific facts), immediately put a line through it and go on to the next choice.
- Ask yourself the same questions regarding each of the three remaining answer choices, crossing out any that are wrong or don't answer the question. (Do this clearly so that you don't mistakenly think an answer choice is still on the table if you have ruled it out. Some people find it helpful to play a sort of "find the wrong answers" game with themselves. The more you rule out, the better. If you like puzzles, this might be a good strategy for you.)
- Now, what are you left with? If only one answer choice remains, select that one and quickly move on to the next question. (Always keep in mind that the MBE is a test of speed as well as knowledge and accuracy, so keep moving.) If you have two answer choices that are both consistent with your conclusion but for different reasons, read each one again carefully and isolate what exactly differs between the two choices. Then, see if one includes faulty reasoning, an internal inconsistency, or an incorrect rule statement, or fails to answer the question posed. Reread the interrogatory to be sure you understand the exact question, and reread the facts as necessary. By process of elimination, choose the best of the remaining answers. Note that the best answer might not be perfect. Sometimes the best answer is supported by a minority rule rather than the prevailing majority rule. In such a situation, if the other choices are flat-out wrong, then the minority position will be the best answer. Select the answer that seems to reason to the best conclusion when applying appropriate law to resolve the issue asked in the particular question.
- When you study answers, you should strive to determine why you chose the answer you did, and, if you didn't choose the correct answer, why it is best. (More on the self-assessment process below.)

Practice by completing a consistent number of MBEs every day, under timed conditions.

"How many should I take?" Students always ask me this question, which is a difficult one to answer. The key is consistency. When I sit down with students to plan their schedules, I don't ask them how many MBEs they can take each day. Rather, I ask them, "How much time do you have each day to commit to a dedicated block of MBE practice?" Once we have a time slot, we can figure out how many should be taken each day.

Let's say someone says, "I can devote a half hour to MBEs every morning. I'll take them while having coffee or breakfast." Someone who is less of a morning person might say, "I can devote one hour for my 'daily MBEs' before bed (after brushing my teeth, so that it becomes an automatic habit)." Some people take them in bed each night before going to sleep, on a smartphone or tablet. Taking them daily at the same time helps make this a consistent commitment.

Once you have determined a good time of day, start with a small number and build up. You will eventually have to complete two sets of 100 questions, each within a 3-hour block.

If you begin earlier than May, doing even five questions each day(in nine minutes) may be sufficient to make daily MBEs a habit. At the beginning of May, increase to ten questions per day in eighteen minutes. (Remember, you will also need at least twenty minutes or so after that to self-assess and review questions you missed.) Work up to seventeen questions daily in thirty minutes by the end of May (with another thirty minutes or so for self-assessment). Your bar review schedule may include a set number of MBE practice sessions to be completed on certain days. Do those as directed. If you can productively include additional practice questions into your schedule, do those as well. By the end of June, most people find it helpful to be answering at least thirty-three questions in an hour every day (or alternate seventeen one day, thirty-three the next, and so on.) And, during July, make time for at least a couple of simulated reviews in which you answer full sets of 100 questions in three-hour blocks. You do not want the actual exam to be the first time you have tried to do three hours' worth of MBEs in a row. (More on simulated exams below and in Chapter 9.)

Be sure to include ample review time whenever you take MBEs. Immediately after you complete a set of questions, you will want to review explanatory answers. Many people double the review time, going over questions that they got right *and* questions they got wrong. Others find it most productive just to review questions they missed or guessed on. *Note: A guess is equivalent to a wrong answer in practice.* If you guess right, you simply got lucky. You should not bank on luck to pass the bar exam, but on knowledge, skill, and preparation.

So definitely study every single answer you got wrong or guessed. And, if you find it helpful and not confusing, study each explanatory answer you got right as well. Use this opportunity to learn and or review the rule of law at issue in the context of the particular question to be sure you answer correctly the next time it appears. (The fact pattern may not be exactly the same, but it will be analogous.)

Another approach is, when you first start taking practice MBEs (during early start or at the very beginning of bar review), slowly and methodically work through sets of these questions, in each subject, one question at a time. See how they are phrased, look at each answer choice, and read the explanatory answer right away before moving on to the next question. After you take at least a small number in every subject area that way, begin taking them under *timed conditions* and continue taking them under timed conditions until the exam, studying explanatory answers to each set just after you complete that set. (Again, study every answer choice or only those you missed or guessed on—whichever you find most helpful.)

The key here, like so many of the other study and test-taking strategies in this book, is to figure out how you learn best and what makes sense to you. Also, realize that what you should do in early start differs from what you must train for in intensive bar preparation.

MORE THAN ONE EXPLANATION: HELPFUL OR CONFUSING? YOU MUST DECIDE FOR YOURSELF.

Eighth-grade algebra. I was doing very well; my best friend wasn't. I noticed that my friend would diligently listen to every word the teacher said. I tuned out as soon as I understood a concept. My friend didn't realize that our teacher explained each concept repeatedly, in different ways, perhaps trying to appeal to different learning styles. Listening to another explanation once I understood something confused me. I convinced my friend to stop listening after "getting" a concept, until the teacher moved on to something else. (And, belated apologies, I too often facilitated this selective listening by passing notes or chitchatting.) Remarkably, though, within a week of trying my approach, my friend's grades shot up. We both ended up with an A in the class, and I ended up with a lifelong learning lesson: not every explanation makes things clearer. I applied this understanding in bar review. Once I "got" something, I moved on.

That said, many of my colleagues suggest that students review every answer, right or wrong, and many of my students have found their MBE practice to be much more productive when they do so. They force themselves to be able to articulate why one choice is the best and the others are not. This can be a great way to review substantive law, as well as develop MBE test-taking skills.

How exactly to review and what you should do when you miss a question are set forth below in self-assessment strategies. But it's important to first reflect a bit more on what you should be taking as practice tests. In addition to asking how many practice questions they should complete, students always ask what subjects they should study. "Should I focus on areas I am weaker on?" "Should I do sets that assess the same subject, or ones containing a mix of subjects (as will be on the actual exam)?" Again, it depends when you start. In early start and through the end of June and beginning of July, you can do subject-specific sets, preferably at or around the same time your bar review lectures cover those subjects. Early start is a good time to do them slowly, to spend more than the 1.8 minutes per question, reading every single answer so that you know why each of the wrong answers is wrong and why the correct answer is "best." In June and July, do your practice tests under timed conditions.

In July, you will want to also be doing mixed sets (questions in different subjects) so that you have several weeks of training to handle them since this format will be tested on the bar exam: questions will be fired at you in random subject order. It takes mental dexterity to switch subjects that rapidly. You must be ready! (Some people focus during the week on whatever subject or subjects their bar review is covering, but do one set of mixed questions each weekend to get acclimated to switching subjects.)

Once you have trained in all of the subjects and have developed your knowledge and skills in answering questions in them, if you have identified one or more MBE subjects that you are weaker in, spend more time on those areas. You do not want to go into the exam "exposed." (Knowing you are prepared for everything will make you feel stronger on test days. Conversely, you will feel particularly vulnerable if you go into the exam hoping an area won't be tested—this is also true for the essay portion of the exam.) But don't feel like you need only to answer extra practice questions in your weaker areas; you should still be training in all of the subjects in order to maximize your ability to do well on every part of the exam.

ARE YOU AVOIDING REAL PROPERTY MBES (OR QUESTIONS IN ANY AREA FOR THAT MATTER)?

Real property questions tend to have the longest fact patterns. They also test a subject that throws many people. Others loathe the constitutional law MBEs. Whatever your Achilles' heel, if you have one, train for that area even harder than for the other subjects! A student came to me in January to create a study schedule for the following July's bar exam. She had taken all of the bar subjects in law school, listed her grades in each course, and sorted them from lowest to highest. We plotted an early-start review based on that information so that she attacked her weakest subjects first and then progressed to those that were stronger, covering every subject once before bar review even started. She went into bar review knowing that her weak areas had been strengthened and it would truly be a review. And, more important, she went into her bar exam prepared and confident.

How to self-assess MBEs

First, be sure to keep track of (on a separate piece of paper) which answers you felt fairly certain about and those you guessed on. Be honest! Again, a guess on a practice exam is equivalent to a missed answer.

When you finish your set, study the answers. Don't just score yourself and add up the totals. Especially in early start and in June, the numbers aren't what counts. The learning is what is critical. (In the end, it does not matter what the score was at halftime. Focus on winning the game.) Proceed to work through every question you missed or guessed on (or every single question if that helps you). Read the explanatory answers. (Again, reputable bar review materials and released questions and answers from the NCBE include instructive explanatory answers that show why each correct choice is the best and why each of the others is not.)

Now, and most important, figure out *why* you missed the question:

- I read the question (the interrogatory) wrong.
- I missed a key word or words in the fact pattern.
- I read one or more answer choices incorrectly.
- I didn't understand what the question was asking, or didn't see the issue.
- I didn't know the law that I needed to apply to the issue to reason to a conclusion.
- I memorized the rule, but didn't understand the underlying principles the question was testing (so I narrowed it down to two possible choices, but missed the best one).
- I knew the correct answer, but entered it incorrectly.

Next, use this information to improve. (After explaining how to do this, I'll give you a chart to do on your own.) Don't spend a minute being down on yourself or frustrated by the fact that you got the wrong answers. That's a waste of time. So long as you know *why*, you are winning this game. (The word *game* does not suggest this is easy. But it can be helpful to view these as challenges, puzzles you are determined to solve.) Practice tests are learning opportunities; your bar-reading skills will become more refined and your reasoning more strategic with every set you do. (They are like weight lifting. Train consistently, and you will get stronger.)

Be very pleased with yourself simply because you are *taking* daily practice tests. Do not obsess about scores. Just keep doing the work and self-assessing. The most important learning is in the review, the deconstruction. This involves developing strategies to strengthen each type of weakness, described as follows:

Reading error?

If you read something incorrectly, ask yourself why. Did you read too fast? Did you drift off while reading? Did you assume some fact that was not in the fact pattern?

Did you read the call of the question incorrectly? Once you know why you missed a question, you can then take steps to change the behavior. Reading incorrectly is one of the most common reasons for missing MBEs, and the easiest to fix. Remember your bar reading skills. Touch each word and say it out loud under your breath as you read with your eyes. It works.

Didn't know or understand a rule?

If, after studying explanatory answers, you can see that you did not know or understand a rule, go look it up and either write it (in your outline or on your paper or electronic flashcards) or say it out loud several times, or both. (If you want to be sure you understand it, try explaining the concept to someone else.) *Expect* to be learning some new rules from practice MBEs, even up to the day before the exam.

USING MBE ANSWERS TO UPDATE FLASHCARDS

Even when you do understand something, often an explanatory answer may phrase a rule more clearly or succinctly, or include an instructive example. Whenever you come across this, get out your flashcards. (Again, *flashcards* here means whatever you have chosen as your "memory tool.") Rewrite the card in question, and replace the older card with your new version. Each practice test sitting is a chance to review or learn more law. Keep a list of concise rule statements (easy to recite in essays) for all subjects tested on the essay portion of your exam. Keep them in whatever format works for you: on paper cards, in digital flashcards that you keep on your smartphone or tablet, or in your outline. Note: Some people learn better by listening, so they also keep audio files of rule statements.

Didn't finish in time?

If you didn't have time to carefully complete each question or didn't finish in the allotted time and guessed on a number of questions, ask yourself why. Did you lose time by focusing too long on one question you got stuck on? Guess and move on if you find you have spent more than 1.8 minutes on a question. Did you drift off while reading? Did you get distracted answering a phone call or going to the bathroom? Each set of questions is an opportunity to incrementally improve your accuracy and speed.

USE QUALITY PRACTICE QUESTIONS

Be sure you are practicing with sufficiently difficult exams. Sometimes older exams are easier than newer ones. And sometimes a bar review's questions may be easier than the questions in the materials of another course.

MBE Self-Assessment Chart for Wrong Answers

Complete this assessment for every question you missed, checking the reason(s) you erred and writing an improvement plan so you do not repeat the same mistakes.

Question # ___

_____ I read the question (the interrogatory) wrong.
_____ I missed a key word or words in the fact pattern.
_____ I read one or more answer choices incorrectly.
_____ I did not understand what the question was asking or see what was at issue.
_____ I did not know the law that I needed to apply to the issue to reason to a conclusion. (If you missed a question because you didn't know the rule, write it now in the space below).
_____ I memorized the rule, but didn't understand the underlying principles the question was testing (so I narrowed the answer down to two possible choices, but didn't choose the best one).
_____I knew the correct answer, but entered it incorrectly.
_____Other: _____

To improve, I will:

_____

_____

_____

Rule(s)/concept/area of law tested in this question that I need to learn/memorize are:

_____

_____

_____

MBE Self-Assessment Chart for Correct Answers

If you are someone who benefits from reviewing questions you got right, complete this assessment for every question you answered correctly.

Question # ___

_____ I understand why I chose the answer I chose.

_____ I chose the correct answer for the right reason.

Note: If you chose the right answer for the wrong reason, write out here why your thinking was flawed:

_____

_____

_____

Rule(s)/concept/area of law tested in this question, and any tip(s) I might use from this question to remember this rule(s)/concept/area in the future:

_____

_____

_____

MBE tips and strategies

Keep this list of tips handy to look at the morning of your MBE, and perhaps again during the lunch break.

- If you have ruled out one or more answers and gone back over the facts and interrogatory and still don't know the correct answer, guess. Come back to it at the end if you have time. You need to complete 33 questions per hour.
- Watch the clock. After one hour, be sure you are on or near question 33; after two hours, question 66. If you stick to this pace, you should be finished or nearly so after two hours and fifty-five minutes.
- Be a smart clock-watcher. Be sure to bring in an approved timepiece. (Verify the rules in your jurisdiction.) And note the exact time each of your sessions starts. Let's say your MBE day consists of an approximately 9:00 a.m.-to-noon block in the morning and a 2:00-to-5:00 p.m. block in the afternoon. If the afternoon session starts at 1:55 p.m., you will finish at 4:55 p.m.; it is therefore important not to think you have until 5:00 p.m. to finish the test. Look at and confirm the time the proctor says, "You may begin." (If that's 2:05 p.m., write on your answer booklet, "End at 5:05 p.m.—begin guessing at 5:00 p.m.") Note that you may begin the morning or afternoon session at a slightly different time each day. Some people reset their clocks at the beginning of every session to noon (that way, one hour will have elapsed at 1:00 p.m., two hours at 2:00 p.m., etc.).
- Have a guessing strategy. If you can't rule out any of the four answer choices for a question or questions, or if you run out of time, bubble in a predetermined letter. Pick your favorite letter, and have the plan in place. (If you are not near question 97 or 98 in the set, recognize that you won't finish in time and implement your guessing strategy. Don't leave any questions blank.)
- Be sure each Scantron response corresponds to the question you are actually answering. Due to nerves on exam day, sometimes students get off one on their Scantron. For example, after bubbling in answers for questions 1–10, you inadvertently skip to 12 when you should have bubbled in 11. If you catch this early, you can fix it. But if you don't notice until 11:55 a.m. that you have just bubbled in an answer choice for question 100 but were actually answering question 99, you will have to redo all of your answers for question 11 on and won't have time to finish.
- Be sure to bubble in the circles on the Scantron completely. Make sure the whole circle is darkened.

Each of these exam tips derives from real people's mistakes. You might not think that people have actually failed because of bubbling mistakes on the Scantron. But it happens with every bar exam. Do not let it happen to you.

THE ESSAYS

Like MBEs, bar essays are made up of relatively short fact patterns, often only a half to single page of text. (Compare that with some law school finals that are several pages long.) You may have anywhere from about twenty-five to sixty minutes per question, depending on the jurisdiction. You must identify issues, state the applicable rules of law, logically apply the law you stated from memory to the given facts, and accordingly resolve the issues you identified in a way that comes to a reasoned conclusion, thereby answering the specific question or questions posed.

The law you are to apply on a particular essay question may be state-specific, federal, modern-majority, or common law. You may pick up additional points for noting influential minority rules, or for comparing a modern trend to the common law rule. Your state bar's website and your bar review will explain which law is to be applied to answer essay questions.

Bar reading is a critical success skill for essays, just as for MBEs. Because you have to produce an *organized* written product rather than just identify the best choice, you must also include time during and after you read the interrogatory and facts to order what you intend to say in a logical manner—in other words, to outline.

On essays, you have to not only understand the rules and how they apply to the facts, but also to articulate those rules in your own words and analyze in writing how the facts prove or disprove the elements of those rules. On MBEs, you must see those connections, but you don't have to write out anything yourself. (This is one reason why doing many practice MBEs does not mean one can slack off on essay preparation. You must do both; they test different skills. This is also why some people find essays more difficult. And, for this reason, nonnative English speakers may have a tougher time with essays than with MBEs.)

YOUR ESSAY AND PT ANSWERS ARE LIKE A PAPER INTERVIEW

Think of your written answers as a paper interview. The graders need to see that you are "lawyer material." After all, it is in their hands now whether to grant you a license that puts you in charge of people's lives and livelihoods. In addition to sounding intelligent and answering thoughtfully, you must present yourself well—in a clear, organized manner. And it helps if your paper looks good, too. Evaluate your work product the way you would your appearance before going to an interview. You'd wear a clean suit that makes you look professional, right? Similarly, your paper should be neat, with an obvious, logical organization. Use headings and subheadings. Avoid typos and especially misspellings of key legal terms. (If you handwrite, write legibly.) Don't scratch through or cross out too many words. Students who fail often show me their papers and say, "But I had it in there." To which I reply, "But the grader could not easily see and understand what you wrote." You are the interviewee. Present yourself as well as you can.

We saw previously that MBEs have a *best* answer choice; your mission is to seek and find it. On essays, you often don't need to know the answer for certain. There may not even be one single answer to an essay question. Rather, the facts provide a vehicle for you to give reasoned arguments as to how both sides would resolve the issues. Think about a personal encounter with someone who saw something happen in a completely different way than you saw it. As you reread and think and outline, you will ask yourself how the plaintiff would use these facts to prevail, and how the defendant would use them.

You may find essays liberating, in that the burden of having to know who is "right" is lifted, momentarily at least. (In a recent alumni seminar, a former student was discussing his first years in law practice. He noted as the biggest change having to *know* (or be expected to accurately predict) who would win, as compared with law school—where he could nearly always just argue for both sides!)

Essay-test tips and strategies[34]

The tips below focus on strategies within a single essay. Before we explore those, let's talk about how to answer sets of several essays in a row. First, answer them in the order they appear. Most everyone else will, and your exam will be compared with others' exams. (For example, if everyone does an amazing job on #1 and a poor job on #3, you will not benefit from going out of order and doing a superlative job on #3 to the detriment of #1. Your goal is to write a passing answer for *each* question.) Answer the questions out of order only if you find yourself blocked when you see question #1. Take a deep breath, and if that doesn't help, just move on confidently to the second question and return to the first one later when you likely have your "flow" back. Second, answer the questions within the suggested time. If you had to answer four thirty-minute essays in two hours, you must budget your time accordingly. (Proctors generally do not notify applicants of how much time has passed.) Cut yourself off (wrap up and conclude) if you exceed the suggested time on a question, finish all the questions, and then return if there is extra time to edit or add to any of your answers. Third, make sure you answer every question; do not skip any.

- Answer the questions asked and only the questions asked. Many students waste time on nonissues. Careless reading is often the culprit. Lawyers must be detailed.

- Whenever you approach an essay question, do the following: (1) Read the interrogatory and the facts; then reread the interrogatory; (2) Read every word, preferably subvocalizing (reading aloud but under your breath, so you can hear yourself while not disrupting others around you), and touch each word (with your pencil, pen, or finger); and (3) Slow down. People next to you will be typing while you are still reading the question! No worries. They are not smarter than you. They may well be failing the exam, writing nonsense, or writing something irrelevant because they do not yet have a handle on the law, facts, or interrogatories. Do not let them throw you. Make certain *you* understand what is and what is not asked of you, and see how the facts fit the analytical steps of resolving the specific question or questions before you write your answer. Have confidence in yourself. Even for a thirty-minute essay, you may want to take a full ten minutes to really see the full picture before clacking away at the keyboard.
- Organize and write an outline (note the main headings and subheadings you will include in your answer). There is nearly always more than one logical way to organize; just be sure that you discuss the issues in some reasoned order (for example, by lawsuit, by event, by asset, by crime, by defendant, or in another systematic manner). Your outline is the road map to your organization, and if you include headings, it will also become the graders' road map; but graders will judge you only on your answer, so there's no need to create an elaborate outline. Bottom line, include in your outline what *you* need to write an organized answer.
- Determine how much time to spend on each call of the question if there is more than one interrogatory (that is, if the question asks about more than one thing). You can almost always assess the time you need to spend on each part by looking at how many facts relate to that question. The more facts, the more time you should spend on writing for that part.
- Cross out words in the fact pattern after you use them, and write about the issues they raise in your answer. Check the fact pattern periodically to see if there are words you have not crossed out and thus have not yet used. Might they be useful? Why?
- Use every fact they give you! This does not mean every word must be restated in your answer. (In fact, if you quote, do so selectively.) It means you should *use* each fact to see if it triggers an issue, provides proof of or refutes some element of a rule of law, or otherwise affects some relevant argument (perhaps a policy argument). And write in plain, simple English that spells out your reasoning so clearly that even a layperson could understand you!
- Focus on the most serious issues first (unless you are writing in another *logical* order, such as chronological order where appropriate). For example, if someone has battered a victim, and that victim dies as a result of the battery, start with the homicidal offenses before even mentioning battery (if that is even relevant at all).

Likewise, when you have a lesser included offense, such as a larceny in addition to a robbery, discuss the robbery first since the larceny elements are essentially subsets of the robbery elements.

- Discuss what *is* a problem or issue first and then quickly address (if time permits) why something is not a problem or issue given the particular facts. (An example of this might appear in a criminal procedure essay about a warrantless search. You want to hit the most likely exceptions to the warrant requirement, thoroughly discuss those, and then—if you have time—perhaps show why the other exceptions would not suffice under these facts; for example, "Here the defendant did nothing to suggest that he explicitly or implicitly *consented* to the search.") Students always ask me whether they should discuss all the potentially relevant exceptions when the prosecution would need only one exception to proceed. My answer is, "Yes, because exams are not the real world." And you typically get points on exams for hitting all of the relevant issues if you demonstrate why they are relevant.

- Write in complete sentences, thoroughly analyzing the facts to resolve the issues. (Note that lists of clear and relevant "bullet points" may be quick to write out and helpful in a particular analysis.) But don't expect a grader to follow your shorthand; "spell out" your thinking.

- Provide a key to any terms or party names that you abbreviate. For example, if you abbreviate "contract" with the symbol "K," write out "contract (K)" or "contract (hereinafter 'K')" the first time you use that abbreviation. You might think this association is so obvious that it's unnecessary to identify it, but the abbreviation "K" is also used to mean "$1,000," so even something so seemingly straightforward may be misconstrued.

- Avoid hammering on one point of view. Each issue often lends itself to both a defense and plaintiff perspective, as the facts can and frequently do cut both ways. If you get stuck trying to advocate in a manner that's too one-sided, you may miss points to be gained from analyzing the opposing party's perspective. Note: If you write about two opposing arguments, conclude your thoughts by noting which side has the stronger position *and why* before moving on to your next area of discussion.

- Write complete (but succinct) rule statements, and then prove up each element of each rule—piece by piece. Lawyers break complex thoughts down into logical parts. Elements are components of the bundle that is a rule, and each part must be proved. This is also true for defenses, as defense theories often have multiple elements that must be discussed. (Always consider defenses when analyzing crimes or causes of action.) Know the difference between tests that include *factors* (all of which need not always be established) and *elements* (each of which must be supported by the requisite level of proof).

- Make sure your exams are reader friendly! Don't underestimate the importance of style. Am I suggesting form over substance? No! I am urging you to pay attention to form *in addition to* substance! The best essay answers tend to identify main areas of discussion with descriptive headings, providing a sort of table of contents so a grader can quickly see that the applicant identified the key discussable issues and relevant rules. At a glance, the grader should be able to see that your answer is set out clearly and logically. (During early start and intensive bar review, work on polishing form and style, as well as mastering content and substance.)

- If you are handwriting your answers, make sure your writing is legible. Note: Even if you don't plan to handwrite, write out at least one or two essay or PT answers by hand during bar prep so that you know you can do it should an emergency (for example, a computer problem or power outage) require you to do so.

- Write using lawyerly language. I don't mean that you should use hoity-toity, silly language ("the party of the first part heretofore contends…."). I mean, rather, that you should write in a professional manner. Below are some examples I have seen frequently when students are concluding essays.
  - Do write: *For these reasons, the plaintiff is unlikely to prevail.* (Do **not** write: *The plaintiff's argument is really not likely to fly.*)
  - Do write: *It is therefore possible that the plaintiff will prevail; however, for the reasons stated above, it appears that the defendant has the stronger argument here.* (Do **not** write: *This is a wash. It is up to the jury. The jurors could decide either way here.*)
  - Do write: *The police arrest may have violated the warrant requirement.* (Do **not** write: *The cops here did not follow the rules, and the defendant was busted without the warrant they should have gotten.*)

- Avoid writing in the first person (do not use "I" or "we"). *Exam graders do not care what* you *think or what* you *believe.* What matters is whether the facts prove, or fail to prove, the particular legal theories you have articulated.
  - Do write: *For the reasons stated above, the defendant will likely prevail.* (Do not write: *I think the defendant will win.*)
  - Do write: *After weighing the facts on both sides, it appears that the plaintiff has the stronger argument on this question because the plaintiff has more evidence and the evidence is more credible.* (Do not write: *I believe the plaintiff has the better argument.*)
  - Do write: *The defendant's spitting on the plaintiff/victim is an offensive action. Reasonable people find spitting to be a rude and even demeaning gesture . . .* Do not write: *The defendant's spitting on the plaintiff/victim is an offensive action. I would be horrified if someone spit on me that way.*

READ YOUR ANSWERS ALOUD.

I often ask students to read their answers out loud. I do this in class and during office hours. Some students will read a paragraph and then stop themselves and say, "This doesn't make any sense." Or, "I'm not sure what I meant here." You have to know what you mean, and what you write has to make sense to you if you want it to make sense to a grader. The same students who might challenge their score by pointing to their written answers, saying that they included all of the necessary points, may realize quickly, while reading aloud, whether what they wrote was logical or not.

Crossover questions

One of the many differences between bar exam essays and law school essays is that some bar questions contain testable issues in more than one area of law. Your evidence professor will give you a final exam that tests evidence rules. A bar exam fact pattern may have a litigation scenario that includes both pretrial civil procedure issues (perhaps a jurisdiction question) and trial issues that concern evidentiary questions, such as whether a document or statement will be admitted and why. A fact pattern that includes issues from more than one subject still usually tells a single story, so certain subjects cross over more naturally (for example, civil procedure and evidence, as noted above; criminal law and criminal procedure; and wills and trusts).

Crossovers tend to be unnerving, as they are often unfamiliar because law school exams don't test that way. (You didn't walk into your torts final to find a family law issue on the exam.) But the idea of subjects crossing is not odd at all when you think about it. The law is not isolated, and neither are people's problems. A client may come to you about a divorce, so she definitely has concerns relating to family law; but she may also have financial concerns that dip into bankruptcy law, there may be a related criminal matter, or she may own intellectual property for which you have to understand perhaps a patent or copyright issue. You don't simply do one search (or open one book), find an answer to one of your client's questions, and let the rest go. Yes, you may end up referring part of a case to an attorney who specializes in that area of law, but you will often need some basic knowledge to even know where to refer the client.

Bar preparation is similar. You are no longer studying one subject at a time. You are preparing to answer any question that they throw at you in any of the subjects, or combination of the subjects, tested on your exam.

Working with numerous subjects simultaneously helps you see how disparate pieces fit together. As we've noted, most law school courses focus on the details—the veins on the leaves on the trees. Bar preparation allows you the opportunity to pull it together and see the bigger picture. That is intellectually exciting! You begin to see parallels and intersections you never realized existed when you were studying one subject at a time, in isolation.

Practice essay writing

Set aside a certain number of hours per week to write essays in full and under timed conditions, as well as additional time to study sample answers and self-assess. Self-critique may be a quick process if you readily see where and how you need to improve. But if a question asks about rules that you don't know or understand, you should take time (if possible) immediately after completing the question to look those up. Invest that time now, after completing the practice test and while the fact pattern is fresh, to learn and see how these rules apply. Don't procrastinate. Why? 1) You may never get back to this question, and then you will remain exposed—with a weak area. 2) The closer it gets to the exam, the harder it is to make time to look things up. 3) Learning a rule in the context of a fact pattern will make it "stick" in your memory more effectively than simply memorizing words in a vacuum.

After completing your self-assessment and looking up anything you need to, add relevant rules or examples to your flashcards, outline, or other memorizing tools.

In addition to writing out essays in full under timed conditions, set aside additional time to outline them and review sample answers. If you do a lot of writing in full under timed conditions and develop your skills during early start and the first six weeks, you can focus mainly on outlining the last two weeks.

How many essays should I write out in full, and how many should I outline? At a minimum, do all of the assigned work in your bar review course. Then do more. (Early start makes this much easier.) Try to complete an essay every other day or so. Take new exams when possible, but it's fine and can be very helpful to rewrite an essay you previously completed to see if you have improved, as well as to cement the concepts and rules that the exam tests.

As is the case for MBEs, make sure you write practice essays in every tested subject. Students often have a tendency to take exams only in the subjects they are comfortable with. Do not fall into that trap. Be sure to hit every subject, *especially* those you feel weaker in. By exam time, you should have written out in full a number of essay exams for each subject that may be tested on the essay portion of your exam. Plan to complete essays slowly and steadily, writing some every week rather than cramming in a bunch of practice essays right before the test.

At first, in early start, look up rules if you cannot write your answers from memory. Closer to the exam, you will need to train under *closed book and timed conditions*, but early practice that is open book is perfectly fine and often very helpful.

Note: When you are quite close to the exam and time is running short, you will gradually shift to writing more essay outlines instead of writing essays in full—still, of course, studying the model answers. Days before the exam, you can even practice by reading and issue spotting in your head and then studying the sample answers. Going through many fact patterns and sample answers will help you review and memorize, as well as see how testable issues tend to arise and repeat themselves. At a certain point, you will hopefully find a great deal of overlap and catch yourself saying, "This question sounds a lot like. . . ."

As you review questions and answers, you can edit your one-page "cheat sheet," ideally so that the main issues in each subject are set out in a logical order that you can memorize.[35]

MAKE SURE YOU CLOSE THE BOOKS.

I often hear students who do not pass the first time confess that they continued to write practice tests open book through July. They never closed the books. Consequently, they never got their timing right and never memorized all the rules they needed to know. (You must have as many rules as possible memorized for instant recall by the time of the exam.) When you begin taking practice tests, spend as much time as is allotted and try to recall everything you can. Then, when you are stuck, look up the information you need to, close the books again, and return to finishing the exam. But, by early July, finish your practice essays entirely closed book. Force yourself to answer the questions as fully as you can, without looking anything up, as if you were taking the actual bar exam. Only *after* you finish to the best of your ability should you study the sample or model answers, self-assess, and look up rules you do not know or understand.

Essays: A closer look at how to read and write them

Read the question you must answer (the "call" of the question), starting at the end of the fact pattern. Then read the fact pattern. Then reread that call. Read slowly and carefully, touching each word and mumbling it aloud under your breath, circling and highlighting key words.

Take notes. Jot down any words that raise discussable issues (more on issue spotting below). You might want to also do a quick chronology, listing key facts in the order in which they occur. That can be especially helpful in certain subjects. For example, in a torts negligence fact pattern for which you are analyzing proximate cause, tracking the chain of causation requires knowing what happened and when. Bar essays may note facts out of order. (Pay attention to dates.) Looking at your own ordered list of events, you will readily see if an event came between the defendant's actions and the victim's injury. You can then assess that intervening event to determine if it was foreseeable or not and complete your proximate cause discussion. Another example is a contracts question in which there are numerous communications between buyer and seller. In order to know the legal significance of each communication, you may need to know exactly what was communicated when (think "mailbox rule"). A final example of when chronological note taking is helpful is for bar takers in community property states. When property was earned (before, during, or after marriage) may change the characterization of that property, and thus who will be awarded certain assets in a divorce proceeding.

Next, create an outline. The best bar exam essay outlines are those that help you create a logical order without taking too much time, as most bar graders will not look at or consider your outline but only your completed answer. Think of your outline as a table of contents to your essay. Start by making sure your outline includes the main discussable issues and possibly relevant subissues, organizing those points into a logical order (often, but not always, tracking the calls of the question). Those taking the bar exam on laptops can often save time by turning their outlines into the headings that serve as a road map for graders, and then fleshing out what they want to say about those points as they write.

Example: A question asks, "Of what crimes, if any, may the defendant be convicted?" Your headings may list the crimes you intend to discuss. When a question asks about the division of assets in a divorce, the headings may be an asset-by-asset list. In a torts question involving multiple parties, the headings may be the various lawsuits: A v. B, B v. C, etc.

Bar writing is logical writing, and it differs in some key ways from law school exam writing.

Earlier you learned that bar *reading* is active reading. Bar *writing* is logical writing. It is often recommended that first-year law students and bar takers write using a style template known by the acronym IRAC: issue, rule, analysis, conclusion. For bar writing, as I will detail below, the acronym IRPC—issue, rule, *proof*, conclusion—may be more helpful.

When law students first hear about IRAC, they sometimes think it stands for "I Really Am Crazy" and wonder why they went to law school in the first place. But

IRAC is just a tool—a template or system—to help students write logically. It forces them to move through steps (like A+B+C=D) and to remember to use the facts to prove or disprove the elements of the rules of law. In law school exams, as distinct from bar exams, the analysis portion is typically richer, deeper, and more thoughtful. You will want to weave into your analysis discussions of cases, analogies, and distinctions, as well as subtleties within the law itself, and how those affect the resolution of the issues at hand. You may mention both majority and minority positions in evolving areas of law, or compare older case law to more modern trends you have studied. And, of course, you must reason to a logical conclusion. Bar writing requires these same logical elements but often stated more simply. Once you understand what is expected and practice every single day, you will likely find bar writing to be rather straightforward.

SOME BAR EXAMINERS PREFER ESSAYS THAT START WITH CONCLUSIONS

CRAC (conclusion, rule, analysis, conclusion) or CRIAC (conclusion, rule, issue, analysis, conclusion): Some jurisdictions prefer that bar applicants state their conclusion and then follow that with a full proof of how the rule is or is not satisfied. This does not change the basic logical structure. (If you are not sure who will prevail until you finish writing, then simply IRAC and cut and paste your conclusion at the top of your discussion.) I suggest writing in an IRAC (or what I call "IRPC") style unless you know your jurisdiction prefers CRAC.

Some people hear the word *analysis* and think of the complex and varied wrinkles in legal theories and reasoning; they picture lengthy, detailed exchanges in law school classes—exchanges designed to break apart and promote an understanding of case law. Others hear *analysis* and think of a layered literary analysis (for example, reflecting on the meaning, style, and value of a novel or poem) in a college English class. As you will see below, a more useful mental picture for effective bar writing may instead require a flashback to middle school geometry and the simple logic contained in a basic proof.

Note: For many students, the term *analysis* conveys a more complex, and often longer, written discussion than is required for most passing bar answers. However, the word *analysis* may well represent what law professors expect on law school midterms and finals. Many law professors wish to see students weave relevant cases into their discussion as they reason to thoughtful conclusions, drawing analogies or distinguishing between the facts in the exam and facts from cases or hypotheticals studied throughout the term. Your professor may also expect a rich policy discussion, possibly noting relevant implications the issues you are discussing might have for third parties, society at large, past precedent, or future evolution of the applicable law. Bar writing is often simpler.

Let's look at the following example as a useful (albeit oversimplified) analogy to bar writing style, what I call and will explain below as *IRPC*.

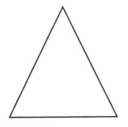

What sort of figure does the shape above represent? **[ISSUE]**

Three-sided figures with sides coming together at three corners are generally known as triangles. An equilateral triangle is a three-sided figure in which all three sides are equal in length and all corners have the same degree angle. **[RULE]**

Here, side A measures *x* inches, side B measures *x* inches, and side C measures *x* inches. The three sides are touching and meet at three corners. Each angle measures *y* degrees. **[PROOF (or analysis)]**

Therefore, the figure represented above is an equilateral triangle. **[CONCLUSION]**

This logic may sound more mathematical than legal, but it is highly instructive for bar writing. Let's consider another IRPC example, this one using an everyday driving scenario in which you will see the same sort of logic but in a situation that more closely resembles a law-type fact pattern. Note here that we will also add a policy consideration to our logical writing ("IRPPC"). Policy concerns, while not essential in bar writing, can be helpful in improving your score. As long as you have written about all the discussable issues, using the basic components of an IRPC correctly for each—*and you finish answering the entire question*—adding policy considerations may indicate a further mastery of the application of the rule of law that a grader may appreciate.

> The defendant and his passenger, Witness X, both testified that the defendant's car was in the left-turn lane, the green arrow was blinking, and it was 3:00 p.m. when the turn was made. Did the defendant's turn from Elm Street onto Main Street on December 1 violate traffic regulations?

Now let's say you know (because you have learned the relevant rule of law) that when the green left-turn arrow is blinking at times other than 4:00 p.m. to 7:00 p.m. on weekdays, left turns are permitted from the left-turn lane at the intersection of Elm and Main. (From 4:00 p.m. to 7:00 p.m. on weekdays, such turns are not permitted even if the arrow is green.) How would we logically deconstruct the validity of the turn in question?

Did the defendant's 3:00 p.m. left turn at Elm and Main violate any traffic laws? **[ISSUE]**

When the green left-turn arrow is blinking at a time other than 4:00 p.m. to 7:00 p.m. on weekdays, left turns are permitted at the intersection of Elm and Main from the left-turn lane. **[RULE]**

The defendant was in the left-turn lane (the proper location to make a left turn). He saw the turn arrow blinking (the signal that it was safe to make his turn). The defendant made the turn in question at 3:00 p.m. (an appropriate time for this type of turn). Note: Since it was 3:00 p.m., it did not matter which day of the week it was, as the only restrictions on turning are from 4:00 to 7:00 p.m. **[PROOF or analysis]** Last but not least, policy would dictate that even if the defendant had followed the technical requirements for turning, he must have also confirmed that it was generally safe to make the turn—that is, that there were no other obstacles, emergency vehicles, or unanticipated conditions that would make the turn unsafe. Assuming the defendant did confirm this, there is no indication that the turn was unlawful. **[POLICY]**

Therefore, the defendant's turn from Elm onto Main appears to have been lawful. **[CONCLUSION]**

This is straightforward, right? It makes sense. It is not mysterious or intriguing. It is not eloquent. It is simple and direct.

One of my professors once explained bar exam writing something like this: "Many of you came to law school from lofty colleges where you theorized and studied literature and history and the like. You read poetry and wrote beautiful essays. You sought to include metaphors and alliteration so your words would flow. You want to continue that sort of writing now, in law school. Your minds are creative. You *want* to think, "Well, I'll start by discussing A; but then let me foreshadow Z; then I'll get back to B; and maybe then toss in a bit of H and J to make things more vibrant." He then hollered, "No!" Everyone in the class jumped. "Cut that out right now! From here on, instead of flowery prose, it's "A+B+C=D. Period." Bar writing, in many ways, is indeed A+B+C=D.

Bar reading and its relationship to bar writing

Both to issue spot and to prove your points, you must read carefully, *and think*, as you read. Let's look at a couple of examples in the context of criminal law. Criminal law fact patterns often include one or more defendants who will have done a series of actions that arguably amount to criminal offenses. You must *use* the facts to demonstrate the proof or lack thereof of the requisite conduct, mental state, or and any other elements of those crimes, and to demonstrate which, if any, defenses apply. As with all law exams, the most important skill needed to successfully answer a criminal law question is careful bar reading. Start with the call of the question, or interrogatory (often presented at the end of the fact pattern). This way, you immediately discern what the question is asking so that you can answer that question or questions—and *only* that question or questions. The questions themselves may also provide an effective organizational structure for your answer. And reading the call of the question first on a bar exam essay often reveals what area(s) of law is or are being tested in that fact pattern so you can begin thinking about potentially applicable rules, which in turn will help you see the holes, gaps, questions, or "issues."

The interrogatory in a criminal law essay may ask something like this: *With what crime or crimes, if any, may the defendant be charged?* or *Of what crime or crimes may the defendant be found guilty?* or *Did the court err in convicting the defendant of any crime or crimes?* By reading the interrogatory first, you will know just a moment into the exam that you are dealing with criminal law. (Bar exam questions will not be labeled by subject.)

After reading the interrogatory, go to the top of the page and read the entire fact pattern, slowly and carefully. Use the active bar-reading techniques discussed earlier. (Read simultaneously with three senses: touch, hearing, and sight. Put your finger or pen on each word as you read it with your eyes, and say it in a barely audible voice.) Circle, underline, highlight, and write notes on or near words that seem significant. If a word or phrase triggers an issue or leads you to see a point you might want to discuss in your writing, note it right away so you do not forget. Mark directly on the question, jot your thought on scratch paper, or type it right into the document that may start as your outline and then become your essay answer. (If your outline is made up of your headings, then you can simply type each section under the appropriate heading.)

Let's practice with the following paragraph:

> Defendant Dufus wanted to burn Vicki's cottage. Dufus set out to burn it, carrying matches and kerosene, and set fire to a chair in the living room. A neighbor smelled smoke and called the fire department. Firefighters came within moments and extinguished the flaming chair. Of what crime or crimes may Dufus be convicted?

The minute you saw the word *burn*, your mind might have immediately recited the definition of arson, after which you would have asked yourself, *Will the defendant be guilty of arson?*

Which definition would you recite? Well, the common law definition of arson is *the malicious burning of the dwelling house of another.* You might have thought of that, or of modern-majority variations on this traditional definition, which relax some of the elements. For example, modern jurisdictions have extended arson to include most any protected structure, not just a "dwelling," and a defendant can in certain circumstances be convicted of arson for burning his or her own house down, not just the property "of another."

You might not have every rule memorized yet, but you must have all the main rules committed to memory by the time of your exam. You must see the word *burn* and automatically recite the definition of arson. All the relevant crimes, causes of action, defense theories, and other testable principles must be as accessible as the passwords you use every day. The applicable rules must be memorized succinctly enough that you can spit them out quickly on essays.

Unlike typical law professors, bar graders usually do *not* want to see treatises on the legal rules. (Many law professors do want to see that you listened to the discussion, read the material, and learned a lot of law during his or her class.) On a bar exam, for instance, you will not get extra credit for knowing and listing all the exceptions to a rule if they don't apply to the facts at hand. And writing too much on particular rules may prevent you from finishing your proof discussion (the most important task!) and reasoning to a conclusion. Shoot for short and clear rule statements.

Back to arson; back to the fact pattern, and to what you were thinking as you read. (I'll paraphrase your potential thoughts in italics.) For this example, just to give us more elements to discuss, we'll use the common law definition of arson: again, "the malicious burning of the dwelling house of another."

> With what crime or crimes may Dufus be convicted? (*OK, let me think.*)
>
> Defendant Dufus **wanted to burn** (*Dufus's desire to burn the cottage proves his willful intent and satisfies the malice or* mens rea *element of arson*) Vicki's cottage (*the dwelling of another*). Dufus set out to burn it, carrying matches and kerosene. Dufus set fire to a chair in the living room. A neighbor smelled smoke and called the fire department. Firefighters came within moments and extinguished the flaming chair. (*The chair was flaming, but did the flames burn or char any part of the structure itself?*) Of what crime or crimes may Dufus be convicted?

"Issue spotting," and what that really means, can confuse people. Start by thinking of issue spotting as looking for those places where the facts raise questions about whether or not an element of a crime, cause of action, or defense has been met. (One former student who for years helped me mentor new bar applicants used to tell students to look at issue spotting like Easter egg hunting. Picture walking through the facts knowing there are issues out there, perhaps just under the surface; you simply need to be alert to see and collect them.)[36] Another way to say this is that the thinking you are doing when you issue spot consists of considering the legal significance of particular facts, asking what they potentially prove or disprove and why, and identifying what additional problems they may raise. One leading bar exam expert suggests that after reading the facts, students think about them from one side's perspective and then consider what opposing counsel might seek to expose as a weakness.[37]

You know that you must mention each element of arson and whether or not it was established under these facts, even an element that does not seem to be in question. For example, these facts say that Dufus "wanted to burn." It seems wholly obvious that the defendant possessed the requisite *intent* for arson. But you still have to *prove* he had the requisite intent (here by referring to the specific facts indicating such.)

Read further. You will notice that only *the chair* burned, not the structure. So you will have to use the facts given to determine whether there was a requisite burning to support an arson conviction. (That's issue spotting.)

Once you read carefully and issue spot, you can start making an outline. Using this simple arson hypo, how might an outline be structured? Let's look at a sample.

Crimes of Dufus
ARSON?

a. Malicious (wanted to burn = willful),
b. Burning (the chair burned; need to demonstrate charring or burning of structure, as smoke damage is not enough), of the
c. Dwelling house (cottage)
d. Of another (Vicki's cottage)

Would you be done if you concluded (which you should, after discussing *all* the elements of arson) that Dufus will *not* likely be convicted of arson? No. Remember that the question being asked is: "Of what crime or *crimes* may Dufus be convicted?" You need to discuss *any and all* of the relevant crimes.

So what should you ask yourself now? You know this: whether Dufus might be guilty of *attempted arson*. To determine that, you have to resolve yet another issue: whether Dufus's action of setting fire to the chair was sufficiently close to the completed offense to find him guilty of an attempted crime. And, to reason to a logical conclusion on that point, you must know the rule or test for attempt in your jurisdiction. (There are several, including those that look at whether the defendant "took a substantial step toward" or was in "dangerous proximity of" completing the offense and those that consider whether the defendant did the "last act" before actually completing the target offense tested. The outcome may differ depending on the test used.)

On a law school criminal law exam, you may be expected to analyze a situation using all the tests you studied. On the bar exam, you will need to prove the attempt did or did not take place using first and foremost the test that controls in your jurisdiction (or, on many bar exams, the modern-majority rule). Only if you have *extra* time should you even consider writing about a minority view, for example. (Note: Some bar examiners stress the need to answer according to modern-majority principles, but may award additional points for noting where your state's laws differ. As part of bar preparation, you will learn what law you are expected to know and use in your answers, and whether or not any additional points may be awarded for more refined comparative knowledge.)

Let's continue our outline then, adding this second possible crime.

Crimes of Dufus
ATTEMPTED ARSON?

    a. Acting with specific intent to burn the structure in question (wanted to burn, yes),

    b. Defendant took a substantial step toward completing this arson (he "set out" to burn the cottage with kerosene (a highly flammable liquid) and matches, went to the cottage, and lit the chair on fire).

Are you done now? Quite likely, yes. *Wait a minute!*, you say. *If the chair burned, then didn't Dufus permanently deprive Vicki of her property? Surely she didn't consent to that. Should I discuss larceny?* You quickly rattle off the elements of larceny: "the trespassory taking and carrying away of the personal property of another with intent to deprive the owner thereof," and you continue thinking, *Ah, but he didn't move the chair at all.*

Let's finish off the outline.

LARCENY?

    • no "taking and carrying away" (asportation element of larceny not satisfied.)

OK, we read carefully. We thought as we read, asking questions about what was potentially in question or at issue while looking at each word. We took notes so as not to lose those thoughts. Then we outlined, placing the points we want to write about in a logical order. Now let's translate this into bar writing.

Note: This is a sample only, using this truncated hypothetical. You may not have time to or need to go into this much detail. This would likely be only one paragraph in a page-long fact pattern, and there would be many other issues to discuss. But this short sample gives you just an idea of how to write, hitting each part of IRPC and making your reasoning explicit enough for a layperson to easily follow your thinking.

Writing Example #1

Crimes of Dufus

The defendant may be charged with several crimes, but under these facts there is only one crime of which he may likely be convicted. [This is a sort of introduction. It shows the grader you read the question and are planning to respond to it.]

ARSON

Will Dufus be convicted of arson? Arson is the malicious burning of the dwelling house of another. Here, the facts tell us that Dufus "wanted" to burn Vicki's cottage and that he "set out" with the tools to do so. His desire to burn the cottage and his going to the target site with those tools prove that Dufus acted deliberately or willfully, therefore establishing "malice" and satisfying *the mens rea requirement for arson.* ("Malice" can be proved by establishing either willfulness or a reckless disregard for the risks.) A cottage is typically a *dwelling house,* and this cottage belongs to Vicki; therefore it would be the dwelling house of another and satisfy the *structure requirement* of common law arson. The *burning element* of arson, however, would not likely be satisfied here since that requires some burning or charring of the structure itself. Here the flames appear to have been extinguished while only the chair was burning—before the fire could reach the floor, walls, or any other part of the structure. Assuming that is the case and no part of the structure actually burned or was charred, despite the fact that Dufus possessed the requisite intent and took some action toward committing the crime, *Dufus may not be convicted of arson.*

ATTEMPTED ARSON

Will Dufus be guilty of attempted arson? A conviction of attempted arson here would require proof of Dufus's *specific intent to burn* Vicki's home, and evidence that Dufus *took a substantial step toward the completion* of that crime. Here, as was noted in the discussion of arson above, the defendant "wanted" to burn Vicki's cottage. His specific intent is evidenced by that fact. Dufus "set out" with "kerosene" (a highly flammable liquid) and "matches" (incendiary devices), went to Vicki's home, and lit a chair inside the home on fire. These actions go far beyond thinking about committing the offense or even simply *planning* to burn the cottage. The defendant went to the site where he wanted to commit the target offense and started a fire in the home, an action very likely to have led to the burning of the cottage had the neighbor and fire department not intervened. The defendant was thus well beyond the zone of preparation and well within the *zone of perpetration.* Because the prosecution has ample evidence of both the specific intent to complete the arson and his having taken a substantial step toward completing that act, *Dufus will likely be convicted of attempted arson.*

LARCENY

Did Dufus's actions in deliberately setting fire to Vicki's chair amount to a larceny? Larceny is the taking and carrying away of the personal property of another with intent to permanently deprive the owner thereof. Dufus may have deprived Vicki of her chair (clearly personal property), and done so intentionally, but nowhere do the facts tell us that Dufus took or carried the chair away. Because Dufus did not move the chair, the asportation element of larceny is not satisfied, and *Dufus will not be convicted of larceny.*

CONCLUSION

For the reasons stated above, Dufus will likely be convicted of attempted arson.

Notice how the writing sample above tracks the logic of IRPC and is written in complete sentences in a way that a layperson could understand and follow the reasoning. In the example above, we *italicized* elements and conclusions to provide a road map for the grader. It would also be possible to set the same answer up with subheadings, as in the example below.

Writing Example #2

Here, we will write the same answer but format it slightly differently, with shorter paragraphs and more frequent headings and subheadings. Which one do you find to be more reader friendly?

Crimes of Dufus

The defendant may be charged with several crimes, but under these facts there is only one crime of which he may likely be convicted.

ARSON

Will Dufus be convicted of arson? Arson is the malicious burning of the dwelling house of another.

Malice or mens rea requirement

Here, the facts tell us that Dufus "wanted" to burn Vicki's cottage and that he "set out" with the tools to do so. His desire to burn the cottage and his going to the target site with those tools prove that Dufus acted deliberately or willfully, therefore establishing "malice" and satisfying the mens rea requirement for arson. ("Malice" can be proved by either establishing willfulness or a reckless disregard for the risks.)

Dwelling house of another
A cottage is typically a place people live (so qualifies as a dwelling house), and this cottage belongs to Vicki; therefore, it would satisfy the structure requirement of common law arson, the dwelling house of another.

Burning
The burning element of arson, however, would not likely be satisfied here. This element requires some burning or charring of the structure itself, and the flames appear to have been extinguished while only the chair was burning—before the fire could reach the floor, walls, or any other part of the structure.

Assuming that is the case and no part of the structure actually burned or was charred, despite the fact that Dufus possessed the requisite intent and took some action toward committing the crime, he may not be convicted of arson.

ATTEMPTED ARSON
Will Dufus be guilty of attempted arson? A conviction of attempted arson here would require proof of Dufus's specific intent to burn Vicki's home, as well as evidence that Dufus took a substantial step toward the completion of that crime such that he crossed over from what might be deemed merely the "zone of preparation" into the "zone of perpetration."

Mens Rea: specific intent to complete the target offense
Here, as was noted in the previous discussion of arson, the defendant "wanted" to burn Vicki's cottage. His specific intent to complete the target offense is evidenced by that fact.

Actus reus: the defendant took a substantial step toward completing the crime
Dufus "set out" with "kerosene" (a highly flammable liquid) and "matches" (incendiary devices), went to Vicki's home, and lit a chair inside the home on fire. These actions go far beyond thinking about committing the offense or even simply *planning* to burn the cottage. The defendant went to the site where he wanted to commit the target offense and started a fire in the home, an action very likely to have led to the burning of the cottage had the neighbor and fire department not intervened. The defendant was thus well within the "zone of perpetration."

Because the prosecution has ample evidence of both the specific intent to complete the arson and his having taken a substantial step toward completing that act, Dufus will likely be convicted of attempted arson.

LARCENY

Did Dufus's actions in deliberately setting fire to Vicki's chair amount to a larceny? Larceny is the taking and carrying away of the personal property of another with intent to permanently deprive the owner thereof. Dufus may have deprived Vicki of her chair (clearly personal property), and done so intentionally, but nowhere do the facts tell us that Dufus took or carried the chair away. Because Dufus did not move the chair, the asportation element of larceny is not satisfied, and Dufus will not be convicted of larceny.

DEFENSES

The facts do not appear to raise any justification or excuse for Dufus' actions, nor are there any mitigating factors.

CONCLUSION

For the reasons stated above, Dufus will likely be convicted of attempted arson.

Notice in this second example that there was no need to *italicize* key terms because the headings and subheadings gave the grader a clear road map.

The purpose of this basic arson example was to take you through the process, from bar reading, thinking and issue spotting, to outlining, and then to writing simply in a logical IRPC (issue, rule, proof, conclusion) style, proving each element of the rules you stated with facts from the fact pattern. If you are reading this well before you even start bar review, it should help give you a window into the strategy of essay writing for bar exams.

Do not assume. Prove it. And say why.

Often one of the toughest things to grasp is how much more straightforward bar exam essays tend to be when compared with the most challenging aspects of classroom questioning. How many times did you go into class thinking you understood the reading only to find the professor threw so many factual variations or subtleties in the law at you that you ended up feeling like you hadn't prepared at all?

It's good to leave law school classes with your head hurting; it means you were thinking![38] But on bar essays, you mostly work with the stated facts, which are presented in a fairly straightforward manner, and show how they prove or disprove elements of rules of law.

Note: I never said bar essays were easy. There are many rules, in many subjects, and you have to read and see the relevance of every word in the fact patterns—and do all of that quickly and in a high-pressure situation. What I *am* saying is that the level of analysis is superficial compared with most law classes. Again, that is why I prefer the mnemonic IRPC for bar exam essays rather than IRAC. It's more often simple *proof* rather than complex *analysis* that the bar essays require. But you cannot skip steps; you must at least note points that may seem obvious to you. (Remember the equilateral triangle example.) And in the Dufus example above, the facts convey that Dufus "wanted to burn" the cottage. How much more obvious could his intent be? It is clearly stated. Nonetheless, in your answer, you must state that the intent element was proved and why (even if that "why" is because the facts stated that "he wanted to burn").

Let's say you read a fact pattern and determine that the main crime the defendant may have committed is burglary. (First, of course, you would recite the rule, "At common law a burglary was the breaking and entering of the dwelling house of another in the nighttime with intent to commit a felony therein.") One element of burglary is *breaking* into the structure. Even when a fact pattern explicitly states that the defendant "broke the door to go inside," you would need to say something to briefly indicate that the facts prove the existence of that element. For example, you might write, *The breaking element is satisfied here because the facts state that the defendant "broke the door" to go inside.* While that may seem self-evident, points are often given on bar essays for stating the obvious in a clear and organized fashion. This shows that you see the relevance of the particular facts and can apply the facts to that law. (This is precisely how litigators help jurors see how evidence presented at trial proves or disproves elements of the causes of action or crimes in question.)

What you do not want to do is *assume*, or arrive at a conclusion without saying why. That is what law professors and bar graders call *conclusory*. (You would not expect a jury to convict a defendant without believing beyond a reasonable doubt that there is sufficient evidence of each and every element of the charged crime, right?) Let's look back at the example of Dufus's attempted arson above. We did not just write, *Dufus wanted to burn the cottage and took a substantial step toward doing so and therefore is guilty of attempt.* We broke down each element (the intent element was easy to prove because the facts stated he wanted to do this, but we nonetheless still noted it explicitly) and then showed how and *why* Dufus's setting out toward the cottage with the kerosene and matches (linking these tools explicitly to the target offense) amounts to a substantial step toward the commission of the crime.

You may think this is obvious, so why bother writing it? Of course kerosene is flammable. On a bar essay, though, your job is *to show why* the exam facts prove or disprove the elements of the relevant rules. I often tell my students, "Walk into the bar exam imagining you have a teleprompter in front of you the whole time flashing the question *Why?*." That will force you to always remember to explain your reasoning and make your thoughts explicit. (And pretending you are writing to a layperson, not a colleague or professor, will also help you note every step of your reasoning more clearly.)

NONTRADITIONAL STUDENTS MAY FIND IT HARD TO "DO THE MATH."

Law students who are professionals in other fields, or businesspeople used to customers and clients seeking quick answers, often find it challenging to slow down and write each step of their thinking. My law students who are doctors frequently tell me, "The patient doesn't want a long story. She just wants the diagnosis and treatment. Basically, she would be thrilled if I didn't say anything other than, 'Take this. It will make you feel better.'" Clients who are paying for services also often want instant answers. Bar graders are more like good math teachers; they want to "see your work," your ability to reason logically, step by step.

Issue-Spotting Exercise

Look at the following sentence: "The defendant entered the Miller office building at dusk through an unlocked door to get the umbrella that he had left, then saw the diamond ring, took it, and walked out into the rain." If the question asks about the defendant's possible criminal liability for burglary, what, if any, discussable issues are raised by the following words? Write your thoughts about these words in the spaces below:

"office building at dusk"

_____

_____

_____

"through an unlocked door"

_____

_____

_____

"that he had left"

_____

_____

_____

"then"

_____

_____

_____

What did you identify as issues? Before identifying any issues, of course, you recited the rule: _Common law burglary was defined as the breaking and entering into the dwelling house of another in the nighttime with intent to commit a felony therein._ Then, you perhaps went on to ask some of the following questions:

1. Does the office building satisfy the "dwelling house" element of burglary? (And, here, you likely reminded yourself that modern jurisdictions have extended this element to include any "protected structure.") And, do the words "at dusk" satisfy the "in the nighttime" element?
2. Does entering through an unlocked door satisfy the "breaking" element?
3. Is the defendant's going inside to get the umbrella "that he had left" sufficient to prove he had the requisite mens rea, or "intent to commit a felony therein"? He may not have had any criminal intent if he walked in to retrieve his own property.
4. Does the word "then" raise a potential issue? It may be relevant to the question of when the felonious intent was formed, timing being critical to culpability.

SOME JURISDICTIONS HAVE SPECIFIC SUGGESTIONS OR REQUIREMENTS FOR ESSAY WRITING.

This chapter has focused on broadly applicable guidelines for and insights into effective bar essay writing. You must research any unique aspects of your exam. Some jurisdictions provide supplemental case or statutory authorities to use in essays; some include essays with problem-solving tasks (which seem a bit like a performance test and essay combined). Enrolling in a reliable bar course tailored to your jurisdiction and studying the website and any information provided by your bar examiners is a must.

Conclusions

Finally, a word about conclusions. While it may not always matter so much *how* you conclude on bar essays (who "wins"), it matters that you do conclude. Bar graders want to see that you can answer the entire question (and all of the issues that it raises) within the allotted time. They will not be satisfied if you merely demonstrate that you can *start* answering the questions, or outline the answers to the questions. (Do not, for example, write a stunningly rich answer to part one of the question and then run out of time for part two.) But two passing answers may contain opposite conclusions—especially when the facts are "gray," meaning there are good arguments on both sides. When faced with such ambiguity, you may, for instance, conclude in a manner that acknowledges this: *Based on the foregoing analysis, the defendant will* likely *be found to have possessed the intent to kill the victim here. If, however, the prosecution is unable to prove intent to kill, also as noted above, the prosecution may well be able to demonstrate that the defendant possessed the intent to cause serious bodily harm or, at the very least, that his actions showed a reckless indifference to human life.* There's nothing wrong with concluding in a way that shows a number of probable outcomes, but you must finish, and do so logically. And again, giving some emphasis to a conclusion, even a brief one (perhaps by underlining it or making it a subheading), shows the grader that you completed the answer.

QUIZ

TEST YOUR HABITS: When I complete a practice exam, I:

    a. never look at it again, and certainly never show it to anyone else.
    b. study it alongside a sample or model answer, comparing and contrasting the two.
    c. show it to a professor, mentor, study buddy, or academic support advisor to review and critique.
    d. do either *b* or *c*, or both, *and* rewrite that same practice exam at a later date and assess improvements.

Many of you, if you are honest, will choose *a*. Hopefully, I will have convinced you by the end of this chapter to act otherwise after completing a practice exam. If you picked *b*, that is good; however, be sure at some point to also have someone else critique your exams, hopefully early on, so that you are not mistakenly thinking your answers are just fine if they aren't. There is also a danger in not studying reliable sample or model answers; you risk cementing your errors. The key is to improve with every practice exam. You do yourself the greatest of disservices if you simply compound your mistakes. That said, if you picked *c*, be sure in the future to *first try to figure out* what *you* think you missed, and then let someone else critique it. Hopefully, what they say will mirror what you saw as errors and ways to improve. Eventually, you will learn what you need to from studying reliable sample or model answers on your own. (After all, you will not have someone critiquing or editing your actual bar exam answers. You must get to the point where you are doing them well, alone, but it is a process getting there!)

How to self-assess your practice essay writing

After completing an essay, look carefully at your own answer and a model or reliable sample answer (such as one released by your state's bar examiners as representative of a passing answer). Sit with both. Assess how they are the same and how they differ. Note the answers' organization and presentation. Note how precise and complete the rule statements are. Are there any rules you can learn more about or rule statements you can memorize more thoroughly? What about application/analysis? Is there proof of the existence or lack thereof of each element of each rule at issue? Was every key fact used? Go through them side-by-side, and, as a clever detective,

- look for what the sample or model answers include that your answer did not contain, and what you may have written about that was not in the sample answers;
- be sure you understand *why* the sample answers included what was discussed and why the sample answers left out things you may have thought were important;
- look for content and style (make sure your answer is reader friendly!);
- look at the rules and be sure you understand them; and
- reread the fact pattern and then look at how the facts were used in discussing each issue in the model answer.

Then, after this basic compare-and-contrast, ask these specific questions:

1. Did I finish within the allotted time?
2. Did I spot the main discussable issues? (And did I see which issues were major and required more discussion, and which were minor and called for less emphasis?)
3. Did I state the rules correctly and succinctly?
4. Did I use facts to show why (*prove*) each element of each rule was or was not established in the question?
5. Did I reason to a logical conclusion for every main issue I raised?
6. Was my answer presented in a manner that was organized and easy to read?

After you have done this first part of self-assessing, find concrete ways to improve. Make every effort to leave each practice session with at least two to three specific ideas about how you can improve. The examples below are just illustrations. Your situation is unique to you. The key is to figure out where you need to improve and to then create a doable plan of action for your success.

CAVEAT: PRACTICE EXAMS MUST HELP YOU IMPROVE!

I have said this before but cannot emphasize it enough: *taking* practice exams is not sufficient. You must walk away from every practice session dedicated to *improve* the quality of what you just produced. If you write essays poorly, or you get the law wrong or your analysis (proof) or use of the facts is insufficient, or your answer is disorganized—and you just keep repeating the same mistakes on future practice exams—you will be cementing and compounding your weaknesses. That is why you have to study quality, reliable answers and learn how to make your answers look and read more like those passing answers. This is also why it can be so helpful to at least periodically have your answers reviewed and critiqued by someone reliable (for instance, ASP, bar support, or bar review faculty).

Improvement area: Action item

- I must read the questions more carefully. (I wrote about nonhomicidal offenses when the call of the question specifically asked about homicide crimes.)

In upcoming exams, I will read the call of the question first, then read the facts, then reread the call of the question before I begin outlining. I will also underline the call of the question, and keep the fact pattern and my outline in front of me as I write.

- I need to manage my time better. (I wrote for 30 minutes on the first interrogatory and didn't have time to write the remainder of my answer.) Note: On a simulated exam, you will write several essays back-to-back, and you will want to watch your timing carefully to be certain you are stopping after the suggested time for each essay so you can finish the whole set in the allotted time.)

I will work on my timing. I will keep a small clock in front of me as I write. During a one-hour essay, for example, I will note when I reach the 15-, 30-, 45- and 55-minute marks. I will try to finish my outline by the 15–20-minute mark. I will strive to have hit all the main issues by the 45-minute mark. And, I will be concluding by the 55-minute mark. (During a 30-minute essay, I will note the 10- and 25-minute marks. I will read and try to finish my outline by the 10-minute mark. I will strive to have hit all the main issues by the 25-minute mark and begin concluding.)

TIMING

It is absolutely critical to have your timing down—*nailed*—by mid-July at the latest. You need to go into your bar exam knowing you can read each MBE question and select the best answer within 1.8 minutes. You need to know you can read, analyze, and write a passing essay answer within the time allotted. Remember, when you appear before a judge, your time will be limited as well. It's part of the game. You must have both speed and accuracy. On essay questions, you will often need at least 10–15 minutes to read and outline (that is true whether the essay is a 30-, 45- or 60-minute exam.) This will help you write in an organized manner and allocate your time appropriately between the issues raised by the question and facts. Note: The times may need to be adjusted if you are a fast reader and slow typist or a slow reader and fast typist. Experimenting by varying the amount of time you spend reading, analyzing, or writing can help boost your scores. Time and again, I have seen bar takers' scores increase significantly when they spend more time reading and thinking and outlining before writing.

- I must type faster. (I have the thoughts in my head, but don't get them out fast enough.)

I will work on improving my typing skills. I will type every day, and make time to type out model answers in full for at least some of the practice essays I write. (This is another good example of why it pays to start bar preparation well before formal bar review. If you determine early in your last year of law school that you are not typing fast enough for the time prssures of the bar exam, you would have time to do something about it, for example take an online typing course. If this is something that you just realize in mid-June is causing a major obstacle you will have a tougher time making the the necessary improvements.)

- I need to understand the law better. (I saw what the issues were, but did not write applicable rule statements clearly.)

I will review the lecture notes and look up areas I do not understand in the outlines. Then, I will either say out loud or copy or rewrite the legal rules several times to help memorize them.

- Facts: I'm not using enough facts.

Cross out terms as you use them in your answer. And learn the law thoroughly. The more you know the law, the better your ability to quickly see how these new facts prove or disprove elements of those rules.

Self-Assessment Chart: Your Turn

1. Did I finish the entire essay within the allotted time? ☐ Yes ☐ No
Improvement Action:

_____

2. Did I spot and write about the main issues? ☐ Yes ☐ No
Improvement Action:

_____

3. Did I allocate my time well as I was writing? (Did I write too much on any one issue such that I gave short shrift to other issues?) ☐ Yes ☐ No
Improvement Action:

_____

4. Did I state the rules correctly and succinctly? ☐ Yes ☐ No
Improvement Action:

_____

5. Did I use facts to show why each element of each rule was or was not established in the question? ☐ Yes ☐ No
Improvement Action:

_____

6. Did I reason to a logical conclusion for every main issue I raised? ☐ Yes ☐ No
Improvement Action:

_____

7. Was my answer presented in a manner that was organized and easy to read?
☐ Yes ☐ No
Improvement Action:

Bottom line: troubleshoot now, during early start or, at the very latest, during intensive bar prep. Do *not* use the actual bar exam to figure out what you need to do better next time. Pass the first time you take the exam. The more practice exams you take, the more opportunities you will have to learn and improve, slowly and surely.

It's normal for improvement to be slow and incremental. Some of you will hit a wall at the end of June and be tired of practice tests. You must keep going, keep plugging away, and don't give up. The breakthroughs and "aha moments" will come, maybe when you're not even expecting them, as long as you keep at it and keep moving forward. By comparing your answers with model answers, you may gain insights that show you where adding even one more sentence or bolstering the factual analysis of one particular issue greatly improves and strengthens the answer—something you may not have seen at first blush. Note those observations. Make them a part of your process. You will get there. Slowly and surely.

Persistence

Keep taking practice tests, and reading and studying those model answers. Even rewriting previously taken practice essays can be helpful. You will see them differently now than you did even a month ago. You will see the ways to improve. And, until the exam is complete, there is time to improve. Even the day before the bar, you can learn valuable things that may boost your scores. Do not give up. Be dogged, determined, and persistent.

You can also try rereading practice exam answers aloud or even handwriting or retyping them out in full from time to time, to "tune your ear" to a complete response. Often doing that just a few times brings home seemingly small changes that can make a huge difference in how effectively your answer responds to the queries and covers the required material.

Reality check: Getting your exams graded by someone else

Throughout this chapter and book, I stress self-assessment. But be sure to *also* complete and turn in as many exams as possible to your bar review for critique. You need to know that you are on track and not continuously repeating problems you didn't even notice. Know, though, that unless you have a tutor standing over your shoulder while you write, there will be a delay in getting feedback—even from the best of bar reviews. (Also, remember that you will go into the exam alone; the sooner *you* see how to improve, the better.) Another reason for *immediate self-assessment* is that powerful learning comes when the fact pattern is freshest in your mind. You will much more and readily see exactly where you erred and understand how to improve. (You will quickly see if you misread a word or didn't see the significance of a key fact. You will easily see if a fact triggered an issue but you didn't know the relevant law. Look up that rule *while the fact pattern is fresh* so that it sticks in your memory.) If you have to reread a fact pattern days or weeks later, when you get back your graded exam, you will waste time getting back up to speed. And, it may be difficult to recall what you were thinking at the time. So, use the grader's critiques to confirm or change your own assessment. When you get an exam back from your bar review, compare the grade and comments to your own assessment. Did they point out things you didn't see, or does the critique confirm what you already figured out for yourself? (If the former, do you see them now? If not, ask for further help.) Either way, you will come out ahead by working to learn from practice tests immediately after completing them.

Self-assess through reverse engineering

For essays, a useful tool can sometimes be to study the fact pattern and sample or model answer, and work backward. In other words, *outline the answer*. Ask what you would have needed in an outline to produce this sort of (passing) answer. Then look *back* to the facts to see how and where the answer got its analysis out of these particular facts. How did this answer use the facts selected to reason to certain conclusions? Usually we move from question to answer. But turning that process around, and moving from answer (end goal) back to the question, can sometimes help you see more clearly where you need to go. Note: This process can also be used on performance tests, as discussed below.

PERFORMANCE TESTS
About performance tests (PTs)

Performance tests serve as the practical portion of the bar exam in a majority of jurisdictions. The work to be completed on a PT is similar to what you might do as a beginning lawyer: draft legal memoranda and write briefs to the court, letters to clients, discovery plans, settlement offers, and more. To complete a PT, you will be called upon to read and analyze a case *file* and a *library* of legal authorities, and draft one or more documents based upon information you glean from those materials. Whatever the exact tasks to be drafted, passing PTs requires demonstrating competency in the ability to

- sort detailed factual materials and separate relevant from irrelevant facts;
- analyze statutory, case, and other legal authorities for relevant principles of law;

- apply the relevant law to the relevant facts in a manner likely to resolve the client's problem;
- identify and resolve ethical dilemmas, when present;
- communicate effectively in writing;
- complete the requested task(s) thoroughly and within time constraints.

These six skills are described in the National Conference of Bar Examiners' MPT information booklet.[39] The California state bar also publishes very useful information about its PTs on its website. (California PTs are similar to, but twice as long as, MPTs.)[40]

TEST YOURSELF

Are you familiar with—and could you draft—each of these documents?

Put a check in the space to the left of each type of document that you would feel comfortable drafting. To the right of each document type, write what the document is, who it is generally prepared for, and what its purpose is. Be sure to learn enough about any document types you aren't yet familiar with to be comfortable with them by the time of your exam.[41]

Task/Document Type
☐ Opening Statement:

_____

☐ Closing Argument:

_____

☐ Memorandum of Points and Authorities to a Supervising Attorney:

_____

☐ Opinion Letter:

_____

☐ Jury Instructions:

_____

☐ Client Letter:

_____

☐ Memorandum of Law:

_____

☐ Trial Brief:

_____

☐ Appellate Brief:

_____

☐ Persuasive Memorandum:

_____

☐ Contract:

_____

☐ Will:

_____

☐ Trust:

_____

☐ Affidavit or Declaration:

_____

☐ Proposal for Settlement Agreement:

_____

☐ Discovery Plan:

_____

☐ Witness Cross-Examination Plan:

_____

☐ Witness Direct-Examination Plan:

_____

ANY LEGAL SUBJECT IS FAIR GAME ON PTS

The performance test library may include virtually any area of law. PTs have involved areas such as health law, sports law, bankruptcy, environmental law, and maritime law in addition to the more familiar torts, contracts, and the like. The good news is that you need no familiarity with the law in advance. As long as you know how to read and brief a case, and read statutes and other sources of law, you are set. The library will have everything you need. And often the law in areas most people are not familiar with is easier to understand than is the law in more routine areas.

You must practice writing PTs in full under timed conditions, rather than just outlining or reading them. They do not involve memorization; they require skills. Training by writing a critical mass of them will give you the confidence to approach whatever might be thrown at you on your exam.

Plan on completing at least eight PTs, written out in full under timed conditions, before your bar exam. Outline several others. That is a minimum. (To be certain you do at least that many, plan a "date with a PT" every Sunday afternoon. And schedule ample time after you complete the exam for self-assessing, as directed below.). Again, it cannot hurt and may help enormously to complete two PTs each week.

PTs are among the most productive work you can do in early start. In fact, some students take bar-writing classes in law school where they are exposed to PTs. If this is you, if you have mastered PT skills early on, you may need to take far fewer practice PTs during the summer. (Again, because PTs are open book and skills based, you really can learn how to do them during school and not wait until bar review.)

Key differences between PTs and essays

There are several differences between PTs and essays. These differences affect how one best prepares for these exams.

1. PTs are open book; essays are closed book. The former are thus predominantly skills based, whereas the latter require skill, knowledge, and memory.
2. PTs have a great deal more material that you must sift through before writing. A bar essay is usually, at most, a page long. MPTs may include a 5 to 15-page file and another 5 to 15-page library, along with several instruction pages. California PTs are even longer.
3. A difference that flows from the previous point: the PT often includes irrelevant material and tests you in part on your ability to distinguish relevant and irrelevant information. Essays tend to have all, or nearly all, relevant facts that often trigger or affect your analysis of discussable issues.
4. You are given more time on PTs than on essays. In multistate jurisdictions, the MEE includes 30-minute essays, and each MPT is 90 minutes. In California, each essay takes one hour, whereas each PT lasts three hours. A longer exam requires more focus and stamina, as well as better time management.
5. There is often more variety among performance test answers deemed to be passing than among passing essay answers.[42]

How to complete performance tests

Although individuals think differently and PTs are set in different contexts with different tasks, it helps to move through the material with a strategic approach.[43]

The logic and timing of completing MPTs (each time allotment is double that for California PTs):

1. Skim general instructions. (1 minute)
2. Study the task memo, and take note of any format memos. (5 minutes)
3. Read/skim the file. (10 minutes)
4. Reread the task memo. (1 minute)
5. Read the library, briefing cases and quickly studying statutes or other authorities. (15 minutes)
6. Reread the task memo. (1 minute)

7. Reread the file, think about the question, and outline your answer. (Outline on scratch paper if provided or on the test booklet itself if scratch paper isn't available.) (12 minutes)

8. Write your answer, going back as necessary to consult your outline and notes in the margins of the file, library, and task memo. (45 min.)

Overview of this system:
Why it works and why it makes sense

PTs are like puzzles. They consist of separate pieces that all fit together. But it takes a while to see how they fit. Though it may seem like the exam provides ample time, the time flies.

A "chicken and egg" approach that moves between different pieces of the puzzle is deliberate. It will make the time you spend on each part of the PT puzzle more efficient. Why? You cannot really understand the significance of facts in the file until you know the law. You cannot readily see how the law applies to or is distinguishable from your client's situation unless you understand the facts. (Law is not relevant in a vacuum, but in how it applies to a given situation.)

The most efficient system is thus to fully understand the instructions, and then gather enough of the facts from the file so that when you go to the library you can readily see not just what the rules are, but their significance to your client's situation. (Hence, skim the file when you first look through it. You can always come back to any portion of it. This is an open book test!) Your goal on this first read/skim is to learn enough about your client so that when you read the library, you will be able to readily see if the legal authorities support your client's position or not, and why. Then, with a basic understanding of the factual and legal backdrop, return to the task memo. You will be surprised how much more sense it makes after you have some context! Also, when you reread relevant parts of the library and file, your reading will be targeted and focused; you will be less likely to get caught up in what you know is a mass of irrelevant information.

Studying the law in a PT library should be like going on a precision mission, not a fishing expedition. It's not like reading cases to prepare for class, during which your professor might ask about any aspect of a case. On PTs, you read to *use* the cases to prepare the documents you are being asked to draft. To this end, your case briefing must also be more targeted.

Once you have a basic understanding of the law and renewed clarity about what you must draft, you can return to the facts and go through the file with a keener sense of what you are looking for. You will much more readily see whether certain factual sources are or are not relevant, and, if relevant, why. When you don't know the law, you will waste time on facts that turn out to be insignificant or even irrelevant.

Always, and at every turn (between each step), come back to the task memo. Such memos are crafted extremely carefully to give you tools to organize and respond to the interrogatory. But again, their importance may not be apparent upon first read. Only after studying the file and library will you really see how helpful these instruction memos are.

Lastly, before writing, think and organize (and outline) carefully so that you can write well. PT answers that are organized and thoughtful score higher than those that are scattered and shallow.

Adjust the timing to fit your strengths and weaknesses

The suggested breakdown is to spend half of your time reading/thinking and the other half writing. So, on the MPT, that's 45 minutes to read, understand, and organize, and 45 minutes to produce your answer. (On the California PT it's 90 minutes for each part). I suggest you experiment with the timing as you are doing practice tests. If you are a very fast reader and slower typist, or vice versa, adjust accordingly. (For example, a typical MPT applicant will read and outline for 45 minutes and then write/type for 45 minutes. If you are a slow reader and a very fast typist, it may be more effective to read for 50 or even 55 minutes, and knock out your answer in 35–40 minutes. Again, if the recommended 45/45 split works for you, fine. But if you cannot understand what you need to write in 45 minutes, a few extra minutes might make an enormous difference. Likewise, if you are a fast reader and thinker but a very slow typist, you may need to devote more than 45 minutes to typing.) Bottom line, watch the clock while you complete practice tests. Experiment with a 50/50 split, then with other time allocations. See if there is a timing methodology that enhances your ability to produce quality work. Remember, the time goes quickly but the material is open book, so don't get bogged down anywhere. Keep moving using this logical approach and keep close track of time. You must get through all the materials efficiently to finish in time with a complete and well-organized answer.

A closer look at each step in the PT approach

We overviewed the process above; now let's break it down.

The instructions

There are usually boilerplate instructions that will be the same or substantially the same as those you have completed in practice. Just take a moment to verify these. They will usually tell you how long you have to complete the exam, what materials are included (usually a file and library, but double-check to make sure they haven't included some other document), and possibly the weight/value of each task if you are to complete more than one assignment. (On the California PT, if a percentage weight is given to multiple tasks, often the only place that is noted is in the so-called boilerplate instructions.) They might also tell you the name of the fictional jurisdiction you are in as well, information you need to assess the precedential weight of the respective authorities in the library. Know what to look for in them that might differ; take a moment and glance at them as you begin.

The second and more important part of the instructions is in the task memo and is specific to this PT. The task memo is *not* boilerplate. You should read every word of it, two or three times. Usually the task memo includes information about your client and specifics on what you are to draft. The task memo may include or be followed by a separate *format* memo telling you how to set up the assigned document. As you read, underline or highlight the exact tasks you are to perform, and as you write, check back in with the task memo to be sure you have completely responded to the assignment. Note, too, that the more closely you read the task memo, the easier it often is to write your response, as there are often organizational hints within the task memo.

The file

After reading the instructional documents, skim the file. Unlike essays, where you have predigested, set facts, PTs provide facts in the form of resource documents such as a letter from a witness, a transcript of a client interview, an office memo, or criminal indictment. Learn who your client is and the issues your client faces. Get a sense of which documents are provided, where they come from, and who wrote them. (Look at the four corners of the document, including letterhead, dates, and footnotes.) Pay attention to whether a document has been redacted or excerpted from something else. For example, there can be a big difference between a transcript of an interview and a summary of an interview; the former, because it includes every word, usually has a lot more irrelevant information.

Get ready to read the library with some sense of your client and the "characters" in this PT role play. (Unlike law school, where you read cases to see all the reasoning and nuances on the opinion, you read cases on PTs to use them to craft your answer. It is much more targeted reading, reading you can only do effectively when you know your client's circumstances.)

On scratch paper, the task memo, or on the table of contents of the file, list the major parties and players, their names, and their roles. Get into the habit of writing this in the same place on every practice PT you write. This way, you will know where to turn to immediately verify who people are if you forget while poring through the file. For example:

- - my client: the professor, Mr. X
- - University of Liberty, "University" = employer and possible D
- - Wanda (witness who observed X's relationships with students)
- - Sally = student bringing complaint

PTS ARE NOT ALWAYS SET IN LITIGATION CONTEXTS.

PT instructions might direct you to produce a transactional document (for example, a contract or a will), so the authorities in the library may not support or negate your client's position, per se, but simply provide information. Nonetheless, your mission in that library is to see how the law relates to your client's situation and helps you draft whatever documents you are to produce.

The library

After your quick look at the file documents (knowing you will come back to it), brief the authorities in the library. Pull out rules. Assess whether each case or statute (or other authority) supports your client's position or not. Note which are binding and which are merely persuasive. Try to determine how the various legal rules in this library fit together.

BRIEFING CASES

If you did not brief cases on your own in law school, master that skill now. (If you bought commercial outlines and relied exclusively on them, you know who you are. If that's you, you must step up now and learn to effectively and efficiently brief cases.) You need to know this for the PT. If you are still in law school and need help learning to read and brief cases, see *Cracking the Case Method: Legal Analysis for Law School Success*, as well as other resources listed in the Bibliography.

Don't get bogged down in long case briefs. You don't have time to brief as thoroughly as you whould in school. Read the case to determine which party is in the position analogous to your client's circumstances, what the court held and why, and whether you can use the case to support an argument or analysis in favor of your client or whether the authority must be distinguished. If a PT is set in a transactional context, you will use case law and other authorities to learn the applicable rules and standards that govern or guide the particular transaction.

Remaining steps in the approach

Now, with the law in mind, review the file and reread the task memo. Again, the documents will make more sense; you will readily be able to note what is relevant and why.

Next, outline the document(s) you are to draft, going back as you need to any document in the library, file, or instructions. (This is the beauty of an open book exam!).

There is no need to write a long or detailed outline. The grader will only consider your final product. I have seen far too many students fail because they tried to follow suggestions of instructors who recommended preparing detailed outlines, charts, and lists. These students get so caught up in preparing their charts that they do not have time to produce passing quality answers. (My favorite way to outline a PT is directly on the table of contents page of the library. Often, the organization will come from a combination of the library rules and the assigned tasks.)

Finally, draft your assignment. Be sure to write for the proper audience in the appropriate tone, and complete the task or tasks requested in an organized, lawyerly manner. If you are writing to a layperson (for example, a letter to a client), be sure to define any jargon you use. If you are drafting a brief to the court, use more formal language. Note: You are often writing to your employer, typically a partner in your firm, but the document may be intended ultimately for your client, the opposing counsel, a private investigator, or another person or entity. Write in a way that is appropriate for the *ultimate audience*.

PTs are deceptive. People think they are "easy" because they are open book and you have more time than on essays. But they are not easy. There is a lot of material to sort through and organize and then use effectively in your answer. The minutes fly. You *must* practice PTs—lots of them—under timed conditions. I recommend at least one PT each week, and in some instances two per week. (My standard advice to students is, "Every Sunday afternoon, you have a 'date' with a PT.") Again, the key to having the time to do a sufficient number of practice PTs under timed conditions is to start early.

Just as with essays, make sure your answer is grader friendly, easy on the eye with headings and subheadings, so that, at a glance, the grader can readily see your organization. Type or handwrite legibly.

Practice PTs and how to self-assess them

PT practice is more time consuming than essay or MBE practice, so students often forget to make time for them. Big mistake. Make sure your study schedule includes a regular time to complete PTs each week.

In some jurisdictions the PT weighs heavily enough that doing well on even one PT can make up for a poor performance on one or more essays. In California, the PT is *only* worth 26 percent of an applicant's total score, but that is twice each essay; therefore, a good grade on one PT may counterbalance a failing score on two essays.

One trick to get more out of each PT practice session is to "spin off" the scenario to review other testable tasks. Let's say you complete a PT set in a criminal context where you are the prosecutor filing a motion to suppress certain evidence. After drafting and assessing that motion, perhaps even on your drive home, talk yourself through how you would have drafted the same assignment if you represented the defendant. Then, "dictate" or write a letter to the client, updating him or her about the upcoming hearing on the motion. Next, reclaim your prosecutor's hat and draft a letter to defense counsel offering a plea bargain. Develop a discovery plan that may be implemented if the motion is denied. Doing such spin-off exercises can give you exposure to different types of tasks (and boost your confidence in your ability to handle anything they throw at you) without having to invest the extra time reading a new file and library. Note: This spin-off suggestion is *not* a substitute for weekly practice PTs but a complement. You can do spin-offs with a study partner. Go for lunch or coffee after doing a practice PT and talk through how other tasks might be drafted using these same facts and law.

PT self-assessment
When you finish each practice PT, ask yourself the following questions:

- ☐ Did I finish within the allotted time?
- ☐ Did I follow the instructions given in the task memo?
- ☐ Did I use all the relevant authorities from the library?
- ☐ Did I bring in key facts from the file to support all the points I made and sort out irrelevant facts?
- ☐ Is my answer well organized and easy to read?

Next, study the model or sample answers. Just as with self-assessing essays, the key is in comparing and contrasting your answer with a passing answer. Outline your answer and outline the sample answer and you will easily see if you missed issues, you discussed irrelevant issues, you didn't understand or write in enough detail about the law, or your writing was disorganized. Then, review them paragraph by paragraph to see how you can improve your own answer. Ask yourself what, if anything, you can do to write more clearly and use the authorities in the library in a more precise and more organized fashion. It is also great to have a quality bar review critique your answer, but that is not a substitute for you yourself seeing how to improve. Self-assess immediately after completing each practice PT, even if you are turning your practice exams in for grading.

PT Assessment Chart: Your turn

☐ I finished in allotted time
Improvement Action:

_____

_____

☐ I followed the instructions in the task memo and any format memos.
Improvement Action:

_____

_____

☐ I used all the relevant authorities from the library, and cited all the cases in the table of contents of the library (I did not have to cite the cases within cases).
Improvement Action:

_____

_____

☐ I sorted the relevant from the irrelevant facts, and I incorporated key relevant facts from the file to support all the points I made.
Improvement Action:

_____

_____

☐ My answer is well organized and easy to read.
Improvement Action:

_____

_____

PT SELF-ASSESSMENT THROUGH REVERSE ENGINEERING

Just as with essays, looking backward from the model or sample answer to the task memo, file, or library can be most helpful in learning to improve PT writing. Outline the answer. Study the task memo. What from this answer came directly (or indirectly) out of the task memo? What points were pulled from the file? How did the answer use the library authorities? How was the answer organized and where in the instructions, file, or library were hints as to what would be a logical organization? Doing this sort of reverse engineering can be especially helpful if you feel "stuck" on how to deal with and organize PTs.

PT strategy tips

The toughest part of the PT is managing the data and your time (there is a lot of material and the time flies). Keep in mind that your notes end up in the trash. You only get credit for your answer. PT facts are numerous; some are duplicative and others are irrelevant. You need to read with a logical system that takes this into account, and practice the approach.

Depending on the exam rules in your jurisdiction, you may be able to use paper clips or different colored pencils or pens to help you organize the PT material. (In California, applicants can tear apart the library and clip cases together with paper clips. You may *not* tear pages from MPTs.) You will *not* be allowed sticky notes, since you could write on them.

Just as I suggest one page cheat sheets for every bar exam essay and MBE subject, I suggest that you draft a PT strategy sheet. Draft it as a note to yourself, with reminders of what you want to keep in mind during your PT. Here below is a sample.

Sample performance test strategy sheet

INSTRUCTIONS: I will read quickly. I'll check for weights of each task if more than one.

Notes:

TASK MEMO: If taking the MPT, I'll fold the corner of, or clip, the task memo page and any format memos. If taking the California PT, I will rip out the task memo and keep it in front of me as I read, outline, and write. *NOTE: The MPT instructions specifically prohibit ripping out pages.* The task memo is the most important document in the PT. I will read it to find out: 1) whom I am role playing and whom I represent; 2) whom am I writing for; 3) what type of writing (analytical, persuasive, transactional) is necessary, and the goal of the task(s); 4) what exactly I am expected to produce by the end of the exam (Is there any guidance on formatting I need to follow?); and 5) whether there are any clues to or suggestions for organization.

Notes:

_____

CASE: Who is the client? What does the client want? What is preventing the client from getting what the client is seeking? If the PT is set in the litigation context, who is suing whom over what?

Notes:

_____

LAW: 1) Try to find the main legal issues and figure out the legal analysis *framework*. How do the library rules fit together? 2) What are the library/legal issues fundamentally about? Is the analysis mainly procedural or substantive, or both? Is it expanding or narrowing a legal policy? Is it building a prima facie case or defense theories? Is it distilling a rule from a long line of cases? Is it arguing why our case doesn't fit some particular statutory scheme? What sort of legal analysis will I have to perform? How can I use the authorities in this library?

Notes:

_____

FACTS: In my initial skimming of the file, *before* I read the library, let me try to determine my client's basic story. In my second read of the file, *after* I read the library, let me think: 1) Knowing what authorities are in the library, and, if possible, breaking down the main legal rule(s) into elements or component parts, I will search for some relevant facts that relate to, by proving *or* disproving, each element. Remember, many facts will be irrelevant or duplicative, so there is no need to use every fact (the way I strive to in essays). Here, I am just looking for some fact or facts that relate to each key component of each main legal rule or principle. 2) Let me take note of inconsistent facts and facts (and sources of fact) that do not seem reliable (credible) and why. I will also keep in mind that I may be looking for additional facts (how to establish and possibly how to prove them.) 3) Again, I must expect irrelevant and duplicative facts. I don't want to get bogged down in anything I don't immediately see as relevant or waste time trying to figure it out. I can always come back to any source in the file or library. It's all right here, open book. Things will become clearer as I have more context. So just keep rereading and thinking and moving between the different pieces of the PT puzzle. Go back to the task memo.

Notes:

PROFESSIONAL RESPONSIBILITY: Look for conflicts and rule violations—actual and potential—and ways to resolve any ethical concerns. Are any lawyers behaving in an unprofessional manner? (Are the lawyers returning client calls and e-mails promptly? Are they explaining the pros and cons of various courses of action thoroughly?) Is there anything being done or recommended that could be accomplished in a more client-centered manner?

Notes:

SOLVE CLIENT'S PROBLEMS: Here, keeping the client's objectives and obstacles in mind, present alternative strategies (give at least two choices), and recommend tactics and strategies as well as substantive courses of action that will help the client achieve the client's goals.

Notes:

CONCLUDE: 1) Finish with some obvious concluding line. 2) Ask myself, as I am outlining and writing my answer: Did I perform the task(s) I was asked to perform? Did I help whomever I'm supposed to help on this project?

Notes:

_____

PT SCORES FOR ALL TYPES OF BAR TESTING

Notice that nowhere in my discussion of assessment did I mention focusing on the scores you receive in bar review if you submit practice tests for grading. In fact, even if you submit your answers to your bar review (which I certainly encourage!), I said it is critical to also do your own self-assessment the minute you complete the practice test. Even if your bar review gets your exam answer back within a day or two, the time the exam is freshest and thus the best time to learn from the experience of writing it is immediately after you finish.

Prepare for this reality: you may get a lot of practice questions wrong. Do not worry; keep working. Students always e-mail in June about how frustrated they are. Many threaten to quit. But it is especially common early on to frequently choose the wrong answer on practice MBEs. Some of you have never even seen this sort of format in a law exam. And bar graders may give very low scores on practice essays and PTs. Don't worry; keep working. Self-assess critically to find any and every way to improve your knowledge and skills. Every wrong answer is an opportunity to get it right on the exam! (That becomes the mantra of many successful students: "Every missed question is an opportunity.")

PRACTICE IS ABOUT THE LEARNING, NOT THE SCORES.

The value of consistently taking PTs is not in the scores, but in what you learn from them—and simply the act of doing them. Michael Jordan seems to have some relevant wisdom in this quote: "I have missed more than 9,000 shots in my career. I have lost almost 300 games. On 26 occasions, I have been entrusted to take the game-winning shot . . . and I missed. And I have failed over and over and over again in my life. And that is precisely . . . why I succeed."

WHAT IS *YOUR* INNER DIALOGUE WHEN YOU COMPLETE PRACTICE TESTS?

What do you tell yourself about the link between doing the practice tests and passing the bar exam? Do you say, "*When* I pass the bar exam . . ." Or do you complete a practice test, look at the results, and say, "How could I be so stupid as to miss that? I'll never pass." If ever you catch yourself thinking or saying, "I'll never pass," stop immediately, reword your thoughts, and adjust your attitude. You will pass. You are not stupid. You are learning. And if you keep learning from everything you do, you are indeed extremely smart. The problem is not making mistakes—it's not learning from them! Watch what you tell yourself. And keep the expectation that you will succeed front and center always, in everything you do, say, and think. Review Chapter 1 on self-talk and how to keep it optimistic.

Caveat: Never do I advocate "doing the ostrich." Ignorance is not bliss when it comes to bar studies. You must concern yourself with critiques and suggestions for improvement. You need to see *why* you made errors, you need to learn as much relevant law as possible, and you need to understand how to analyze and write more effectively.

If practice test scores are consistently lower in certain areas, *use* that as information on where and how much you may need to improve. Do not let scores on any practice tests have a negative effect on your self-confidence. But do not ignore those scores either. It is tempting to settle into denial and *hope* that the scores will simply improve with time. No! Test scores do not just miraculously increase. *You* improve your scores. Get busy figuring out what is lacking and how to continually bolster your progress.

Conversely, do not let higher scores on practice tests inflate your ego or lead you to conclude that you can stop doing them. No! Continue to work to improve until the last "time" is called on your exam. A bar review grader may have inflated a grade on an essay. You may have guessed on a multiple-choice question and gotten lucky. You can always do better. There is always room for improvement. (In an area such as constitutional law, for example, even if you have mastered all the rules and your essays provide solid analysis of the facts given those rules of law, you can still improve by weaving in policy concerns.)

A solidly IRPCd answer that has hit every discussable issue is like a cake without frosting. It's a good cake, and you must strive to bake that sort of well-prepared cake. (The bar exam is pass/fail. All you have to do is pass. You do not have to "get an A.") But, if you have time, go ahead and "frost" that cake with "bonus" issues. Perhaps you might make a subtler point that if some fact were slightly different an entirely different outcome might result, or you might weave in commentary on policy implicated in one or another approach to resolving an issue, or you might compare legal frameworks (especially if your jurisdiction awards points for knowing the state and federal distinctions). For instance, in a contracts question for services or land that is governed by the common law, there may be an analogy to a UCC provision that, while not binding, is nonetheless instructive. That would be frosting the cake. But again, only frost the cake *if you have time.* Do not go in search of "bonus points." However, *if you have hit everything* that is straightforward and a main issue, and still have extra time, by all means say something further that is thoughtful and relevant if it comes to mind.

What if you think something might be at issue, but you are not sure? My rule on this is that if it takes you longer to think about it and figure out whether it's relevant than to just get it out logically on the paper and move on, write it. You will likely not be marked down if something is not correct. It will simply take time from points that are definitely at issue. The more practice essays you complete, the more you will see what sorts of points tend to be main issues and which are more "bonus points."

––––––––––––––

So are you convinced? No matter how difficult or time consuming, in order to pass the bar exam you must practice, practice, practice! Louis Pasteur said it best: "Chance favors the prepared mind." Of course it sounds better in the original French: *Dans les champs de l'observation le hasard ne favorise que les esprits préparés.*[44] Your chances for success multiply geometrically the more prepared you are. Give yourself the best odds possible. If you want to pass the bar exam, prepare as well as you can. And the best preparation includes consistently taking practice tests under timed conditions and studying sample answers so that you constantly work to improve.

THE HOME STRETCH: ELIMINATE DISTRACTIONS AND EMBRACE SUCCESS

- The home stretch: a week at a glance

  - Envision success to achieve success

  - Eliminate distractions and focus fully

  - Simulated exams as the "dress rehearsal"

  - Simulated-exam assessment

  - The days before the exam: getting ready

  - Plan the event: what you will do on test days and nights

  - Getting dressed on exam days

  - Set out ahead of time what you plan to bring into the test site with you on exam days

  - Bathroom breaks on the bar exam

  - Listen to the instructions and proctors

  - Be careful what you eat before and between each testing session

  - Be careful where and with whom you eat

  - Manage your stress and don't be thrown by curveballs

  - You may not feel like it, but you are ready

  - A walk through your bar days

- Handy lists for bar days
  - Top-ten test-taking tips for essays
  - Top-ten test-taking tips for MBEs
  - Top-ten test-taking tips for PTs

The saying "It's always darkest before the dawn" applies to the home stretch of bar review. This chapter gives you tools to keep going, even when you feel you cannot. It will help you see that you are almost there. Stay the course.

THE HOME STRETCH: A WEEK AT A GLANCE

- Eight weeks and counting: clear your calendar and make your study plan if you have not already. Work on skills-based learning as well as staying on track in your substantive law portion of bar review.

- For skills training, get on a daily regimen of MBE practice, daily essay writing (open book, at first, if need be), and weekly performance test drafting. Do not be freaked out when a pile of books arrive, and when you open the website and see endless subjects to cover. Two months is a long time if you use it wisely.

- Book whatever travel and lodging you may need for the exam if you have not yet done so. The earlier you plan the better rates you will likely get.

TO STAY OR NOT TO STAY (IN A HOTEL), THAT IS THE QUESTION

Some applicants live far enough away from where they sit for the bar exam that there is no question; they must stay in a hotel. Others either live close by or have friends or relatives who can drive them each morning to the exam site. People always ask where they should stay, and my advice is stay wherever will make you more relaxed. A student came to me recently trying to decide where to take the bar. (Some states have multiple sites; others have only one location.) Her parents lived close to one site and she could save several hundred dollars by staying with them. My question was simple: will you feel at your best staying with them? This particular student thought carefully and decided that her parents would be supportive, she would have meals cooked and feel nurtured, and not having to drive a long distance would be much less stressful. I have talked with many other students who have come to completely opposite conclusions, realizing that even if they live very close by, they need to be alone in a hotel to totally focus, away from any family or friends. Do what is best for you. (And try not to make the decision based on cost alone. I know that everything adds up, and you may feel guilty adding to the debt by something "frivolous" like staying in a hotel. It is not. If you are thrown by coming home on bar nights to an atmosphere that distracts or undermines you, you will pay far more dearly than for a few nights of treating yourself to a hotel. If you need it, do it. You are worth it. Done.)

- Seven weeks and counting: assess your skills. Where are you weak? Adjust your daily schedule to correct those weaknesses while continuing to strictly follow your bar review schedule. Do not get overwhelmed by the quantity of material. Think of how much you learned in one day before certain final exams. You have seven full weeks. Make the most of every day, one step at a time, one day at a time. Reread the parts of this book's earlier chapters that discuss anxiety. Any time it all feels like too much to handle, use the tools you have learned to move through paralysis to power.

- Six weeks and counting: stick to your bar review. You chose a reputable bar review. Trust the process. Avoid distractions. Keep your focus. By now, it should be an absolutely dedicated habit to be doing daily MBEs and essays, and weekly PTs. Don't be concerned about the scores you are getting on them yet; just do them in full under timed conditions, self-assess, and implement strategies to improve in any way you can. The focus is on continuous improvement.

- Five weeks and counting: combat burnout. You may feel fried. If you have put in three really solid weeks, you should be tired. This is perfectly normal. Still, you have a long way to go, so hang on. Push yourself. Slow and steady wins the race. Take off a couple of evenings to do something enjoyable that will take you away for a moment from bar study, then get back to it bright and early next morning. Stick to your schedule.

- Four weeks and counting: July 1 arrives; the July date you have known about for years is now just weeks away. Just seeing the new month on the calendar and phone will kick you into high gear. Pace yourself. Take off July 4 to celebrate. This is also the time to take care of some business. Make sure that all your travel and hotel arrangements are set for the bar exam, that you have your admission ticket, and that you know the rules on what you will be allowed to bring in to the exam.

JULY IS HIGH GEAR

You are in *high gear* now. It's July. Only a few weeks until the big show. Don't be alarmed or freaked out when you see the date. Be at your peak, in both mind and body! Don't forget to sleep and eat healthy foods. Being strong in body, mind, and spirit is just as important as memorizing rules. At the actual exam the person next to you may know more law than you. No matter how much you study, that is possible. But, when all is said and done, if he or she is too tired to be an active, detail-oriented bar reader, all the memorized rules in the world won't help. Yes, you must know your stuff. But you must also go in ready to read critically, understand every word of every question, and use that information to think and reason carefully to logical conclusions. On that score, it's a level playing field. You may go in with a different mastery of legal knowledge, but the facts will be new to everyone in that room. And the person who stayed up all night before the exam to pack in more rules may not be awake and alert enough to read the facts critically and intelligently answer the questions asked.

- Three weeks and counting: do a simulated exam—not as a referendum on how you will do on the real exam, but as a learning tool. Work on improving wherever you still need to. Stick to your schedule.
- Two weeks and counting: draft your "cheat sheets." Put each subject on one page. This will force you to identify the most critical areas in each subject and master the applicable rules in a logical order, and it gives you something to "hold" if you want to do any last minute review. (Students frequently tell me they learn so much just from *preparing* their "cheat sheets.")
- The last week: reread the rules so you know what you can bring in, and assemble your clear plastic bag. Decide what you will wear and eat, and what you will do each day before and after the exam. Review your one page sheets. Keep doing your daily MBEs as you have every day for at least eight weeks. And keep outlining essays and reading sample answers. Be good to yourself. Sleep well, eat well, exercise regularly, and get ready for battle.

The key to July, in no uncertain terms, is to use the time you have as productively as possible. Work steadily and confidently, day by day, study session by study session, improving slowly and steadily, the key still being *improvement*. Also, get in the habit of focusing for longer stretches. Try to focus for at least three hours straight (I call this studying in "bar blocks.") If you study for four-hour bar blocks, then focusing for three hours may seem easy. For many people, it can be physically grueling just to sit for that long with no breaks. (Train as if you are training for a marathon; this includes getting enough sleep, eating right, and exercising. Do it.)

Be sure to continue doing practice tests in all three areas: MBE, essay, and PT. If the time is too short, do a smaller quantity but still do daily sets of MBEs. With essays, continue writing out some in full, still under timed conditions. But, especially as you get closer to the actual exam, alternate between writing essays in full and simply taking time to read, issue spot, *and outline*, and then study the model answers. You can cover more essays in less time. Note: Outlining is *not* a substitute for, but a complement to, writing answers out in full. Exposure to as many fact patterns as possible during this last month, though, is essential.

Hopefully, you will be reviewing fact patterns along with summary outlines, so that your mind learns to see the main issues as they tend to arise in each particular area of law. A good bar review program will help you to get these in order, but you must tailor them to work for you—make them your own. Remember, this month you are transitioning out of the big outlines into condensed outlines and eventually to your memory alone. You will eventually have to close those books entirely. Your summary outlines provide a bridge to help you make that transition.

Be sure this month (July) to shift your body clock (if it is not already there) to "Bar Standard Time" (BST). If you are a late-night or early-morning studier, know that the hours you must be "on" are loosely between 9 a.m. and 5 p.m. Make the shift now, slowly and surely, so that by July's end you are on BST, and functioning well with it.

Another must this month is to keep the flow going. Nerves are good, to some extent. Often in July they turn into adrenaline and become more empowering than paralyzing. But if ever the nerves throw you (in practice or on the real exam), know what to do to get back on track. (Reread the section in Chapter 7 on anxiety and how to unblock nerves and counterattack with power.)

As you study model answers, envision yourself writing answers that flow as logically as they do. Realize how much easier it is to read an exam that is clear than one that is disorganized. Make your answers simple to follow, with key points labeled for the grader. Make it easy for graders to see and understand what you have written. State what you have to say plainly and obviously. Do not try to sound particularly witty or funny. The grader may not share your sense of humor.

Visualize yourself in the exam. Every day, take a moment to picture yourself thinking and typing, having your words flow. Every time you do a practice test, visualize doing it in that test setting. Picture yourself in that exam room, calm and confident. Breathe deeply and slowly. Believe you *can* pass. Positive thinking is critical! Tell yourself every day you *can* do it. Say it aloud several times each day.

SHOULD I POSTPONE TAKING THE BAR UNTIL THE NEXT ADMINISTRATION?

By the end of June, there are always students who question whether they should take the exam. They made a good-faith commitment to pass and began bar review with all the right intentions, but something interfered with total immersion. Sometimes the student or a close family member falls ill or, because of job or personal responsibilities, the student was unable to give bar review his or her all. To determine whether it is best to defer taking the exam (which, in some circumstances, it may be), it is critical to distinguish whether this is just nerves or whether the student is grossly underprepared. (Discuss this with a trusted mentor or ASP faculty member who can help you see where you are.) I almost always have to talk people "off the ledge" around the beginning of July. Just about everyone feels overwhelmed, and feels like they will "never learn it all." *That is normal.* It is not a reason to defer. Other people genuinely are not where they need to be by the end of June, will not have time to catch up in July, and would be better served by waiting. (There is no magic formula to say where you need to be, but if, for instance, you have not listened to or understood a great deal of the bar review lecture material, or if you have done few practice tests, you may well have fallen too far behind to catch up.) If you find yourself in this position, look honestly at July and see if you can make up the time to master what you need to learn. If not, consider deferring and putting yourself on an extended study plan to slowly and surely get ready for the next administration. There is no shame in this decision, so long as it is well reasoned. You will still be considered a first-time passer if you wait until February and pass then. Again, normal nerves hit everyone, but going into the exam knowing you have not adequately prepared is a setup for failure.

Envision success to achieve success

See success in your mind's eye. If you are a verbal person, write a short description of your goal(s). Write as specifically as possible. If you are a visual person, develop an image of yourself in the successful role you are working toward. First, get a good picture of yourself in your cap and gown, with all the graduation regalia. Sit with those visuals. Let it sink in deeply how the image symbolizes the realization of years of hard work. (In most schools, graduation is held before bar review begins, so you can keep a graduation photo on your desk or computer while you study for the bar.)

Next, imagine yourself in the room of applicants, reading questions; finding issues; and writing solid, strong, logical analyses. Calm, confident, and strong, you are!

Now, picture yourself standing before a judge being sworn in to the state bar—being asked to take that oath to uphold the laws of your state. See your own smile and the pride of those who come to witness.

Then, see yourself as a lawyer. Stand before the mirror and introduce yourself as a lawyer. Use the words, "Hello, nice to meet you. My name is _____ and I am an attorney here in [your state]." (Revisit Chapter 3.)

Eliminate distractions and focus fully

When you started working, you *reduced* distractions; when you are closing in on your goal, *eliminate* them. During this last month, shut virtually everything down. Review the passages on distractions in Chapter 4. Until it's over, give this exam your single-minded, total focus.

That said, do not start the last laps too early. It's only in this final stretch that you must zero in on the ultimate goal. When you first set your goal, you needed to get in the work groove—plan how to achieve, and work slowly and steadily toward success. If you put in too much effort too early on, you tend to peak and burn out before the exam. (In plain English, if you spend twenty-hour days studying in June and are ready to take the exam on July 1, you have peaked too early.)

During the home stretch, you must cocoon. In those last weeks and days it must be all bar exam, all the time. You must learn to be self-centered in a way that allows for success. (If you want company or need a study break, do what it takes to ensure that these are positives. Avoid any negative thing or person, as much as possible. Reread Chapter 6 if you need help getting away from naysayers, or stepping back and taking a break from people you love but just don't have time for now.)

For many of you, this part will be extremely difficult. Others will get in the way—intentionally or accidentally. Distractions and procrastination enticements will come in every shape and size. You may feel guilty spending so much time on yourself. Don't. You have to. This is what is necessary to achieve great things. You have worked too hard to lose the edge now. You must remain in high gear. This is your Super Bowl, your Mount Everest, the day you make your Broadway debut. It is whatever feels huge and awesome to you. And it's fast approaching.

ARE YOU AFRAID? GREAT! THAT MEANS YOU'RE HONEST AND REALISTIC.

This is a huge challenge. It is doable but not easy. Do not feel weak because you are nervous. Fear can be a good thing! (Especially if you redefine it and use it productively.) Redefine fear? Yes. Try calling it *respect*. (Do you hear Aretha? I do! And if that's not power, I don't know what is.) It sounds pretty different to say "I have a healthy respect for the challenge," rather than "I'm afraid," right? With the first phrasing, you sound like an athlete facing a worthy opponent. Control the fear; don't let it control you. Let it not paralyze but propel you forward, toward the success you deserve! Use fears to boost productivity. When fear meets adrenaline, you can turn it into its productive counterpart: powerful energy. Use the power to be *on* big time—highly alert and extremely motivated. (See the discussion on combating anxiety in Chapter 7. Also, there are a number of articles noted in the Bibliography that discuss anxiety as a key factor in bar exam failure.)

"COURAGE IS RESISTANCE TO FEAR, MASTERY OF FEAR—NOT ABSENCE OF FEAR."

— MARK TWAIN —

Simulated exams as the "dress rehearsal"

Make a simulated exam part of your plan (either with your bar review, with your law school ASP program, or independently). Taking a simulated bar exam can give you a much-needed reality check. If you identify weak areas, study those. You can see what times of day you have the most energy and when you are dragging. The real exam will seem less daunting after making it through a trial run. You gain the confidence to believe that you can intelligently reason through anything they throw at you.

A simulated exam helps you plan logistics. You will see how long you can physically sit and write before you need to stand up and stretch, you can decide what you should eat for lunch for maximum efficiency, you can plan some warm-up exercises before the exam begins (outlining one essay or going over your one-page approaches). And simulating the exam helps you to practice your timing so you stay on target and finish.

DON'T LET YOUR SIMULATED EXAM FREAK YOU OUT.

Do not get psyched out. Simulated exams help you when they provide an opportunity to make necessary adjustments before the real thing. For many reasons, however, simulated exams are *not* necessarily a referendum on how you will actually perform on the bar. They are an opportunity to get lots of useful information. Use that data wisely. Use the time left to improve!

You don't have to take the real thing today. It's still some time away. (It may not feel like a lot of time, but think about how much you were able to learn in one day before certain finals! There is still a lot you can clarify.)

- Your simulated exam may have been harder than the real exam.
- The real thing is a pass/fail test; you don't have to get an A.
- The simulated exam can help you strategize ways to plan actual exam days to maximize energy and efficiency.

Simulated Exam Assessment

After completing a simulated bar exam, ask the following questions:

Did you bring in a watch? Could you see a clock from where you were sitting while taking the practice test? Did you budget your time well? (For example, let's say you had to complete three essays in three hours; did you actually spend one-and-a-half hours on essay #1 and find you had next to no time left by the time you got to essay #3?) You may need to watch the clock more carefully and be vigilant in limiting your time on each question. Note your thoughts and observations—points you want to remind yourself about timing:

_____

_____

Were you tired after lunch? What foods did you eat at lunch? How much did you eat? Perhaps you can eat a bit less and take some of that lunch hour to walk and burn off some stress or listen to motivating music. Thoughts on food and fatigue:

_____

_____

Did you "blank out" on any questions? If so, get a plan ready to work through a temporary "brain freeze" should one occur next week. (See more on test anxiety in Chapter 7.) Thoughts on dealing with test anxiety:

_____

_____

Were there any subjects you hoped would not be on your exam? Look at those again now. Try not to go in with an exposed weakness.

_____

_____

The days before the exam: getting ready

- Review your condensed outlines—the "cheat sheets" we talked about earlier. Put the big outlines on the shelf. (Use them to look up rules if you realize you still don't know something after erring on practice questions, but no more reading long outlines. No time left to do that.)
- Memorize rules. You have been memorizing slowly and surely for months. Now is the time for your final push. Aim for instant recall of all key rules.
- Read numerous fact patterns and model answers. Read them aloud. Retype some of them. Tune your ear to success.
- Visit the test site ahead of time, if possible. Even the day before, walk by and see if you can at least look in the room and get a feel for the surroundings. The "vibe" in the room will be stressful. There will be lots of nervous energy. People may be snippy, or downright rude. Don't let anything faze you. It's all about the exam and you. Keep your own head clear. Stay *calm* and *confident* (your "two Cs" on bar days.)
- Keep your daily routine. (Drink your coffee or whatever you have when you wake up just like you do every day. Continue to exercise. Eat regular meals.)
- In the days before the exam, if you cannot focus on any sort of review or study, then exercise, eat well, and sleep. Or go to a movie! Do whatever will get your body and mind ready for peak performance.

NO ONE KNOWS *THE* RIGHT THING FOR *YOU* ON THE DAYS BEFORE THE EXAM.

Some people will say study. Others will say, "Whatever you do, do not study." It does not matter what others say. It's *your* exam. Do what works for *you*. Does reviewing more essays, more MBEs, and your one-page sheets calm you or make you more nervous? What have you done successfully to prepare for other big events or challenges in your life? (Think perhaps of the LSAT or SAT, a big game you played in, or theatrical production you starred in.) Do whatever works to get you focused for success.

Plan the event: What you will do on test days and nights

The more control you have over your environment, the more you will feel in control on the exam. (If you are taking the exam at an unfamiliar test site, you may want to get there a day or two ahead of time to acclimate.)

Psyche out positively. Do what you need to do to be in peak form. You are preparing for battle; your keyboard (or pen) is your sword.

Determine well ahead of time what you can and cannot bring with you in the exam room. Have snacks or meals waiting for you in your room or a plan as to what and where you will eat at the breaks.

Sleep. Get as good a night's sleep as you can on nights before test days. You may be tempted to stay up all night studying just a bit more. There is always more to study! But now you are definitely at a place of diminishing returns. Stop. Sleep. And, rest if you cannot sleep. Why? Let's say you go in well rested, but the guy next to you stayed up all night and indeed learned or memorized some key rules of law that you don't know or remember. Is he better off? No. You are. Much of the bar exam is reading comprehension and analysis, skills you will perform more effectively if you are well rested.

For some, it helps to think of the test not as several days long but as a number of distinct sessions, each of which is about as long as many of your law school finals were. (Take the California bar, for example. In its current format, as of the writing of this edition, the exam lasts three days. That sounds so long! But if you think of it as six three-hour tests, it sounds more doable.)

THE BAR EXAM MAY NOT BE THE HARDEST DAY OF *YOUR* LIFE.

A secret for working students with families: a day where all you have to do is sit and work, uninterrupted, may feel like a break. Several of my students who are professionals with young children confess this. The bar is supposed to be the hardest of all, but compared with these students' day-to-day lives, it is much more straightforward. There is one responsibility and one only, unlike work days where the juggling never seems to end: demands from bosses and clients, spouses, parents, and children; not to mention leaky faucets, broken car parts, computer viruses, and bills to pay. I am reminded of a cartoon that a friend expecting one baby sent a friend expecting twins. The cartoon showed five women, each phoning another. The woman with one baby phoned the woman with two babies, the woman with twins phoned the woman with triplets, and so one. Each one simply said, "How was your day?" It's truly all about perspective.

Getting dressed on exam days

First, dress in layers. One day they may crank up the air conditioning in the exam room, but the next day it may feel like a furnace. (Someone might have complained the day prior or there may be a power failure and the air conditioning breaks down.) Expect the unexpected, and remember your task: be fully present and clear-headed, and read and answer every question to the best of your ability. It can throw you if you are too hot or too cold. Dressing in layers gives you a bit of control over your environment.

Second, dress for success. For many of you, that may mean dressing as comfortably as possible—for example sweats, jeans, maybe leggings. (Shorts and flip-flops are prohibited in some locations. Check your rules to see if there is a dress code.) Other people feel more powerful dressing in business attire, as if going to work. One former student said she wore a suit; it made her feel like an attorney and she wrote with confidence. Whatever you put on, make sure you feel good and strong.

DRESSING TO INTIMIDATE

Many years ago, I met some former students on the evening of the last day of their bar exam. They regaled several of us with tales of bar exam lunches. Among other stories, they described a group of people seated at a nearby table, wearing sweatshirts from a highly prestigious law school. They were, seemingly, drinking beer. She had no way of knowing what school they were really from, or whether the "beer" in their glasses was indeed alcoholic. Nor does it matter. Her perception was that they were staging bravado to try to intimidate other exam takers. (People often tell of leaving a morning session only to have another applicant ask something like, "Did you see the business organizations crossover issues on that contracts question?" knowing full well that it was a straight contracts question without any business organizations issues at all.) As with many of life's greatest challenges, the bar exam may bring out the best in people, or their most competitive, nastiest side.

Third, wear your lucky socks! OK, I'm joking a bit here, but not entirely. If you have some piece of clothing or tradition that makes you feel lucky, go with it. You are not alone. You are in good company with some of the nation's most successful lawyers.[45]

Set out ahead of time what you plan to bring into the test site with you on exam days.

Determine what you are allowed to bring into the exam with you and get it all ready so you know you're not missing anything. Be sure to bring your paperwork: admission ticket, identification, and anything else you will need. Many jurisdictions require you to bring everything in a clear plastic bag. No purses, backpacks, or briefcases. Bar examiners are very strict about what you may bring in and what you may not. No fooling around. Can you imagine failing the bar because you inadvertently wore the wrong kind of watch? It has happened. Do not let it happen to you. Read the rules carefully. (And read them all. The rules on the MBE day may differ from the rules on other days.)

I have read the bar rules and am allowed to bring in the following (perhaps include black ink pens, ear phones, paper clips):

_____

_____

_____

I am not allowed to bring in (for example, Post-its, wallet, food):

_____

_____

_____

Now, what will be in your clear plastic bag?

_____

_____

_____

Bathroom breaks on the bar exam

If you need to use the restroom during the exam, that's fine. Don't try to hold it and get distracted with discomfort. Do make the most of the break, though, by reading the next question before you go, then mentally outlining while you are gone. Return, thoughts organized, and get back to work.

Listen to instructions and pay attention to what proctors say

You will get instructions on when to start (and they may make you wait a while). They will tell you when to stop, and they may rattle off a host of other details. Listen carefully. Be polite and attentive to proctors. They are in charge. A proctor may tell you that you must wait to go to the bathroom or leave the room. (Do not get up and leave the room without permission.) Do what they tell you.

Be careful what you eat before and between each testing session

Remember, use practice test days and simulated exam days to figure out which foods for which meals make you most productive. Some people find the best bar exam breakfasts are small but healthy meals, with protein and carbs but nothing too greasy, spicy, or unusual. (Do not eat anything that smells spoiled or in any way seems like it might not be fresh.) For bar lunches, again don't eat too much or anything that makes you sleepy. (Many people avoid turkey sandwiches for this reason.) Some popular lunches are peanut butter with bread and salad with chicken or beef for protein. It can be wise to avoid big desserts and excessive caffeine on bar days, focusing instead on foods for lasting energy. (For example, you do not want a sugar high at lunch that falls into a groggy low in the middle of the afternoon session.)

Be careful where and with whom you eat

The restaurants at test sites are often very crowded. (They may have to serve hundreds of people at once.) You can avoid the crowd and get the food you want without a long wait either by bringing a lunch with you, or from your hotel's room service (especially if you can order the lunch in the morning so that it's ready when you are allowed to leave for the break). If you are staying in a hotel room that has a refrigerator, you might consider stocking it with healthy to-go options. This is a good choice if you have dietary restrictions. (One of my students who keeps kosher found it much easier to bring her own food than to have to worry about the food at or near the bar exam site. I have also heard that from students who were vegans or on gluten-free diets.) Another student who had heard my tips and packed her own lunch was particularly happy because she and a number of other applicants seated near her were kept in the exam room for a while after others were released for lunch because of some issue that had occurred during the morning session. Those seated next to her who did not have lunches simply did not get to eat during that break. There was no time left to order and wait for food at the restaurant.

Some people do well eating with friends who are also taking the bar; some avoid other bar applicants completely. Will your classmates make you more nervous? If so, stay away from them. Stay away from anyone who does not make you feel great during exam days. (Remember Chapter 6, lose the naysayers—something even more important during actual bar days than it was during study days.)

Manage your stress and don't be thrown by curveballs.
Listen when the proctors are giving instructions. During the exam, breathe and sit up tall. During breaks, listen to power music or close your eyes and rest.

Expect the unexpected: an earthquake or power outage during the exam, or the person next to you getting up and walking out, never to return. Strange and disconcerting things happen during exams. If something unplanned happens to you, adapt. Do what you need to do to continue on as unfazed as possible. These will be your crazy bar horror stories. Remember this book's introduction: we all have one!

"'COME TO THE EDGE,' HE SAID. THEY SAID, 'WE ARE AFRAID.' 'COME TO THE EDGE,' HE SAID. THEY CAME. HE PUSHED THEM . . . AND THEY FLEW."

— GUILLAUME APOLLINAIRE —

The exam is your time to push off that edge and fly, to soar to success. Keep in mind not just the fears you may feel when you're poised to jump, but the excitement and empowerment that come with meeting the challenge. You are close to that edge now. You are ready to go. Sure, it's scary. It's supposed to be. But you are ready. You can fly.

Some things to remember when you go in: the fact patterns that will be placed before you are all stories. They may be about contractual agreements entered into and broken, marriages fallen apart with assets left to be divided, crimes of passion. Read them like puzzles; every fact is there on the paper for you. Let it be interesting!

Think of yourself as walking through the ultimate cocktail party, where each cluster of people tells you stories and problems. For each, you have advice: good, solid, sound, and rationally reasoned answers! In your mind are rules that help unravel how each of those stories can play out. If they might well go one way or another, say that. ("Defendant will argue; plaintiff will argue; and the likely conclusion will be . . .") Read your exam questions, your "bar stories," and feel the incredible power that comes with knowing you can do that unraveling. You can and will pick each fact pattern apart and put it back together in a logical way that answers the questions asked. (Have you ever thought about *the bar exam* as a cocktail party? I know there is an alcohol pun there. Unintended. What is intended is something I have been reiterating from page one. You can view this experience as punishment if you so choose, or you can see it as a welcome challenge. You can grow and learn from every aspect of preparation and performance.)

Take in and appreciate the feeling of richness that comes from having this many rules at your command. It's like being ready to run a marathon knowing that all your muscles are strong. The intellectual flab has melted away these past two months, through the long hours of mental work out. There are few if any times in your life when you will have this many rules in this many subjects memorized, at your fingertips, and ready to go. In daily work as a lawyer, one may almost always look up information. Here, all the rules you need will be packed into your memory in a usable place, ready to be called upon.

Appreciate how strong your wings are. When day one of your bar exam approaches, push off despite the fears. Push off with as much confidence as you can muster. You are ready.

A walk through your bar days

The famous race car driver Bobby Unser once said, "Success is where preparation and opportunity meet." Your opportunity comes when you walk into that exam room and stays with you until the last "time" is called. When you start your engines, be ready to succeed!

Exercise: Notes to yourself for bar days

Alright, let's say it's Tuesday, day 1 of your bar exam. What is your plan of action (POA) this morning? What do you want to eat at breakfast? At breakfast, do you want to outline one or two essays to warm up, so that the ones you see on the exam are not the first of the day, so your mind is limber? You have your timing down; you have your approaches and your systems for reading and answering the types of questions that will appear on this session. What else do you want to remember before going into the first segment of your exam? (What language will you use to talk yourself out of anxiety if nerves turn to panic? Remember, you will be nervous and that's OK. Just use it as energy to power through. But you have also trained and have a plan about what to do to combat nerves if they start dragging you down.)

_____

_____

_____

What will lunch look like? Whom do you want to lunch with? What will you try to eat?

_____

_____

_____

What is your POA for the afternoon session? What might be tested? Essays? A PT? What would you want to look at or listen to at lunch to get you pumped up for the afternoon? Do you want to tell yourself anything going in?

_____

_____

_____

Have a great dinner. Do not experiment with any foods that might make you ill. Do not drink excessively. And remember, no matter how you think you did, the first day is over. (I always think of the Cat Stevens song "Tuesday's Dead" on Tuesday evenings of the bar exam. Bar exams often start on Tuesdays.) It's all about the future now. Do not look back. Do not second-guess yourself or allow in any doubts. I have seen far too many students fail because of a perceived "defeat" early on that they carried into later sessions. This also applies to individual questions. Let go of whatever is done and do your very best on each and every minute that follows. It is not over until the last "time" is called. And, success on this exam is *not* about perfection. It's a pass/fail test. This *is* your Olympics, but here winning bronze is every bit as good as gold.

What will you do this evening?

_____

_____

_____

Now day 2. Wednesday, MBE day. What do you want to do this morning? (Look over your one-page sheets for MBE subjects, do a few MBEs as warm-ups over breakfast?)

_____

_____

_____

Day 2 Lunch?

_____

_____

_____

Afternoon? 100 more questions.

_____

_____

_____

Day 2 Dinner?

_____

_____

_____

Day 3, if you have one on your bar (truly _the_ home stretch)
What will the morning of day 3 look like? What do you want to remind yourself?

_____

_____

_____

Day 3 Lunch?

_____

_____

_____

Day 3 Afternoon? The very last lap. Keep that energy high. Just being fully awake and focused will give you a great edge because others around you will be dragging. What do you want to tell yourself going in?

_____

_____

_____

After the bar, maybe head to a bar, one that serves drinks! Or go to a nice dinner? Or sleep? Or . . .

_____

_____

_____

Handy lists for bar days

Below are "Top Ten Tips" lists for each type of testing: essays, MBEs, and PTs. These summarize the main strategy points made earlier and are meant to be lists you can grab and look at just before the bar, and possibly during nights or breaks between bar sessions. Just as you did with your one page "cheat sheets" for each subject tested, personalize these strategy sheets. Add your own notes and reminders about particular parts of your exam.

Top Ten Test-Taking Tips: Essays
Ten: Finish the question

A final heading with the word _conclusion_ in it can signify to graders that you finished. So can wording in your final paragraph such as _in conclusion_ or _in sum_.

Nine: Avoid abbreviations, slang, and humor

Let your grader's focus be on seeing the main and important points you have made. Do not distract or confuse the grader. (Remember, you are on an "interview," so write in a lawyerly tone.) Avoid the first person. Focus on what the facts _prove_ and why, not on what you think.

Eight: Avoid canned speeches

Graders do not want to see that you can spit back lengthy, memorized portions of your outline. (Regurgitating law statements is something most people can do.) Graders want to see that you *understand* the law at issue here in this particular exam and how the facts in this fact pattern prove or disprove elements of applicable rules of law.

Seven: Avoid irrelevant discussions

You will not impress a grader by discussing issues that do not bear on the problem at hand or are not raised by the facts given.

Six: Give arguments for both sides

Often, facts cut both ways. (Stated otherwise, different inferences can be drawn from the same facts.) Keep in mind the phrase "Plaintiff will argue on the one hand . . . defendant will argue on the other hand. . . ." Remember that the A (analysis) in IRAC, or, as we discussed in Chapter 8, the P (proof) in IRPC, is more important than the C. (And remember that you may conclude in a qualified manner, "it appears on balance that the plaintiff is likely to prevail"; as long as you have substantiated the reasons in your analysis and discussed thoroughly what both sides will argue, you do not have to "know" who will prevail.)

Five: Answer the question or questions asked!

If the question asks for the theories upon which Patty might recover, do not address the claims, however interesting they may be, of Paul.

Best advice here is to read the call of the question first. Read it again after reading the facts, and read it periodically as you proceed through writing your answer to be sure you are being responsive.

Likewise, if a question asks about guilt or liability of two defendants, it is often wise not to lump them together; it is usually better to separate them and assess the differences and similarities. Note, though, where the same legal standard applies in two different lawsuits or to two different defendants, you do not need to write the law out twice. You can say "see above," and incorporate your discussion.

Four: Key in to the difference between "racehorse" questions (those with many issues) and "think-'em" questions (those with fewer issues).

Exams may have many issues that you need to discuss fairly quickly in order to analyze each one and still finish in time. Other exams have a smaller number of issues that require more-in-depth analysis. Be able to distinguish between these types of exams so you can handle each effectively, and still complete the exam.

Three: Make your logic explicit

Avoid writing in a conclusory manner. Make your reasoning complete and transparent. Proceed step by step, showing what the rule is and exactly why the facts satisfy or fail to satisfy the rule. Do not assume the grader knows what is in your head.

Two: Analyze all the discussable issues

A discussable issue is a question raised by the facts. Note that what makes an issue relevant to discussion in a typical bar exam is not whether the moving party will or will not prevail in a particular legal claim. Analyzing why a rule is not satisfied, given the facts present and facts lacking, may be just as important to your success on bar exams as showing how, in another cause of action, the moving party may prevail. Be sure to spot and discuss all of the significant questions the facts raise.

One: Write in an organized manner

Make the grader's life easy. Let the grader see that you can take a complex set of facts, and proceed through your analysis of them in a logical manner. Where legal rules break down into elements, or tests break down into components or factors, organize your reasoning using these as tools.

Top Ten Test-Taking Tips: MBEs

Ten: When you are close to the end of the morning or afternoon MBE session guess on any questions you don't finish or don't know.

Nine: Try to reason through to the correct answer from reading the interrogatory and facts without first looking at the answer choices.

Eight: Look for and cross out answer choices that have internally incorrect or inconsistent statements.

Seven: Look for and cross out answer choices that didn't answer the question asked. (There will be a best answer. One thing that makes an answer the best choice is that it focuses on the exact thread in the question. So, once again, read and reread the question.)

Six: Make sure you are bubbling in the correct answer number and answer choice on the Scantron.

Five: Cross out answer choices you know are wrong, and have a system to keep track of questions you have to guess at so that you can come back to them if you finish early and have extra time.

Four: Watch the clock and do thirty-three questions each hour.

Three: Read the answer choices carefully. (Review Chapter 8 on "bar reading." Read with your finger or pencil, your eyes, and your voice at the same time.)

Two: Read the facts carefully, using "bar reading" techniques.

One: Read the interrogatory carefully, again using "bar reading."

Top Ten Test-Taking Tips: PTs

Ten: Complete the task or tasks requested in the task memo. Let the grader know you finished.

Nine: Avoid abbreviations, slang, and humor. Do not distract or confuse the grader.

Eight: Use every main case cited in the library.

Seven: Be aware of who your client is and what your client needs or wants. Look for this information in both the task memo and the file.

Six: Use the appropriate tone for your audience. Know whom you are writing to and why. (Adopt a more formal approach when writing to those outside of your office, especially the court, and, if appropriate, a more casual tone when writing to another lawyer on your team.)

Five: Outline before writing. Find a logical way to organize. (Remember, there is often more than one effective way to organize so do not spend time worrying that you haven't found the roadmap. Create your own. But know that organization is critical.)

Four: Remember that much of what is in the file is irrelevant or redundant. Do not feel obligated to find a way to use every fact in the file.

Three: If you are asked to draft more than one document and the instructions make clear how much each is worth, respect those percentages and apportion your time accordingly.

Two: Use headings. Even in a task that does not normally include headings, such as a letter or closing argument to the jury, use headings and subheadings so that the grader can easily see (and has guideposts to) your organization.

One: Read the task memo carefully and read it several times. (Review this after the file, after the library, and again while you are drafting your outline and maybe even your answer.) If ever you feel stalled, reread the task memo. It is the most important document in a PT.

10

CELEBRATE YOUR ACHIEVEMENT, AND ACKNOWLEDGE AND THANK THOSE WHO HELPED YOU (THEN SET YOUR NEXT GOAL!)

- You did it. You completed your bar exam! (Now you wait, and wait, for results)
  - Just before results come out
- You did it. You passed the bar exam. Congratulations. (Now set your next goal!)
  - What if you passed but a close friend or classmate did not?
  - Finding a job (if you don't already have one)
  - Interviewing strategies
  - Transferable skills
- Bar exam success takeaways: What can you say you learned from preparing for, taking, and passing this exam that will help you in the future?
  - Keep learning and keep all doors open

FEELING GRATITUDE AND NOT EXPRESSING IT IS LIKE WRAPPING A PRESENT AND NOT GIVING IT.

— WILLIAM ARTHUR WARD —

This sounds silly; after all, you don't *know* yet that you passed. But it is really important to validate your hard work and acknowledge the support of those who helped you! Plan ahead so that a trip or some special celebration awaits after you finish the exam. It will keep your family or significant other on board (and willing to wait for you). It helps them stay on your side. It gives everyone something to look forward to and helps you see that light in the distance.

YOU DID IT. YOU COMPLETED YOUR BAR EXAM! (NOW, YOU WAIT, AND WAIT, FOR RESULTS.)

Enjoy your after-bar celebration. Having a big reward to look forward to will help you get through June and July. You don't want to be working so hard each day that you feel like it will just never end. (*Poor me, gotta study, then gotta work, then more work, then when I pass the bar it's even more work.*) No! No way. If life feels like all work and no reward, you will lose your stamina. You need to keep up the energy, and keep it flowing until they call time on that last day of the exam. Have something fun planned when it's over to celebrate *having done your best*. You can live with whatever results arrive when you know you gave it your all. *You owe it to yourself to leave the exam able to honestly say, "I did my best."* Think about that if you are ever wondering, *"Should I do one more practice test today?"* (If you can productively keep going, the answer is yes, of course you should. Push yourself while you have the chance, while you are training for the exam. You do not want to say that you could have and should have done more.)

Note: An after-bar trip does not have to be costly. If funds are tight, consider camping or even a local outdoor day trip, picnic, movie day, or other fun escape.

Just before the results come out

If the months before the exam are hard, those last days before results are released are crazy nerve racking. (*Huge* understatement.) But wait you must. At the appointed time, you will log onto your state bar's website with ID number in hand, and with a click you will know.

If you passed, which I very much hope you did (!), then you may be looking for a new job or possibly working hard at one already. If you did not pass this time, you will need to pull every ounce of confidence together to learn from this experience and train for success in February.

Be especially kind to yourself just before the results come out. It's horribly stressful. Go see a funny movie. Take an afternoon off for a hike or walk. Have a bubble bath and champagne. Distract yourself with positives. You are smart and worthy, regardless of this one test result. Surround yourself with good and positive people who will love and support you no matter what.

If you are a friend or family member of someone awaiting results, be even more kind. Dredge up every ounce of respect and compassion you can find. Back off, and wait to see what that person wants from you. Give them space. Provide comfort and laughter when that is called for. Be a positive distraction. Realize that even if your loved one is not expressing it, he or she is consumed with getting on that site and finding out, one way or another.

YOU DID IT. YOU PASSED THE BAR EXAM! CONGRATULATIONS! (NOW, SET YOUR NEXT GOAL!)

Your swearing-in ceremony will mark this achievement. Throw yourself a party or let someone else throw you one! This is a big accomplishment. Be very proud. Whatever you do with it, as long as you remain ethical, this is a lifetime stamp of credibility. Guard this license.

If you did not pass, skip to Part II of this book.

What if you pass but a close friend or classmate didn't?

As you prepare to look up your own results, and get ready to hear news from friends and classmates, prepare for the possibility that someone you care about didn't make it. Given pass rates generally, it's likely that at least someone in your circle or even your study group won't see his or her name on that pass list. It's rough to be the one who didn't make it when friends did but it is also painful to console people who you know should have made it.

Some face that challenge of having to retake the exam easier than others, especially people who may have been working full-time or otherwise knew they had not given it their all. But it's never easy. It almost always means a game plan must be devised, a way to prevail must be developed, and then a new strategy for success must be realized.

Think of news generally. In so many ways, this bar exam news mirrors the way all of life's news comes. One day it's a call from someone offering you or a loved one a promotion, the position you always dreamed of, a vote of confidence, a moment in the sunshine, an opportunity for change. Maybe it's a call to say a new, healthy baby was born. Then, another day, it's a call from a close friend, your age, who has just been diagnosed with cancer and is facing surgery, chemo, radiation, and the challenges of trying to rebuild a semblance of normalcy when their very core has been shaken.

Is it hyperbole or offensive to equate bar results with news of a life-threatening illness? It isn't meant offensively, so if it's taken that way, I apologize. What it's meant to acknowledge is how important this news is. Unless you have taken the bar exam, it's hard to convey just how big it feels. You work and dream of law school for a long time, then you work for three or four of the hardest years ever, then you study intensively, giving everything you have for another several months before taking a grueling, multi-day exam. After that, you wait even longer for results.

Many who are unfamiliar with law and law school think the bar exam is just another test. It is not. While it should not be, people will make it a referendum on your personal success. It's bigger than any test you have ever taken and likely ever will.

Be as supportive as you can. Remember, many successful lawyers have failed the bar once, if not more than once. Stick around for your friends.

Finding a job (if you don't already have one)

If bar pass rate statistics did not scare you, current employment data may. But just as fear was not helpful on the exam itself, do not let it paralyze your job search. Note: most of the following are thoughts for those who are *not* graduates of top-tier schools, but some of the ideas may help everyone. And, these are just some suggestions. There are many excellent career-related resources you can and should consult.[46]

- Consult quality books, articles, blogs, and other career resources.
- Get a career mentor. (Reread Chapter 6 on finding a bar mentor.) Look for someone who will brainstorm with you about job hunting, help keep you on track, and help keep you from getting discouraged.
- Go on lots of interviews. The more you do, the more confident you will be! The nervousness you may feel on a first interview should dissipate after going on a few. So get going!

How to get an interview?

- Carefully and regularly read as many online job postings as possible.
- Go to law school career centers. (As an alumnus, you should have access to great resources through the career counselor and career center at your law school. Other law schools in your area may also have open-door policies. Ask around. And be polite! Storming in and displacing frustration about the job market onto these people will make them less inclined to want to help you.).

- Tell everyone you know you are looking for a job and ask them to keep their ears open.
- Write to law firms or lawyers whose work interests you (and ask for an informational interview. See if they will just meet you for coffee to tell you about what they do. After talking, if it seems appropriate, ask if they know of anyone who might need to hire a new lawyer.)
- Ask one of your former law professors to meet with you. See if he or she has ideas on where you might apply for a job. Profs often stay in touch with students and hear about people doing interesting work. Some may do their own consulting work in law firms or nonprofits.

FIND A CAREER MENTOR.

A career mentor is someone who can help you strategize about finding job opportunities or whether to take a job opportunity that comes along. The person can also help you plan steps to advance in your career or change jobs, if that is your goal. Throughout my professional career, I have regularly sought the advice of trusted colleagues who were either older and more experienced or would have a different perspective and thus help me think of points I had not considered. I meet with a mentor when I am offered a new professional opportunity, and talk regularly about how best to grow within the work I pursue. I encourage you to ask experienced lawyers, professors, or other professionals you trust to help you think through possibilities; to help you in finding suitable jobs if you are in job search mode; and to help you advance in whatever position you are in or transition to some other opportunity, if that is your goal. Think carefully about potential career mentors. Does he or she have insight into the field you are interested in? Will he or she push a particular agenda or help you decide what you want? Will the person be jealous that you have these opportunities and not be helpful at all? Certain people may be helpful at one point in your career but you may need to look for another mentor at a different stage. Reach out. Decide for yourself what you think is best, but listen to the wisdom of those who have gone before you.

Some interviewing strategies

Again, many of the quality resources on employment opportunities for lawyers have extensive and helpful advice on both live, in-person interviews and telephone interviews (which are increasingly common.) The list below represents just a few points to keep in mind, after you get your foot in the door for an interview:

- Make the best impression possible.
- Dress well—and appropriately! How you look is part of how you sell yourself. Make sure your clothes fit well, fit in, and are clean.
- Arrive on time (better still, arrive early).
- Bring an extra resume with you. Bring a writing sample, if appropriate. Put those documents in a portfolio or binder in which you also include some blank paper if there is anything you want to note.
- Study up ahead of time on the people who will interview you. Google the institution and the individuals. Study the company, organization or law firm. Determine its philosophy. Find out what cases individuals have worked on. Read anything they have published. Get their resumes. Find out where they went to school. Note any points you may have in common with them.
- Develop two lists of questions: 1) what the interviewers may ask you, and 2) what you will ask them! Prepare your responses to what they will likely ask you. (How do you stand out? Why will you be successful? How will you help their office, practice, company?) Next, try to list at least three things you want to know about them. Asking questions is important—it shows your enthusiasm, curiosity, and intelligence. Pay close attention to the answers, so you can follow up, too.
- Send a thank-you note after the interview!

Volunteering

While waiting for bar results, you can boost your legal resume by volunteering in a legal clinic or for a lawyer in a law office. You can perform many helpful tasks without a license, including intake interviews and legal research. Depending on who the supervising attorneys are and how much time you have to give, they may even allow you to draft motions or come to court to listen to arguments and help out. Many organizations need part-time help on weekends or evenings, so this is something you can do even if you are working a full-time, nonlaw job or law job you know will not be permanent. To find places or people who need volunteers, call your local bar association or law school career placement center. You can also call or send resumes to organizations directly and find alumni from your law school who may have worked on an organization and can give you an introduction. Part of the reason for volunteering is to gain experience with legal work. Another reason is to get to know some lawyers and have them see that you are responsible and show up when you say you will, you have a logical mind, and you are willing to pay your dues. Lawyers tend to know lots of other lawyers, and a good word from a colleague may add an invaluable touch to even the most distinguished of resumes.

Transferable skills

To prove that you can perform well, think of skills and qualities of an effective lawyer.[47] List specific experiences that evidence your possessing these attributes. Consider what you do in and outside of school, including with work, family, community, professional, or political organizations you belong to or volunteer for. Think also about hobbies you pursue. In the spaces below, write examples of experiences that demonstrate your skills. Be as specific as possible. This is just for your brainstorming. You will translate this into a cover letter and perhaps into talking points for an interview.

I have good research skills:

_____

_____

I communicate well:

_____

_____

I reason well:

_____

_____

I am organized and responsible:

_____

_____

I am technologically competent (savvy):

_____

_____

BAR EXAM SUCCESS TAKEAWAYS: WHAT CAN YOU SAY YOU LEARNED FROM PREPARING FOR, TAKING, AND PASSING THIS EXAM THAT WILL HELP YOU IN THE FUTURE?

You have passed the bar exam. You have proved to yourself and the world that you can pull a ton of disparate material together *in your head* and write about it logically, reason, and think. This is impressive. This is important. You have shown yourself able to withstand significant pressure without imploding.

A former student, a recent law school graduate for whom law was a second career, asked me to write a letter of recommendation. He sent the following documents: his resume, the cover letter he had written to the person I was to write to, the job description, and some information he wrote directly to me about why he wanted the job and why he thought his background would help him thrive on the job. He joked that he was now giving *me* an assignment that looked a lot like a PT! The more I thought about it, the more accurate he was.

What did we say in Chapter 8 was the most important piece of the PT? The task memo. The first thing I did was read the student's request several times, and follow up confirming when he needed the letter and how (by mail or e-mail). I then had to figure out the appropriate tone for this audience. Whom was I writing to? Who am I? Whom do I represent? I had to sort through a bunch of documents that contained much information that was irrelevant to this job. His resume alone was nearly five pages! I had to decide on my format. (And I rewrote the letter numerous times after printing it to ensure that the format was clear and pleasing to the eye.) *I am a law professor, but my letter will be less credible if it is not formatted in an easy-to-read manner*, I reasoned. I had also decided that less was more. His own documentation gave all the facts and his qualifications; my piece was to give one unique angle: how I had gotten to know this student in class and why the skills he possessed would be an asset to this employer.

I thought further about the analogy of this letter to a performance test. There were also implicit ethical obligations and professionalism concerns. It is not in my contract with my employer to write letters of recommendation for my students. I am not required to do it. But it is something I consider part of being a professional educator. (Recall that I mentioned in Chapter 8 that you might get points in a PT for identifying not only ethical obligations but good practice, such as returning calls promptly.) As a professional and a lawyer, I must make sure that what I write is accurate (I cannot lie), but to be effective, it must also be persuasively phrased to show that my former student is a fine candidate (or the best candidate, if that is my belief). And if, for some reason, I felt I could not endorse the person for the position, I would politely decline the request as quickly as possible so that person could seek a letter from someone else.

My student was right. This "simple" task of writing a letter of recommendation was a lot like a performance test! Do not think for one minute that developing the skills you are working so hard to master to pass the bar exam is in any way, shape, or form a waste of your time. You will use these skills. They are important. And succeeding on the exam will make you stronger, more articulate, more efficient, and more powerful!

It is a gift, a treasured opportunity, to be able to challenge ourselves, commit to success, and work to achieve it.

Keep learning and keep all doors open

Read what is happening in the world and in the legal community at large. Don't get pigeonholed in one specialty. Expanding your knowledge and awareness will bring new clients and may help you serve your existing clients more effectively. Additionally, you will be better prepared if you need to, want to, or are given an opportunity to change jobs.

Stay connected. Network. Stay in touch with people. Talk regularly with your career mentor about planning your next steps.

And keep asking yourself what *you* want; try, to whatever extent possible, to be the master of your own professional destiny. Take what comes along when that makes the most sense, but do not shy away from opportunities to try something new. Trust yourself. You have climbed Mount Everest. You have achieved. You have the success strategies. You are a success story. Keep on writing your future, with confidence.

PART II

REPEATING THE BAR EXAM:
THE NEXT TIME IS
THE LAST TIME

INTRODUCTION TO PART II

This part of the book is called "Repeating the Bar Exam," *not* "Failing the Bar Exam." Be careful about dwelling on the words *failed, fail,* and *failure.* You have not *yet* passed. But if you are committed to achieving the goal of passing and have not given up, you have not failed. Giving up *would* be failure. This is a temporary setback. Commit to a permanent victory. Plan to pass the next exam you sit for. Decide that now, and work toward that end.

Note: All readers are urged to read the entire book. The strategies and tools in the first part will help you achieve success on your next bar exam. And, first timers, force yourself to think in concrete terms about what failing the bar exam really entails. You will be more motivated to take the first time as seriously as possible and do everything in your power to pass.

I have helped thousands of repeating students. It is not an easy place to be, but it is common. You are not alone. You are not a freak. And you are not stupid. There are tools that can help you refocus:

- Accept but do not absorb the shock. Do not let this be a referendum on what you believe about yourself or your ability to pass next time. Take the break you need to be angry, frustrated, scared, or whatever you feel. Then, as the expression goes, get back on the horse and ride on to success on the next exam.
- Analyze your scores. And when you get your exam answers back (in jurisdictions that return the papers), determine why you did not pass and what to correct for success next time. If you need help doing this analysis, hire a reliable bar-review expert or ask an academic support faculty member at your law school to help you make that assessment.

- Did you put in so many hours that you were no longer effectively studying but daydreaming, falling asleep, or tuning out as you read? Were you otherwise distracted?
- Were there areas of law you didn't get and hoped would not be on the exam?
- Did you skip the practice writing, or skimp on it? (Did you outline but not write exams in full under timed conditions)? And if you did do practice questions did you do all types (essays, multiple-choice tests, and performance tests)? Did you analyze the model and explanatory answers? If you did not study sample answers, you did not maximize the opportunity to perfect your skills from practice; you went through the motions but didn't realize the benefits.
- Get on an effective study plan. Figure out which parts of your study schedule worked last time and which did not. Be honest. There is no point in doing otherwise.

"ONLY THOSE WHO DARE TO FAIL GREATLY CAN EVER ACHIEVE GREATLY."

— ROBERT F. KENNEDY —

11

WHY DIDN'T I PASS THE BAR EXAM?

- Diagnosis and treatment plan
- What did you do that you should not have on your last exam?

THERE ARE NO SECRETS TO SUCCESS. IT IS THE RESULT OF PREPARATION, HARD WORK, AND LEARNING FROM FAILURE.

— COLIN POWELL —

DIAGNOSIS AND TREATMENT PLANS

Do any of these reasons people commonly fail the bar exam fit your situation?

1. You were not worried enough.

You got by in law school—maybe not top of your class but you passed everything and graduated. You thought you would knock it out on the bar exam. You thought, *It can't be that tough*. But it was.

Solution:

If the bar exam was harder than you expected, you need to train more rigorously this time. This exam is a different ballgame from law school, physically and mentally. Bar exams last for days and are exhausting. In law school, each final exam covered one subject alone; the bar covers a host of subjects, all of which require you to memorize and quickly recall many rules. And bar applicants are more stressed-out than you may have anticipated; you may have been thrown by the psyche-out factor. Get on a new study schedule now. Review all of Part I, especially Chapters 4–7. If you can, take off time from work to study so you can give the next months total concentration.

2. You were too worried.

You were filled with so much anxiety that you could not relax enough to learn the material. You couldn't absorb the rules because you were completely stressed.

Solution:

This time, plan to sleep more, take more breaks, and do more physical exercise. You cannot study effectively for twenty hours a day, and you don't need to in order to pass.

Just be diligent, disciplined and give it a good six-to-ten-hour day. (Remember: Any time estimate is just that. I cannot tell you how long it takes to learn something. Bottom line: use every day as productively as possible. Slow and steady wins the race.)

3. You did not really learn the law.

You did not know enough law. You may even have memorized rules but didn't understand them and therefore did not know how to effectively apply them under the time pressure.

Solution:

Get that, accept it, and hit the books. You *will* learn the rules this time. If you don't understand the explanation of a certain concept in one source, try another. As a lawyer, if you did not understand the client's problem, would you wing it? No. You'd learn what you needed to know (or refer the case out if you must).

4. You learned law, but did not train by doing hundreds of practice tests under timed conditions.

Solution:

Imagine an out-of-shape person wanting to be fit. He or she reads dozens of books on fitness, watches fitness videos, and reads fitness blogs, but does not exercise. That's what reading outlines without doing practice tests will get you: well read but not ready to perform! Remember the Olympic metaphor: the essays, MBEs, and PTs (if you have one on your bar exam) are three separate "events" that you are competing in. Train for them.

5. You were "The Dreamer."

You went beyond the scope of the fact patterns. You read into things. You assumed facts not in evidence.

Solution:

The graders want you to answer the questions asked and use the facts given. So, next time, read slowly and carefully. Stay away from "what ifs." Analyze the facts they give you. Use those facts and only those facts to prove your points. (Review Chapter 8.)

6. You have weak reading-comprehension skills.

You really don't understand what you are reading. Either you are nervous, trying to read too fast, or have not developed your reading skills thoroughly enough.

Solution:

The bar, like all standardized tests, is largely a test of reading comprehension. Reading is the success thread that runs through every form of testing. Your reading skills must be in top shape to pass. Work on reading and self-assessing. (Study Chapter 8.) Read aloud and touch each word as you read. Do many practice tests and study the model answers so that you see where your reading is not careful or precise enough. (If you have time and want a good exercise, try reading and summarizing, in one to three sentences, all the articles in the opinion section of the newspaper or a news blog each day—this will develop your comprehension skills and keep you informed at the same time!) Last, get help if your reading weakness is due to an ESL issue.

7. You are a practicing attorney in another jurisdiction.

You are licensed to practice in another state. You may have been practicing for years. You took and passed at least one other bar exam but are having difficulties passing this one. First, acknowledge that you may be angry at having to take the exam in the first place. You are an attorney, after all. You are licensed. You have done your time. You shouldn't be asked to take another test. It's been a while since you were a student and you resent this imposition. (Note: This same challenge may be true if you are an accountant, physician, engineer, or any other professional who went to law school as a second or third career.) Next, you are knowledgeable in the real world. You might know too much. You think of too many practical issues.

Solution:

Try pretending you are back in school. Reread Chapter 8. (Try pretending you are back in math class, long before law school.) Be sure to spot the major issues and write a complete and logical analysis for every question. This is not shorthand to help you resolve a client's problem. This is longhand. Prove your skills for the grader. "Show the math." Also, lay off the jargon unless terms are used in the problem. Don't use flash to impress graders; it won't. Write in simple IRPC style (issue, rule, proof, conclusion)—in short, complete, plain English.

8. You write illegibly.

If the graders can't read what you wrote, they won't. (See Chapter 8) They will not assume you wrote the right things. They will not give you the benefit of the doubt. The burden is on you, not the grader.

Solution:

Use headings and subheadings. Leave clear margins; leave spaces between paragraphs and double spaces before and after headings and subheadings. Underline, bold, or italicize key terms sparingly. Make your presentation easy to read! Be sure also to practice with exam software ahead of time.

9. You don't manage time well enough.

You didn't bring a watch or clock with you to the exam, and/or you didn't look at it. Either way, time ran away without you. You were caught with moments to go and unanswered or barely answered questions.

Solution:

Even one question left unanswered is enough to fail you—especially if it's a performance test question that is worth a big percentage of your total grade. Practice a lot, and under timed conditions, with a big, easy-to-read clock. (Check your state's rules on what sorts of clocks or watches, if any, you can bring in. If, for some reason, you are not permitted your own timepiece, find the clock in the exam room and check it frequently.)

10. You are not ready to or don't want to be a lawyer.

Maybe you went straight from college to law school, and are still a little overwhelmed. Maybe you know too many lawyers who hate their jobs. Or maybe you are too focused on the difficulties in finding a law job.

Solution:

Quick fix: Put it all out of your mind. Pass the exam. Then decide what to do to earn a living. One step at a time. (See Chapter 2 for more thoughts on this challenge.)

11. If none of those reasons fits your situation, maybe you were simply unlucky. Some people do just have a bad day or bad luck. If so, dust yourself off, and get back to work. Pass the next bar exam!

WHAT DID YOU DO THAT YOU SHOULD NOT HAVE, LAST EXAM?

Your turn: If you are repeating the exam, why are you here and what steps will you take to ensure (not just *hope*) that this is your last exam? Did you get distracted with personal issues, spend time in chat rooms, or worry too much? Did you find yourself thinking, *"People like me always fail the bar exam"*? Did you hope it wouldn't matter that you didn't know the law in certain subjects as well as you should have?

Take a moment now and jot down some things you did that you now see hurt you.

_____

_____

_____

_____

_____

What didn't you do that you now realize you should have done?

Did you skip the supplemental bar review that would have given you the extra guidance or motivation on essay writing that you knew you needed? Did you skip or not do practice tests under timed conditions? Did you do practice tests but skip the crucial step of analyzing the sample answers?

Note several things you should have done last time, did not do, and are committed to doing next time:

_____

_____

_____

_____

_____

Were you healthy and strong enough to focus for the entire exam?

Do you need to exercise regularly this time, and take better care of yourself?

_____

_____

_____

_____

_____

Do you need to see a doctor about anything?

_____

_____

_____

_____

Did you have a mentor?

Did you have support from the people you love or live with? Were there any detractors? Did you deal with any naysayers as well as you could have? (See Chapter 6.) Did you get "buy-in" from whomever affects your day-to-day life? Were you working and did your employer know you were taking the exam (and support you in that effort)? And did you have a credible, helpful mentor with whom you regularly talked or e-mailed?

Jot down any thoughts about lack of support you may have felt last time, and what you can do this time to bolster your support system.

_____

_____

_____

_____

_____

Was your computer working properly?
Did you have any technical problems? Did you fear having such difficulties?

_____

_____

_____

_____

Was your machine in good working order? Did you practice with the software you had to use during the exam?

_____

_____

_____

_____

_____

Use your scores to help determine why you did not pass.

Were you weak on the law? All subjects or certain subjects? What must you do to learn what you need to between now and the next exam? Were you weak on essay or performance test writing? Do you need a supplemental writing course? Were you weak on MBEs? Do you need an intensive MBE review? These are among the many questions you need to ask yourself, so you can move forward and create a bar exam success plan tailored for you to pass the next exam. Note: In some places, you just get back scores when you fail the exam, while other jurisdictions will allow you to review your actual exam. If you have an opportunity to look at your exam, take it. And if you do not see clearly what is wrong and how to improve, get help from a reliable expert reviewing your answers.

After reviewing your scores or answers (if you have access to them) on the last bar exam, what are your preliminary conclusions?

_____

_____

_____

_____

_____

I FEEL LIKE I WAS KICKED IN THE TEETH

- Get up and dust yourself off
  - Avoid psyching yourself out
  - Accept where you are and refocus on success on the next bar exam
  - Assume responsibility: do not try to shift the blame
  - Put it in perspective
  - Dealing with others who learn you did not pass, especially during the holidays

"TO BEAR FAILURE WITH COURAGE IS THE BEST PROOF OF CHARACTER THAT ANYONE CAN GIVE . . . YOU WILL FIND THAT PEOPLE FORGET THE FAILURES OF OTHERS VERY QUICKLY . . . MY LAST PIECE OF ADVICE IS NOT TO LET ANYONE SEE YOUR MORTIFICATION, BUT WHATEVER YOU FANCY PEOPLE ARE SAYING ABOUT YOU TO GO ON WITH YOUR ORDINARY LIFE AS THOUGH NOTHING UNPLEASANT HAD HAPPENED TO YOU."

— W. SOMERSET MAUGHAM —

One of the biggest barriers repeat takers face is moving past the hit to your confidence. Even for people who accurately diagnose what needs to be fixed, it may be rough to shake off bad feelings. Remember, *you* are not a failure. You never have been. You never will be. This is not a referendum on who you are or what you are capable of. It is news; not good news, but news that can inform you if you let it. You can learn a great deal about what path to take next on your road to success.

Learn from your past; don't let it define you. If you weren't frustrated, you would not be normal. How can someone invest so much and not be frustrated? You put in years of study—your time, your money, your sweat, and your pride. But you are not alone, and you can turn it around. You did not pass this past bar exam, but you did not fail as a person. Once you get over the disappointment, you can turn this into a challenge, and go into problem-solving mode to figure out how to pass next time. If you think success means never failing, think again. Learn from this so-called failure and make it your step to success on the next bar exam.

GET UP AND DUST YOURSELF OFF.

What do you do when you trip and fall? Do you lie on the ground, give up, and say, *"I will never walk again"*? Do you lose confidence in your ability to walk? Of course not. Usually, you get up, brush yourself off, and are on your way. Even after a bad fall, even should you be hurt seriously and need medical care, what follows is healing. Except in unusual circumstances, as long as the will to succeed is there, anyone you talk to who tripped up on the last bar is a person who can walk forward and pass the next exam.

You do not even get the opportunity to *take* the bar exam without a huge investment, and many steps of proving yourself worthy. If you were a person who at the first stumble simply left the path and looked for a smoother trail, you would not have finished law school, let alone applied for and sat for an entire bar examination. The fact that you got far enough to even take the bar exam is itself evidence of your potential. Your job is to get up, get going, and realize that potential.

If you were the sort of person who gave up easily, it is doubtful that you'd have chosen law school to begin with. Learn from past experiences. Turn this into a strength!

Avoid psyching yourself out

To pass the bar exam, *think* about passing. Believe you can pass, that you deserve to pass, and that you will pass. Don't let in the idea that you could fail again. I recently participated in a defensive driving class for teenagers, led by professional race car drivers, and found an analogy to bar passage. The race drivers reminded the students that to drive safely and avoid crashes, you must keep your eyes focused on the road where you want to end up. Even if you swerve or your car loses control, keep looking where you want to go. Do not look at what you fear you may crash into. They led the students through one exercise, a slalom course with cones scattered on the pavement. We were to drive fast, weaving in and out to avoid as many cones as possible without losing control of the vehicle. Their advice on how to do this was to focus on the open road in the distance, beyond the cones. We would see what we needed to avoid hitting the cones with peripheral vision. Stay focused on where we wanted to end up, they said, and we would get there. (If we looked at the cones, they warned, we would likely hit them.)[48] Don't look at the obstacles in your way. Look at the open road of the future ahead. It is common for people who failed a bar exam to believe they will fail again. Turn that belief around. Focus on success.

THINK *FALL* AND YOU WILL FALL; THINK *FAIL* AND YOU WILL FAIL.

I went skiing for the first time in several years and was out for about an hour having fun and did not fall. Suddenly, I began thinking, *I haven't fallen yet. I wonder how many times I will fall today. Wouldn't it be great if I didn't fall at all. I hope I don't fall. What if I got hurt?* You can guess the rest. I soon thereafter went sprawling! When I hadn't been thinking about it, I was fine, but as soon as the thought of falling entered my mind, I fell.

Accept where you are, and refocus for success *on the next bar exam.*

The first question many people ask is, should I take this very next bar or wait out an administration? Most often the answer is take it again as soon as possible. If your scores were close and you can devote serious time to studying for the next exam, the answer is definitely yes. Momentum will help. Your memory will be fresher in relearning and reviewing the material now than it will be six to eight months from now if you delay until the next exam. If your scores were very far from passing, indicating a serious deficiency in all or a number of areas of law, or if you know that this upcoming bar you are otherwise occupied with commitments that cannot be postponed, then you may be better off delaying and putting yourself on an extended study plan. This decision—whether to retake the very next exam—is one you must make quickly, though, to avoid missing filing deadlines or paying late fees.

Take a few days to absorb the shock and to mourn, and then consider the advantages you now have, repeating the exam:

- The more you put in last time, the easier it will be for you to learn what you need and pass this next time. You may think you forgot everything you knew six months ago but you didn't. Depending on how far and where you fell short, you may be close, and with daily practice exams, you may get there fairly easily. Or you may have to really work hard in one area, but be pretty strong in the others. The key is to learn where you are and where you need to get to. Don't allow the frustration to take over. The bar exam is doable. And, again, it may not even be as much work as it was the first time around. Do not decide that the bar exam is insurmountable. It is easier than law school. You can do this.

- You have data from which to create a smart, strategic plan to improve. Use that information!

Were you weak in a particular subject? (If that subject is an MBE subject, look to see if you were weak in that area on both an essay and the MBEs.) If you were only weak in one or a small number of areas, you may not need to take another full bar review. You might just need to get some supplemental materials in that one area and get on a "maintenance" plan for the rest of the exam.

Were you weak in certain skills? Perhaps the MBE was easier for you, and you did well on it, but your essay scores were low. This may mean you know and understand the law, but do not articulate it well enough or have not trained sufficiently in using facts to prove or disprove rules of law, and your analysis is insufficient. You may benefit from a supplemental writing course while you continue to work on daily MBEs on your own.

Did you just blow the performance tests? Many people do not practice these as much as they develop MBE and essay skills, and find that they fall down on this portion of the exam. Consider a supplemental performance test course, or a book designed to help you write effective PTs.

Now remember, your review for February must still cover everything. You wouldn't dream of thinking something like, *I only failed by a couple of MBE questions, so I'll just focus on those and I'll do fine.* No. You are taking the whole exam again, so your focus is on a comprehensive study approach that covers everything that is tested on your bar exam. You may give more attention to certain subjects than others, but you are studying everything carefully.

Did you get tired? When? In the afternoon? Every afternoon? Was day 1 more difficult or less difficult than day 2?

You should not be as nervous as the first-time takers around you. You know what to expect. You have what I call the *been there, done that* edge! You will stay calm and focused this time. With your *slow and steady wins the race* attitude, you will do it.

Accept responsibility. Do not try to shift the blame.

Get rid of any thoughts resembling this: *Those stupid graders just must not have seen what I wrote. I know it was all there. I'm not even going to look at my old tests . . .* Replace such thoughts with this: *I will look critically at what I did and what I did not do last time and I will take the steps necessary to pass this time.*

Too many people spend precious time and energy blaming others for their failures. (*My professors in law school didn't cover that. My bar review didn't give me enough helpful critique on my writing. My ASP professor didn't warn us how hard it would be.*) All of these thoughts are a huge waste of time.

You need to get out the anger, sure. You need to move past the disappointment, of course. But take responsibility. This was your exam. And the next one will be your exam as well. Decide what you will do differently. You make the changes.

SPENDING MORE MONEY

One of the toughest parts about retaking the exam is deciding what sorts of courses to take, and spending more money on preparation tools. Do not react impulsively. Do not just throw money at the problem without thinking carefully through where and what kind of help you really need. But, then, after you see what you need, do not skimp. If you need another course, take one. People will prey on your fears. Don't "jump" at everyone who promises that they can help you. But do take care of yourself.

Put it in perspective.

There are plenty of wise sayings. The adage "That which doesn't kill us makes us stronger" comes to mind. Or Babe Ruth's wonderfully inspiring "Every strike brings me closer to the next home run." Wise sayings do not take away the pain, but they really might help if you let them. Seeing your name on the pass list was the home run you sought. But if last time was a strike, the key to future success will be to get closer to the home run. Reframe this from a failure to a setback. Turn things around. As soon as you can pull yourself out of the anger, frustration, and sadness, focus on success this coming February.

Dealing with others who learn you did not pass, especially during the holidays

The timing of bar results is such that those who do not pass the July bar will most often prepare to retake the exam the following February, which means they will be studying during the holiday season. The holidays (Thanksgiving through the New Year) are often a difficult time, even without bar results in the mix. It may be very hard this year to eat, drink, and be merry with family and friends. For those of you who are now formulating your game plan to turn things around in February, gala festivities can sometimes be devastating, either because of your own beating yourself up or because others make offensive or insensitive comments.

Try not to let bar results ruin your holidays. You are in control. Use these top ten suggestions to help you cope:

1. **Expect that these holidays will be particularly hard.** Knowing that this may be a stressful time will make it easier than if you are blindsided by the negativity you feel when confronted with cheer at a time you are not feeling cheery.

2. **Limit your time at holiday gatherings.** You should have a study schedule anyway, and you should have already canceled or be actively working on canceling or limiting as many things as you can to clear your path for studies in the next months. So accept those few invitations that will make you feel good (or better), and turn down all the others. For events that you do attend, plan to go for an hour or two only. Leave on a high note, and get back to studying or go to sleep so that you can get an early start on studying the next morning.

3. **Unless cooking and entertaining inspire you, excuse yourself from hosting any holiday gatherings this year.** If it is a must that you host, make things as easy as possible. Take every shortcut you can. Buy prepared foods, let others bring dishes, and be sure you have help with setup and clean-up. (Excuse yourself while others clean up so that you can study, or sleep!)

4. **Surround yourself with positive people**. Avoid negative comments and negative vibes. This is a must! If there is anyone, anywhere or in any part of your life, who is communicating to you directly or indirectly a lack of faith in your ability to pass the bar exam, get away from that person, minimize contact with that person, or put him or her off until March. It is a must to believe in yourself, to believe that you can and will pass the bar exam, and to surround yourself with like-minded people who will lift you higher. Avoid those who drag you down.

5. **If someone starts up a conversation, probing you on your results, end it quickly.** Ready yourself with responses to change the subject, and if necessary, politely excuse yourself. A direct response that can cut off probing may be something like, *Yes, I missed this past July. My focus is on the future now, so that's all there is to say about last time. Thank you for your concern.* Then launch right into a question about that person, to be certain the subject is changed.

COOKING THERAPY

Some people find meal preparation cathartic. If this is you, cook away this holiday season. The methodical, repetitive action of chopping vegetables can be particularly soothing, and you can let out aggression without hurting anyone. If you peel or chop onions, you may end up crying. And once those tears begin, don't be surprised if you have a bar exam meltdown. It's a good time, if you have to have one. No one looks "wimpy" because of onion tears! So let loose. If crying helps, jump up and volunteer to be the chief onion chopper.

6. **You do not need to discuss the past.** If you want to—if it helps you to talk about it—go ahead. But if you do not want to talk about it, it is your choice. Change the subject, or politely excuse yourself and walk away.
7. **You do not owe anyone any explanations.**
8. **Do not drink and drive.** Of course, that is advice for any occasion, but there are a couple of problems at holidays just after you learn bar results. One, people might try to get you drunk to make you feel better, and two, you may drink more than usual to drown your own sorrows or escape.
9. **Be sure to exercise.** If nothing else, take walks. Schedule them. Don't skip them. Walk off the stress of it all.
10. **Sleep**. Do not neglect your sleep. Things tend to look gloomier when you are tired. To keep your spirits up and your study skills sharp, get lots of rest.

Armed with awareness and some solid strategies to avoid those parts of the holidays that might otherwise have gotten you down, you can move effectively through November and December, already on a powerfully positive study plan. You will begin the new year with the groundwork in place for the intensive, quality work you will do in January and February, in a diligent and disciplined manner, to pass the February bar exam.

13

RETHINK "FAILURE" AND USE YOUR PREVIOUS EXPERIENCE AS PREPARATION FOR SUCCESS

- You have the "been there, done that" edge. Use it!
  - Complete your new strategic plan
  - Changing your approach

YOU HAVE THE "BEEN THERE, DONE THAT" EDGE. USE IT!

Whatever you did or did not do preparing for or on the last bar exam, now is the time to face up and make the necessary changes. Figure out what you need to do for success next time.

You can understand the major rules and theories. You got through law school, right? There may be weaker subjects but there is nothing tested on the bar exam that you are incapable of understanding.

- Maybe you need a different approach or a different professor or study guide to explain certain concepts. Perhaps you should try a new bar review this time.
- Maybe you were tired when bar review classes were held, or you were distracted by others in the classroom if you took a live class.
- Maybe you need substantive lectures (and even writing workshops) that are recorded or online so you can listen again and review points you did not clearly understand the first time.
- Maybe you need to do some serious practice writing and submit your exam answers for real critique—not just a number grade at the top of the page, but actual comments that tell you where and how to improve.
- Maybe you need your own tutor or bar coach—someone who will not just help you in a room of hundreds of other applicants, but guide you to the success you know is within your reach.

Whatever you decide, believe you *can* do it this next time. Reach out, and make the effective changes that will take you to success next time. From pass rates alone, you know that many applicants did not pass. Probably some of your classmates and friends did not pass. Again and always keep at the forefront the knowledge that this is not a reflection on your ability to pass the next bar exam.

Complete your new strategic plan

Create a smart, new strategic plan. Consider targeted improvement. You may not need a full bar review again. You may want to invest in a different entire full-service bar review course.

Change your approach

The approach you will take to study for a second bar exam must differ from the first.

- If you did all the "right" things but not enough of them, do more this time.

- If you studied passively (reading outlines and listening to lectures) but didn't do many practice writing exercises under timed conditions, change that. Get cracking!
- If your focus was heavier in subject areas you were comfortable with, study the weak ones more thoroughly this time.

In addition to study changes, what other changes will you make? Consider a few life changes that might really help:

- Get more sleep.
- Minimize time spent on e-mail, texting, and web use generally.
- Keep a more regular, disciplined study schedule that starts earlier in the day.
- Approach this exam differently; take it seriously enough to give it your all, but not so seriously that you freak yourself out with stress.
- Avoid all people other than those who believe you can pass and with whom you feel strong, smart, and capable.

Take a moment and write what you know needs to be in your strategic plan to pass this February.

_____

_____

_____

_____

_____

_____

Now go back to Chapter 2, and create your new bar exam success plan. Start fresh, adding in the points you made just above. Reread all of Part I and replace the words *first* or *first time* with *this next bar exam*. Commit to success on the February bar exam. You can do it.

CONCLUSION

Hopefully you now see the bar exam as something challenging but doable, and you are ready to realize your potential and achieve your goals. When you pass and are equipped with a law license, still a powerful and permanent stamp of credibility (so long as you guard it well), you *will* be better able to find a job, some job. You may join the many bar members who, despite tough economic times, are still earning a good (or at least decent) living. Or you may look outside of the law altogether, but you will do so with proof of your capability to read and think critically and perform under intense pressure.

Seeing your name on the pass list brings an incomparable high. It also shows that you can accomplish whatever you set out to do. Making it across this "finish line," with credentials and license in hand, you will have opportunities to take your place and help lead us to a better 21st century. Think of the exam as a very heavy door. It takes all the strength you can muster to open it, but once opened you never have to open it again; you can simply keep climbing the steps on your pathway to ever-greater success, to those extraordinary places that lie on the other side of challenge.

Remember these strategies for success whenever you embark on a new challenge. (You will undoubtedly, hopefully, have many new challenges and opportunities!) These tools will help you. They will move you forward. And you will take each step with the knowledge that you are most capable. You have what it takes. You are a success.

ENDNOTES

1. *See* Yakowitz, J. *Marooned: An Empirical Investigation of Law School Graduates who Fail the Bar Exam.* 60 J. LEGAL EDUC. Volume 1, see generally (August 2010).

2. *See* D. Riebe, *A Bar Review for Law Schools: Getting Students on Board*, 45 BRANDEIS L. J. 269, 273 (Winter 2007). "The purpose of the bar exam, as a part of the broader process of licensing attorneys, is consumer protection. The bar exam protects consumers by ensuring that new lawyers are minimally competent to practice law, thus preventing unqualified practitioners from being 'let loose on the unsuspecting public.' The ABA further justifies the bar exam, asserting: Bar examinations… encourage law graduates to study subjects not taken in law school. They require the applicant to review all he has learned in law school with a result that he is made to realize the interrelation of the various divisions of the law—to view the separate courses which he took in law school as a related whole. This the curriculum of most law schools does not achieve. Also it is the first time many of the applicants will have been examined by persons other than those who taught them, a valuable experience in preparation in appearing before a completely strange judge."

3. *See* L. Trujillo, *The Relationship Between Law School and the Bar Exam: A Look at Assessment and Student Success*, 78 U. COLO. L. REV. 69 (2007). Other works reaching similar conclusions in the Bibliography.

4. The ABA/NCBEX Guide to Bar Passage has a wealth of information about bar exams nationwide. http://www.ncbex.org/assets/media_files/Comp-Guide/CompGuide.pdf. *See also* http://www.nationaljurist.com/?q=content/bar-exam-guide.

5. W. Somerset Maugham, The Mixture As Before in *The Treasure* (W. Heinemann Ltd., 1940).

6. G.R. Blair, *Goal Setting for Results: Success Strategies for You and Your Organization* (The Walk the Talk Company, 2003).

7. A. Hamilton, J. Madison, and J. Jay, *The Federalist Papers* (originally published by J. and A. McLean in 1788 and reprinted recently by ABA Publishing in the ABA Classics series).

8. Yoda, fictional character in Star Wars, *The Empire Strikes Back* (1980), film series created by George Lucas.

9. A phrase typically associated with economic growth and popularized in a 1963 speech by John F. Kennedy.

10. Professor Paul Bergman.

11. There is extensive stereotype threat literature. Among the first was by Steele and Aronson in the *Journal of Personality and Social Psychology* (1995), and most recently in the *ABA Journal* by Stephanie Francis Ward (2012). Other related works on race and gender bias in bar exams appear in the bibliography.

12. The term "preventive law" was popularized by the late Louis M. Brown, Esq. (More on Brown and Preventive Law movement he launched at www.preventivelawyer.org).

13. *See* D. K. Rush, H. Matsuo, *Does Law School Curriculum Affect Bar Examination Passage? An Empirical Analysis of the Factors Which Were Related to Bar Examination Passage between 2001 and 2006 at a Midwestern Law School,* 57 J. Legal Ed. 224, 225 (2007). See also the Bibliography.

14. *See* D. DeBenedictis, *Bar Exam Insiders Debunk Myths about Test,* The New Lawyer Supplement to the Los Angeles and San Francisco Daily Journal (20 Nov. 2012); *see also,* Bradley D. Bonner, *Removing the Veil of Secrecy from the Bar Exam,* 34 Aug Wylaw 18 (2011).

15. Professor Robert Hull.

16. *See supra,* Note 4.

17. Professor Bracci.

18. *See* www.ncbex.org/multistate-tests/mbe/.

19. All credit for the "Batman" speech to Joy Nonweiler.

20. *See generally* www.ncbex.org/multistate-tests/mpre for a variety of information and preparation resources. Be sure to read the most current version of the Multistate Professional Responsibility Examination Information Booklet.

21. *See supra,* Note 4

22. Legaledtech attorney Craig Gold first alerted me to this issue. I have since heard many law professors and employers echo the same point.

23. Credit to Yvette Lloyd for this idea.

24. This reference is from a television commercial that aired frequently on American television during the Summer 2012 Olympic Games in London. It pictures athletes reflecting on their training saying things like, "I haven't watched TV since last summer," and "I haven't ordered dessert in 2 years," and "You know that best-selling book everyone loves? I haven't read it." The athlete then concludes, "Hey, I've been busy."

25. John Quincy Adams, from 1802 speech commemorating the landing of the Pilgrims in Plymouth.

26. "I Fought the Law." Song written by Sonny Curtis, popularized first by the Bobby Fuller Four (1966) and then by The Clash (1979).

27. A. Lamott, *Bird by Bird, Some Instructions on Writing and Life.* (Pantheon Books,1994.)

28. D. Carnegie, *How to Stop Worrying and Start Living*, (originally published by The Chaucer Press, Ltd. 1948)

29. Among other books on thriving in law school, D. Tonsing's *1000 Days to the Bar: But the Practice of Law Begins Now*, (2003) has excellent suggestions on how to effectively memorize, as well as many other helpful ideas for law students.

30. Professor Steve Bracci has been teaching students nationwide about the need for active reading on bar exams for decades.

31. Credit to Professor Steve Bracci for this strategy.

32. Thank you to Rabbi Chaim Seidler-Feller, whose Torah study classes since law school taught me this multisense method of critical reading.

33. If you are still in law school, to help you understand logical inferences and make your reasoning explicit, be sure to read at least one book by UCLA Law Professors D. Binder and P. Bergman, such as D. Binder, P. Bergman: *Fact Investigation: From Hypothesis to Proof*, (first published in 1984 by West Publishing); *See also* P. Bergman, *Trial Advocacy in a Nutshell* (West Publishing).

34. The following are excerpts from informative suggestions for successful essay answers from the Maryland State Board of Law Examiners, applicable to most all bar exam essays. See "Description and Tips on the Written Test for the General Bar Exam" on the website for the Maryland State Board of Law Examiners at http://www.courts.state.md.us/ble/pdfs/gbtips.pdf.

The policy of the Court of Appeals of Maryland governs the preparation, administration, and grading of the examination. The Court states:

> "It is the policy of the Court that no quota of successful examinees be set, but that each examinee be judged for fitness to be a member of the Bar as demonstrated by the examination answers. To this end, the examination shall be designed to test the examinee's knowledge of legal principles in the subjects on which examined and the examinee's ability to recognize, analyze, and intelligibly discuss legal problems and to apply that knowledge in reasoning their solution. The examination will not be designed primarily to test information,

memory, or experience." Presentations at the University of Maryland and the University of Baltimore: During the month of March of each year, the Board of Law Examiners meets with students at the local law schools to discuss the structure of the Bar examination and to explain the characteristics of a good answer to a Bar examination question and how to prepare to take the examination. Contact the Board's office to determine the next scheduled presentation. The Board lists below some general suggestions for your guidance. These suggestions represent an effort on our part to state what is generally of importance in analyzing the facts of a question and preparing your answers.

1.   The Examination is not a test of how much law you know. It is a test of your ability to analyze, recognize and intelligibly discuss legal problems, and to apply your knowledge of legal principles to their solutions. Your answers should demonstrate your knowledge and understanding of how to apply the principles and theories of law to the facts given, and to reason logically and in a lawyer like manner to a sound conclusion.

2.   Some individual questions may involve more than one subject area. For instance, the facts presented may present ethical issues which you must be able to recognize and resolve consistent with the Rules of Professional Conduct and the legitimate interests of the client.

3.   Read each question carefully and in its entirety; perform the factual analysis necessary to give you an understanding of the relationship of the parties, the resulting rights and duties and the significance of the facts set out. Many candidates are unsuccessful because of faulty or insufficient factual analyses. Decide upon an orderly and logical organization of your answer. Then begin to write your concise and complete answer.

4.   Follow instructions. If you represent the Plaintiff, argue the facts and the law, to the extent possible, consistent with the legitimate objectives of the Plaintiff. If you represent the Defendant, advocate for him, to the extent possible, anticipating the thrust of the plaintiff's arguments. If you are required to prepare a memo for a judge, prepare the memo in accordance with the instructions and discuss, if necessary, the merits of both sides. Do not define terms unless requested to do so.

5. Extracts are provided to help you. Use them.

6. Each question contains the facts sufficient to raise all pertinent issues. Assume sparingly. Do not assume away facts, and do not assume facts not given. Do draw inferences from facts which may be ambiguous.

7. As a general proposition there is no preferred formula for the answering of questions; we suggest that you use the logic and analysis appropriate to the facts given and for the question posed.

8. Use proper, clear, and effective English. And please write legibly. We cannot grade what we cannot read. (Emphasis added.) We believe that the properly prepared applicant, with a proper understanding of the examination and a lawyer-like approach to the questions will demonstrate his or her competence with not too much difficulty. Best wishes for success.

35. *See* PASS Contracts for examples of such logical approaches (www.passlaw.com).

36. Ross Mitchell.

37. All credit here goes to colleague Steve Bracci, one of the nation's leading bar exam experts.

38. Though it is now out of print, find a copy of Professor Arthur Miller's 1982 book, *Miller's Court*. With many rich examples, this book written in plain English for lay people is an excellent resource for law students; it takes readers through the twists and turns of an effective Socratic questioning session. You will see why it makes sense that your head hurts from law school classes! Another brand new book that will help your head hurt less in law school is *Cracking the Case Method: Legal Analysis for Law School Success*. This book tells you how to handle law school class discussions, questioning, and arguments, how to brief cases, and how to thrive as you learn how to "think like a lawyer." Both of these books are referenced in the Bibliography, as well as a number of other books helpful in succeeding in law school.

39. The MPT Information Booklet and a great deal of other useful information is at www.ncbex.org/multistate-tests/mpt/.

40. www.calbar.ca.gov.

41. Straightforward information on how to draft many of the documents that have appeared as tasks on performance tests in P. Bergman & S. Berman, *Represent Yourself in Court: How to Prepare and Try a Winning Case* (www.nolo.com).

42. One of many articles regarding differences between grading MPT and essays, http://www.ncbex.org/assets/media_files/Bar-Examiner/articles/2011/800411Bosse.pdf.

43. *See* PASS The Performance Test for strategic approaches to answering performance tests (www.passlaw.com).

44. *See* L. Pasteur, *Lecture*, U. LILLE (December 7, 1854).

45. *See* B. Weiser, *In a Field of Reason, Lawyers Woo Luck Too* (NY TIMES, February 17, 2011).

46. Professor Richard Hermann (among others) authors a blog and has published more than a dozen excellent books on legal career-related issues.

47. M. Schultz, S. Zedeck, *Identification, Development and Validation of Predictors for Successful Lawyering* (A.B.A. J., July 2012 at 39).

48. www.putonthebrakes.com.

BIBLIOGRAPHY

BOOKS

Bergman, *Trial Advocacy in a Nutshell*, (4th ed., West Publishing 2006).

Bergman, Berman, *Represent Yourself in Court: How to Prepare and Try a Winning Case* (Nolo.com, 8th ed. to be published in 2013).

Bergman, Goodman, and Holm, *Cracking the Case Method: Legal Analysis for Law School Success* (Vandeplas Publishing, 2012).

Binder, Bergman, *Fact Investigation: From Hypothesis to Proof*, (first published in 1984 by West Publishing).

Espinoza, Ukleja, Rusch, *Managing the Millennials: Discover the Core Competences for Managing Today's Workforce* (John Wiley & Sons, Inc. 2010).

Furi-Perry, *The Millennial Lawyer* (ABA Publishing, 2012).

Hegland, *Introduction to the Study and Practice of Law* (West, 5th edition 2008).

Hermann, *From Lemons to Lemonade in the New Legal Job Market: Winning Job Search Strategies for Entry-Level Attorneys* (Lawyer Avenue Press, 2012).

Marietti, *Rice First Year Law Student: Wisdom, Warnings, and What I Wish I'd Known in My Year as a One L* (Kaplan Publishing, 2008).

Miller, *Miller's Court* (originally published by Houghton Mifflin, 1982).

Moore, Binder, *Demystifying the First Year of Law School: A Guide to the 1L Experience*, (Wolters Kluwer Law & Business, 2010).

Nerison, *Lawyers Anger and Anxiety: Dealing with the Stresses of the Legal Profession* (ABA Publishing, 2010).

Stropus, Taylor, *Bridging the Gap Between College and Law School: Strategies for Success* (Carolina Academic Press, 2009).

Susskind, *The End of Lawyers? Rethinking the Nature of Legal Services* (Oxford University Press, 2010).

Tamaha, *Failing Law Schools* (University of Chicago Press, 2012).

Tonsing, *1000 Days to the Bar: But the Practice of Law Begins Now* (2003).

ARTICLES

AALS Survey of Law Schools on Programs and Courses Designed to Enhance Bar Examination Performance, 52 J. LEGAL EDUC. 453 (2002).

Alphran, Washington, Eagan, *Yes We Can, Pass the Bar. University of the District of Columbia, David A. Clarke School of Law Bar Passage Initiatives and Bar Pass Rates: From the Titanic to the Queen Mary*, 14 U.D.C. L. REV. 9 (2011).

Bonner, *Removing the Veil of Secrecy from the Bar Exam*, 34 AUG WYLAW 18 (2011).

Clydesdale, *A Forked River Runs Through Law School: Toward Understanding Race, Gender, Age, and Related Gaps in Law School Performance and Bar Passage*, 29 LAW AND SOCIAL INQUIRY 4 (2004).

Cochran, *Hope, Again: Hope Theory in Bar Exam Preparation*, 48 DUSQUENE L. REV. 513 (2010).

Cross, *The Bar Examination in Black and White: The Black-White Bar Passage Gap and the Implications*, 10 NAT'L BLACK L. J. 9 (2003).

Day, *Law Schools Can Solve the Bar Pass Problem—Do the Work!* 40 CAL. W. L. REV. 321 (2004).

Handy, *Blacks, The Bell Curve, and the Bar Exam*, NAT'L BAR ASSN. MAGAZINE (1996).

Jarvis, An Anecdotal History of the Bar Exam, 9 GEO. J. OF LEGAL ETHICS 359 (1995).

Jellum, Reeves, *Cool Data on a Hot Issue: Empirical Evidence that a Law School Bar Support Program Enhances Bar Performance*, 5 NEV. L. J. 646 (2005).

Kaufman, LaSalle-Ricci, Glass, Arnkoff, *Passing the Bar Exam: Psychological, Educational, and Demographic Predictors of Success*, 57 J. LEGAL EDUC. 205 (2007).

Kidder, *The Bar Examination and the Dream Deferred: A Critical Analysis of the MBE, Social Closure, and Racial and Ethnic Stratification*, 29 LAW AND SOCIAL INQUIRY 547 (2004).

Matasar, *The Viability of the Law Degree: Cost, Value, and Intrinsic Worth*, 96 IOWA L. REV. 1579 (2011).

Morriss, Henderson, *Measuring Outcomes: Post-Graduation Measures of Success in the U.S. News & World Report Law School Rankings*, 83 IND. L. J. 791 (2007).

Riebe, *A Bar Review for Law Schools: Getting Students on Board to Pass Their Bar Exams*, 45 BRANDEIS L. J. 269 (2007).

Rush, Matsuo, *Does Law School curriculum Affect Bar Examination Passage? An Empirical Analysis of the Factors Which Were Related to Bar Examination Passage between 2001 and 2006 at a Midwestern Law School*, 57 J. LEGAL EDUC. 224 (2007).

Trujillo, *The Relationship Between Law School and the Bar Exam: A Look at Assessment and Student Success*, 78 U. COLO. L. REV. 69 (2007).

Ward, *Belief in Bias Can Block Your Success*, 98 A.B.A. J. 62 (2012).

Wightman, *LSAC National Longitudinal Bar Passage Study*, (1998).

Wurtzel, *A Badly Run Business Begins with the Bar Exam: An Opinion*, originally published as ablog post on the online review of the Brennan Center at NYU Law School (2010).

Yakowitz, *Marooned: An Empirical Investigation of Law School Graduates Who Fail the Bar Exam*, 60 J. LEGAL ED. 1 (August 2010).

Zeigler, Ingham, Chang, *Curriculum Design and Bar Passage: New York Law School's Experience*, 59 J. LEGAL EDUC. 3 (2010).

INDEX

F

Facebook, 73

Failing bar exam

diagnosis/treatments for, 279–282

not finishing in allotted time and, 185

reasons for, 279–282

Failure, rethinking, 299–300

Family challenges, bar exam and, 120

Family support. *See* Positive and supportive people

Fear, redefining, 245

Feasibility, memorizing, 113

February takers, xviii

First-time passage, 3

Flashcards, 107, 110, 159, 185

Flowcharts, 111

Focus, increasing

exercise and, 92

sleep and, 92–93

Ford, Henry, 46

4L student, xix

Friend support. *See* Positive and supportive people

G

Generational communication divide, 72

Goal setting

believing you will pass exam, 13

decide what you want, 10

denominators for passing bar, 23–25

juris doctor *vs.* esquire, 11–12

language to use, 14–15

mistakes and, 22–23

self-doubt sources and, 15–20

statistics and, 17

stereotypes, eliminating, 20–21

writing goals and, 15–16, 26

Goldwyn, Sam, 59

GPS to bar passage. *See* Success plan, developing

H

Hamilton, Alexander, 11

Hard work, 59–61

dos and don'ts of, 61

Health and staying focused, 92–93

Heartbreak House (Shaw), 110

Holiday season tips, 294–295

Home stretch. *See* Bar review, home stretch of

Hornbooks, 103–104

bar review outlines as, 111

case reading and, 33

coursework selection and, 36

Hotel *vs.* staying with family, 239

Humor, 163

Hybrid learning, 144

I

Inspirations, drawing upon, 63–65

Intensive bar review, xix

Interviewing strategies, 268–269

IRAC (issue, rule, analysis, conclusion), 197–198

IRPC (issue, rule, proof, conclusion), 197

example of, 199

Issue, rule, analysis, conclusion. *See* IRAC (issue, rule, analysis, conclusion)

Issue, rule, proof, conclusion. *See* IRPC (issue, rule, proof, conclusion)

Issue spotting, 174, 202–203, 210–211

I will language, using, 13–15

ABOUT THE AUTHOR

Sara Berman is a graduate of UC Santa Barbara and the UCLA School of Law and has been a professor since 1998, joining the Concord Law School faculty as a pioneer in online legal education in 2000. She is also the Assistant Dean for Academic and Bar Support at Whittier Law School in Costa Mesa, California. Berman's courses include criminal law and procedure, torts, contracts, remedies and community property, as well as legal writing, study skills and bar exam success seminars. Professor Berman conducts bar review lectures nationwide for Kaplan Bar Review, preparing students for both substantive and skills portions of bar exams in numerous jurisdictions. Her publications include *The Criminal Law Handbook: Know Your Rights, Survive the System*, and *Represent Yourself in Court: How to Prepare and Try a Winning Case*, both co-authored with UCLA Law Professor Paul Bergman and published by Nolo.com, as well as numerous law-related articles, bar exam, and academic support course materials. She is one of the founders of PASS Bar Review and Academic Support (more information and Professor Berman's blog can be found at www.passlaw.com).